Investment Trusts Explained

Investment Trusts Explained

YOUR GUIDE TO SUCCESSFUL INVESTING IN CLOSED-ENDED FUNDS

MICK GILLIGAN
IN ASSOCIATION WITH KILLIK & CO

Harriman
House

Harriman House

HARRIMAN HOUSE LTD
3 Viceroy Court
Bedford Road
Petersfield
Hampshire
GU32 3LJ
GREAT BRITAIN
Tel: +44 (0)1730 233870

Email: enquiries@harriman-house.com
Website: harriman.house

First published in 2025 by Harriman House, an imprint of Pan Macmillan
EU Representative: Macmillan Publishers Ireland Limited, 1st Floor, The Liffey Centre, 117-126
Sherriff Street Upper, Dublin 1, DO1 YC45
Associated companies throughout the world
www.panmacmillan.com

Paperback ISBN: 978-1-80409-127-2
eBook ISBN: 978-1-80409-128-9

British Library Cataloguing in Publication Data
A CIP catalogue record for this book can be obtained from the British Library.

01

Printed and bound by CPI Group (UK) Ltd.

Cover design by Heat Design.

KILLIK & CO

IN THE 1980S the Thatcher Government sought to encourage people to save through the stock market. It was on the back of this that Killik & Co was founded in 1989 to offer professional advice, services and market access to the growing numbers that were new to the stock market as well as to traditional private investors.

That premise still holds true today, and Killik & Co remains focused on private individuals and their families. However, we also believe that we have a role in helping to educate the public about financial matters that are not well understood. It is our belief that people are often fearful when they don't understand a subject, and that is particularly true when it comes to investment trusts.

Many invest via funds such as unit trusts. Although they have a place, investment trusts offer a structure which is arguably superior. They can hold investments for the long term, unlike unit trusts which must be ready to liquidate investments at short notice. The investment trust's ability to borrow also makes them well placed to generate superior returns.

The wealth management landscape has changed markedly since 1989, with consolidation leading to fewer, but larger firms. This is not always good for the customer, as larger entities often seek greater uniformity and eschew investor-led decisions. This consolidation has caused larger firms to shun investment trusts, which are less well suited to portfolio standardisation.

Killik & Co remains independent and proud to facilitate the investor seeking investment trust exposure in their own portfolio. It is for these reasons we have produced this book, *Investment Trusts Explained*. I hope you find it an interesting read and a useful source of reference. If so, we will have succeeded in our objective of broadening the understanding of investment trusts.

Paul Killik
Killik & Co
Smart advice when it matters most
www.killik.com

CONTENTS

Part 3: How to Invest in Investment Trusts (Strategies / Techniques / Approaches) **179**

ACKNOWLEDGEMENTS

To Andrea, Cara and Neamh. Thank you for your love, understanding and great sense of fun.

And

To those who helped me, with my gratitude.

The production of this book was truly a team effort. There are many people to thank.

I would firstly like to thank Alvin Hall, financial educator, broadcaster and author for his time and counsel at the outset.

A big thanks goes to Merryn Somerset Webb for her foreword. Merryn has long been an advocate for investment trusts through her time as editor at Money Week, in her Bloomberg columns and on her *Merryn Talks Money* podcasts. Her experience as a non-executive director on several trust boards has also given her valuable insights into the workings of these excellent investment vehicles.

I would like to give a particularly big thank you to Tim Bennett, Killik & Co's Head of Education and an excellent sub-editor. Tim helped to declutter my paragraphs and knock my syntax into shape.

I also would like to thank Gordon Smith, Head of Fund Research at Killik & Co and Andrius Makin, co-manager of our Managed Portfolio Service. They helped to lighten the load on the day job as well as sanity checking my copy.

I would also like to thank my colleague Stephen Timoney for challenging several of my assumptions, as well as Paul Killik, Craig Manning, Sarah Threadgold and Leelee Blackwell for their input.

Thanks also to my colleagues Will Stevens and Sarah Hollowell for their input on financial planning and tax related aspects of the book as well as Natasha Ward for help with chart formatting.

I would also like to thank some former colleagues. Priyan Rayatt, now an Investment Funds Director at Marex, for his forensic attention to detail in checking much of the data-heavy sections. Jonathan Jackson for sanity checking much of the content. Monica Tepes, now a non-executive director on two investment trust boards, was very helpful in checking the sections that relate to governance.

Nick Britton and his colleagues from the AIC were incredibly helpful with their expertise and guidance, so thank you. I would also like to thank my old university mate Max Anderson, author and travel writer, for casting a non-financial eye on my copy and providing some great suggestions.

And finally, I would like to thank the guys at Harriman House. Craig Pearce, my publisher, for getting in touch all those years ago and for overseeing this project. Thanks also to Tracy Bundey, Neil Burkey and Charlotte Smith.

I would like to dedicate this book to my brother Martin, a gentle soul who left this world far too early.

FOREWORD BY
MERRYN SOMERSET WEBB

I F YOU WERE to make a list of the greatest conceptual innovations of all time, you might not think to add the limited company to it. That would be a mistake. It should be at the top. Before the introduction of the limited liability structure in the UK in the mid-1850s, investing in anything was fraught with almost unimaginable risk – if the company failed shareholders were personally liable for all its debts. With it, your losses as a shareholder became limited to the amount you originally invested. Clearly no shareholder would want a company to fail and of course would therefore always want to keep a reasonably close eye on those hired to run it (the directors). But if it were to fail, as a shareholder your only problem would be the loss of your stake. That its debts might not be paid back in full became a problem for those who had lent to it (a risk they should have understood when they made the loan). This might sound like no more than a legal tweak but turned out to be rather more. With losses capped and the risk of a bad investment being utterly life destroying gone, investors could take on rather more overall risk – investing in more companies and more exciting (occasionally mad) ideas. Without the structure and the organisational capacities of companies, notes my old *Financial Times* colleague Martin Wolf, 'the unprecedented economic development seen since the middle of the nineteenth century would have been impossible.'

You could say the same for the development of investing. The corporate structure, it turns out, also creates a close to perfect investment vehicle, one that the well off of the 19th century fast learnt to love. Most investment structures are designed to gather assets and to make money for fund managers. A limited company, the purpose of which is to invest in other companies or assets – which is all an investment trust really is – is not. Trusts are owned by their shareholders. Those shareholders appoint a board of directors to run the company – and the assets – for their benefit and their benefit only. It is democratic by design. It gives the manager freedoms he or she simply doesn't have with an open-ended fund. And over the long term it works – investment trusts tend to outperform open-ended funds invested in the same way. There's a reason that 17 of the big-name trusts ordinary investors love (think City of London, Alliance Trust and Law Debenture for starters) have all been around since long before 1900.

That said, it doesn't always look like it is working – the last few years have been pretty tricky for example. With the UK market being out of favour globally, wealth managers moving away from the sector and some trying bits of regulation, discounts have moved out (shares in most investment trusts are trading at prices below their net asset value per share) and there have been few new launches.

But one of the key strengths of the sector is its ability to use the corporate structure to constantly reinvent itself. Over the last year directors have really begun to show how they can support shareholders over fund managers. They have reacted to the discounts with share buy back programmes, with mergers with better (or at least stronger) trusts and in a large number of cases by actually winding up trusts that look like they aren't ever coming good. And when directors haven't stepped up to the plate in time, they have found activist shareholders appear on their registers to force them into it. This is not a sector that allows complacency – but it is one that always finds a way to use its structure to sort itself out.

Look if you will to Alliance Trust Plc, one of the greats of the sector and a favourite of mine. It was initially formed in 1888 from the merger of land and mortgage firms, one of which provided direct loans to new immigrant farmers in the US. Its shareholders then were the jute traders and shippers of Dundee. Today, 140 years of shape shifting later, Alliance has weathered a series of crises; has a rather wider pool of retail investors and a totally different investment focus (high conviction listed equity investing); has merged with another trust (it is now called Alliance Witan); and, having paid a rising dividend every year for the last 57 years, stands as an example of just how fantastic a vehicle investment trusts are for long-term investors. They should be a part of all serious portfolios. If they aren't part of yours, this excellent guide is the one for you.

Merryn Somerset Webb,
Autumn, 2025

PREFACE

Warming up

THIS BOOK IS about one of the most innovative and accessible investment vehicles that exists in the UK – the investment trust. It explains what they are, how they operate and how you can use them to help you achieve your financial goals.

In simple terms, investment trusts are a type of UK fund, which is to say a legal structure for pooling investors' capital. So, along the way I will explain their history and how their original purpose remains relevant in the context of other types of funds. This will help you to better understand their advantages and disadvantages, plus how they can offer an edge over other types of investment vehicle.

Like most investments, investment trusts come with risks, some of which are specific to their structure. I will explain what these are, how to identify them and highlight ways to avoid many of the most common investment mistakes.

Some of the information and analysis that I provide along the way is undoubtedly technical. For instance, this book makes multiple references to annual reports and comparative data. Annual reports are publicly available for all stock market-listed companies, including investment trusts. So, you can access many of the same ones that I quote from. To ease you through the book, I have moved the more in-depth examples, along with some of the more detailed number crunching, to the appendices.

Helping investors

In that context, it is fair to say this book is not aimed at complete financial market novices. I imagine most readers will already have investments, whether focused on individual shares, or more likely mutual funds, such as unit trusts and open-ended investment companies (OEICs). As such, I assume a basic understanding of how the stock market works.

That said, even more experienced readers may find a few of the concepts that I cover challenging. Rest assured, however, that I will try to convey any market jargon using plain English and plenty of examples. Experienced investors, who already understand the more complex terms, should find that this book helps them to better understand investment trusts, especially when it comes to the more esoteric types. One of my main target readers is the seasoned mutual fund investor that has yet to fully venture into the world of investment trusts. At the time of writing there is some £1.2 trillion invested in actively managed UK mutual funds, compared to just £230 billion in investment trusts. If this book helps to redress that balance, even in a small way, then one of my primary objectives will have been achieved.

I should also point out that what follows is aimed squarely at long-term investors rather than short-term traders. As such, this is not a guide to getting rich quickly, but rather a guide to using investment trusts to build wealth over an extended period of time.

Providing structure

To help you on this journey, the book is split into three main parts plus the appendices and tables. The first provides context, the second outlines the necessary tools needed to do proper analysis and the third provides practical investment guidance. All are followed by appendices and tables. Here is a slightly deeper dive.

Part 1: Introducing investment trusts

I open with a simple explanation of what an investment trust is and how it differs from other types of funds. Along the way, we will revisit the launch of the very first investment trust in the late 19th century. I will also highlight how society benefits from their existence before concluding with an outline of the different structures.

Part 2: Lifting the lid

This section illuminates the most important features of investment trusts. These include discounts, premiums and gearing – their ability to borrow to enhance returns.

It also introduces the different stakeholders involved in the creation and operation of a trust. These include shareholders, an independent board and the investment manager, responsible for managing the trust's portfolio on a day-to-day basis. Here, you will also find my guide to analysing financial statements.

Part 3: Diving in

This section illustrates several important financial concepts that can be used by investors to enhance long-term investment returns when buying and holding investment trusts. It explains how you can use compounding to good effect, benefit from *pound cost averaging* to manage volatility and understand the valuation of certain types of investment trust. I also consider the importance of liquidity, alongside the other factors that can influence investment returns. Investor psychology features here too, as well as how to invest tax efficiently.

Finally, we will look at specific investment trusts and categorise them based on how suited they are to helping you achieve certain financial objectives, whether capital preservation, income generation, growth, or a combination of these goals.

Perhaps most importantly, I will then attempt to answer a vital question for fund investors: do investment trusts outperform mutual funds? You'll have to read on for my answer!

To get the most from this book you should be prepared to spend some time on research. That's why Part 3 ends by flagging several useful sources of relevant data.

Part 4: Appendices

Throughout the book, readers will find references to various studies I have undertaken. These include a comparison of how investment trust fees differ from those of mutual funds. More detailed information about these, including my methodologies, is contained in this section.

I also look at investment trusts that hold hard-to-value assets, consider different ways of arriving at a valuation and explain and quantify how buying back shares at a discount, or issuing new ones at a premium, can enhance net asset value per share.

The final parts of the appendices provide the full methodology that underpins my comparisons between investment trusts and mutual funds, including their relative performance.

Part 5: Tables

The concluding section ranks investment trusts for comparison purposes, based on criteria such as age, size, liquidity and gearing.

Since writing

Writing a book takes time. The world doesn't wait for you to finish. The investment trust sector is a very dynamic one, and so is constantly adapting to events. The information in this book is accurate as of 31/12/2024. Some things have changed since that date, and where these are material changes, I have added a footnote.

INTRODUCTION

I'VE BEEN FASCINATED by the stock market since I was youngster. Looking back, this must've been obvious to my parents who bought me a stock market board game when I was 13. I remember it had three charts – a Quote Board with prices, a Turns Chart and best of all, Market Trend Cards featuring dramatic 'bulls' and 'bears'.

Truth is, it was a fairly odd gift for a kid growing up in Enniskillen, County Fermanagh.

Located in the most westerly part of Northern Ireland, Fermanagh is a beautiful county of rolling hills, and a vast expanse of water called Lough Erne. Back then, it seemed a million miles from London's Threadneedle Street with its noisy trading floors. In the local newsagent where my sister worked, you could count the number of customers who bought the *Financial Times* on one hand. To my knowledge, there has never been a stockbroking firm in Fermanagh.

But it didn't take long before investment trusts – the subject of this book – made an impact on my home county.

The UK's first renewable infrastructure investment trust, Greatcoat UK Wind came to the London stock market in 2013 and in the process bought several wind farms. One of them was Tappaghan, overlooking the village of Lack in the north of Fermanagh. Meanwhile, HICL Infrastructure, the first social infrastructure investment trust, which launched on the London stock market in 2006, acquired a concession to maintain the Southwest Acute Hospital, just outside Enniskillen.

As you'll discover in these pages, investment trusts sometimes get to the places other funds fail to reach.

Starting out

I made my first stock market investment as a student. It was the late 1980s and Britain was in the initial stages of a series of government privatisations. I applied for some shares by filling in a coupon in the newspaper. I'm pretty sure they were British Gas shares. I held onto them for less than a fortnight, as I didn't have the money to pay for them on the settlement date.

My next foray came in 1988. The London stock market had yet to recover from the 1987 crash. In the space of four days in October 1987, the FTSE 100 Index (which represents the largest 100 publicly traded companies in the UK) dropped by more than 20%. In just over a month, the market fell by 35%.

To a contrarian like me, that seemed like a great time to set up a share dealing account. I imagined there must be plenty of bargains after such a steep decline. I was living in Lincoln, the cathedral city in the east of England, at this stage. Having spotted the brass plate of a stockbroking firm in the city centre, I walked in and said to the receptionist that I'd like to open an account. She looked me up and down before politely informing me that the firm 'wasn't taking on any new customers'.

It was somewhat fitting then, that many years later I'd end up working at Killik & Co, a firm launched in 1989 to address this very issue.

Killik opened offices on the pavements of London neighbourhoods, actively seeking to attract young savers, educate investors, and offer broking accounts with no minimum investment levels. That accessibility ethos remains in place to this day.

Growing interest

As share dealing became more widely available, I took full advantage. My investment horizon lengthened from two weeks to several years as I bought and sold stocks. However, as my investment pool grew, I also became less comfortable with the regular and sudden drops in individual share prices – I wanted to insulate myself from the volatility.

That's when I came across investment trusts, separate companies listed on the stock market which seek to generate income or capital via a diversified pool of investments.

By the time I joined Killik & Co in 2001, I was responsible for analysing a wide range of funds, including investment trusts.

It's investment trusts I have most enthusiasm for – I believe they're superior to the alternatives in terms of achieving long-term capital growth and generating income. For the last 25 years, I've analysed hundreds and hundreds of them, and held meetings with most of their management teams. I've also made thousands of buy and sell recommendations and invested hundreds of millions of pounds on behalf of investors.

The fund research team I'm part of manages portfolios on behalf of clients and the bulk of these are invested in a combination of index funds and investment trusts. I also eat my own cooking in the sense that the bulk of my own personal investments are made via investment trusts.

Shining a light

So, why author another book on the subject now, given the number of good ones already available?*

Well, my aim is to redress an important imbalance. Although investment trusts were originally devised as a way for investors of moderate means to invest and grow their wealth, the truth is that UK private investors now have a vast choice of funds to choose from. Many default to mutual funds, commonly known as unit trusts or open-ended investment companies (OEICs). Although these have their merits, many of the actively managed versions have seen their asset-raising-ability far exceed their capacity to deliver attractive returns.

At the time of writing there's some £1.2 trillion invested in actively managed UK mutual funds, compared to just £230 billion in investment trusts. I believe that this imbalance is more a function of commercial incentives in the financial services sector than it is about what's right for the end investor.

Over the years, the media's done a decent job in highlighting and promoting investment trusts to private investors. However, what I'm seeking to do is to not just provide a comprehensive guide to this world, but to also shine a light on certain aspects of the sector that have not garnered sufficient column inches. These include the basic tools that should help investors to gauge the value of interesting but tricky-to-value assets, whilst avoiding the duds. I am also keen to highlight the issue of fees and how certain trusts could better align management and shareholder interests.

---

* I recommend *Put Not Your Money in Trust* (Newlands, AITC 1997), *Investment Trusts* (Baron, FT Publishing 2020), *Investment Trusts: A Complete Guide* (McHattie, McHattie Group 2021) and *The Investment Trusts Handbook* (Davis, Harriman House 2023).

I hope this book goes some way towards educating those investors who have yet to properly consider investment trusts. I hope it fills in important gaps in the existing literature. And most of all, I hope it helps you in your investment decisions – to play the game a little better!

PART 1

WHAT ARE INVESTMENT TRUSTS AND WHY DO THEY MATTER TO YOU?

CHAPTER 1

WHAT ARE INVESTMENT TRUSTS?

"Put not your trust in money,
but put your money in trust."

—**Oliver Wendell Holmes, Sr.,**
US physician and poet

THE TERM INVESTMENT TRUST is somewhat misleading. This is because these vehicles are, in fact, companies. And whereas most companies manufacture a product or carry out a trade, an investment trust company exists to make and hold a portfolio of investments. However, that simple purpose overlooks a rich history and an excellent structure for generating investment returns.

Some of the earliest versions of the investment trust invested in railroads in North America. Fast forward to today and their reach spans established stock markets around the world and encompasses everything from fintech start-ups to frontier markets, infrastructure projects, windfarms and investments in outer space. What investment trusts have in common is that they allow investors to buy their shares to gain access to a wide range of underlying investments. A ready-made portfolio if you will. So, we'll start off by considering how this works in a bit more detail and look at some of the key features and benefits associated with what has sometimes been labelled 'one of the City's best kept secrets'.

The basic concept

It is a pity that the investment trust is still an enigma to many private investors. They are an often-overlooked gem. That's despite these vehicles having existed for more than a century, quietly accumulating and compounding wealth on behalf of those who know about them.

Their story began in the 19th century when they emerged as a novel solution to the problem of pooling investment capital for the rapidly industrialising British economy. The very first one, the Foreign and Colonial Government Trust, was established in 1868. This laid the foundation for a new way of investing, providing individuals with an opportunity to access a diversified portfolio of assets, often including foreign securities, without the need for substantial capital or expertise. It also set the scene for today's hugely diverse investment trust market. A quick tour of the basic principles will highlight why the market has grown so rapidly.

Imagine a world where you and some friends would like to buy several businesses. None of you can afford to do so by yourselves. None of you wishes to be responsible for the day-to-day running of them. Furthermore, no-one in the group wants to take on the full risk associated with any of them failing. In that context, a single investment structure, which could pool capital such that each person buys a little bit of every business and also appoints someone to independently oversee the underlying investments on a day-to-day basis, is pretty appealing. That, in a nutshell, is what an investment trust does. Figure 1A displays the roles of the three key stakeholders in an investment trust: the shareholders, the board and the investment manager.

Figure 1A: Investment trusts, roles of the three key stakeholders

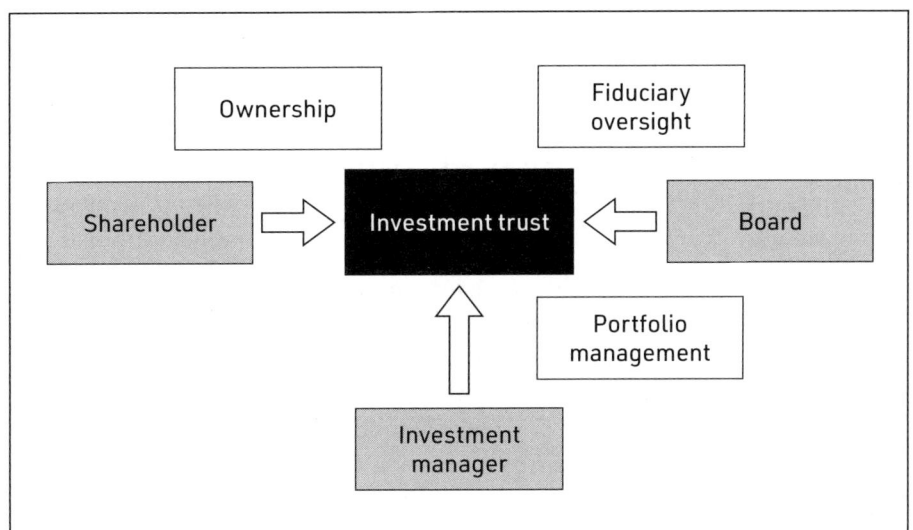

The modern City jargon used to describe such an arrangement is a 'collective investment scheme'. That is the broad term used to describe any vehicle which takes in money from a wide range of people and invests it in a portfolio in return for a certificate of ownership.

Key features and benefits

So, what makes investment trusts so appealing? The answer lies in the advantages they offer when compared to both direct investment in individual securities and other types of collective investment vehicle.

Before we get to those, here are a few key facts. Investment trusts usually raise capital from investors through an initial public offering (IPO), during which a fixed number of shares are issued. Once the IPO is completed, these shares are fully tradeable, such that investors can buy or sell them like any other stock. Unlike their better-known mutual fund counterparts, 'unit trusts' and 'OEICs' (open-ended investment companies), investment trusts are known as 'closed-ended' funds. This means that having issued shares, the number available to trade is usually fixed. They remain 'closed' to new capital. Their subsequent value is determined by the actions of buyers and sellers. As such, the price at which they trade on an exchange can differ from the value (per share) of the trust's underlying portfolio. This leads to the potential for listed investment trusts to trade at a 'premium' or 'discount' to their net asset value (NAV), an important aspect to which we will return.

One of the most significant advantages of investment trusts is their ability to offer investors access to a diversified portfolio of assets. Unlike direct investments in individual stocks or bonds, where investors assume the risk that a single company or issuer could flounder, or even fail, investment trusts hold a broad range of assets. This hugely reduces 'single stock' risk and thereby enhances the overall stability of returns, a critical factor in long-term wealth accumulation.

They can also use leverage. This term just means borrowing money to invest. This can potentially enhance returns in a rising market environment, as the trust benefits not only from the performance of its original assets but also from those purchased with this borrowed money. This is something that not all fund structures are able to do. That said, poorly judged leverage also introduces an element of risk, as it can magnify losses in a declining market. Nonetheless, given that stock markets tend to go up in more years than they go down, prudent leverage can add value to equity portfolios over long time horizons.

"One of the most significant advantages of investment trusts ... is their ability to offer investors access to a diversified portfolio of assets."

The fact that investment trusts have fixed ('closed') pools of capital helps in this regard. It means that the portfolio managers, responsible for the investment strategy day-to-day, can take a very long-term view as they don't have to worry too much about investors demanding their money back at a moment's notice, forcing a sale of assets in order to pay them back. This is not a luxury afforded to the managers of other structures such as unit trusts and OEICs.

Many investors also turn to investment trusts for regular long-term income. This is typically generated from the dividends and interest income earned by the trust's underlying assets. Consistency is achieved through an ability to set aside excess ('reserve') income, and profits, in one year and use them to supplement payments in a future one. This is a very valuable feature when the objective is to provide a growing income stream, perhaps to someone in retirement.

Managing risk

The investment manager is central to both the overall strategy and the day-to-day operation of these vehicles. They conduct analysis, assess market conditions and make informed decisions aimed at optimising returns and managing risk on behalf of external investors. The goal is to achieve the trust's objectives, which are usually stated in its prospectus. That document is effectively the legal contract between the investment trust board and the external shareholders.

Further, the existence of an independent board of directors helps to safeguard the interests of those shareholders and is a key differentiator over almost every other type of pooled investment vehicle. The board's role is to oversee the investment manager's underlying portfolio and ensure that any investments chosen are suitable to meet the aims and objectives of the trust.

The board can also help to enhance the profits to shareholders which are generated by the trust's own investments. It can do this by, for example, buying back its shares in the open market when they are undervalued. It can also increase regular dividends or make one-off special payments.

> "The existence of an independent board of directors ... is a key differentiator over almost every other type of pooled investment vehicle."

Whilst investment trusts offer all of these advantages, they are not without their risks. As noted earlier, the use of leverage (borrowed money) can magnify losses in a declining market. Further, the trust's investment returns rely on market conditions and on the skills of an investment manager. Both of these can undergo periods of poor performance. Many trusts aim to provide income but there is no guarantee of a consistent payout. And even though investment trust shares are traded on stock exchanges, they can still experience periods of illiquidity, making it challenging to buy or sell at an investor's desired price.

A valuable quirk

Those caveats notwithstanding, as mentioned earlier, one of the distinguishing features of investment trusts is their propensity to trade on the open market at a discount or premium to their underlying NAV. That NAV is simply the value of all the underlying assets once borrowings and accrued costs have been netted off. The deviation arises because investment trust shares are bought and sold on stock exchanges, where supply and demand dynamics influence their price. As such, when an investment trust's shares trade at a price below the NAV of the assets it holds, they are said to be trading 'at a discount'. Conversely, if its shares trade at a price higher than the NAV, they are trading 'at a premium'. Pure mechanics aside, the existence of these valuation anomalies can confound investors, so it is important to understand why they arise.

Discounts and premiums are in fact perfectly normal and arise for various reasons. A trust may trade at a discount because investors have become pessimistic about its prospects, its portfolio holdings or the asset class it specialises in. Conversely, a premium may emerge if investors are enthusiastic about a particular investment strategy, anticipate future gains or become attracted to a trust's specific income distribution potential. Canny investors in this space therefore often view discounts as an opportunity to buy into the underlying assets cheaply – meaning for less than their intrinsic worth. Premiums, on the other hand, may deter new investors or prompt existing ones to consider selling on the basis that the same assets are available for less elsewhere.

> "Canny investors in this space therefore often view discounts as an opportunity to buy the underlying assets cheaply."

Something for everyone

To wrap up this chapter and to help you truly understand the scope of investment trusts, we will finish with a few examples.

To kick off, it is perhaps no surprise that one of the most famous and consistent investment performance vehicles still in existence has a lot in common with investment trusts. Berkshire Hathaway is the investment company managed by Warren Buffett, widely considered to be one of the most successful investors of all time. And whilst not an investment trust it nonetheless shares some key characteristics. Berkshire Hathaway holds a portfolio of investments, uses leverage to enhance its investment returns, takes a long-term investment perspective, has a board that can decide to buy back shares if that is deemed to be a better use of capital than making further investments, and makes its shares available to be bought and sold via a stock market. Sound familiar?

Closer to home, there are now countless examples to choose from. Take 3i Group, currently the largest investment trust on the London stock market. Its origins go back to 1945, when the government and major UK banks formed the Industrial and Commercial Finance Corporation (ICFC). This was a key component of a post-war effort to provide capital to small and medium-sized businesses businesses that struggled to borrow capital from banks and were too small to raise money via the stock market. ICFC typically provided finance in the form of a loan or an equity stake.

ICFC expanded in the decades that followed its formation and in 1983 was renamed Investors in Industry (III), hence the name 3i. It duly floated on the London Stock Exchange in 1994 with a value of £1.5bn and has grown to around £35bn in size today. 3i Group now invests internationally, with stakes in firms ranging from BoConcept, the Nordic design brand, to the George Best Belfast City Airport.

For those investors who want to target a specific theme, such as clean energy, there are plenty of options. For example, Greencoat UK Wind is an investment trust that was established in 2013 to acquire a portfolio of UK windfarms. The opportunity materialised when the UK energy regulator OFGEM incentivised suppliers to reduce their carbon emissions between 2008 and 2012. Many constructed windfarms to help them meet their targets. However, once fully operational, whilst many electricity suppliers were happy to receive the power being generated as a result and sell it on to customers, they did not want to retain ownership of the windfarms themselves. Enter Greencoat, which came to the London market in March 2013, raising £255m in an oversubscribed IPO, as the first listed renewable infrastructure fund. It immediately acquired a seed portfolio of six windfarms, albeit with the day-to-day operations carried out by power companies such as Scottish & Southern Electricity and RWE. Greencoat now holds more than 40 windfarms that stretch from Caithness in the very north of Scotland to Romney Marsh near Rye in Kent.

Those are just a few examples of the vast range of opportunities this sector has to offer. Those opportunities would usually be challenging to access or normally only be the preserve of large pension or sovereign wealth funds. These days there are investment trusts focused on emerging markets, technology start-ups, infrastructure projects and more niche sectors such as drug discovery.

Wrapping up

In conclusion, investment trusts are a versatile and time-tested investment vehicle with a long track record. They offer many benefits, which include diversification, professional management expertise, income generation and access to niche markets. And although they also come with their own challenges and risks, they continue to evolve to meet the changing needs and preferences of investors. Before we explain any more about investment trusts, it is important to place them in context with other types of collective investment funds.

Summary of key points

- An investment trust is a company which holds a portfolio of investments.

- Investment trusts began in the 19th century when they emerged as a novel solution to the problem of pooling investment capital for the rapidly industrialising British economy.

- Investment trusts offer some key advantages when compared to other types of collective investment vehicles.

- An independent board of directors helps to safeguard the interests of investment trust shareholders.

- Investment trusts can use leverage (borrowed money) to invest, which can magnify gains when assets rise in value but also can magnify losses when assets decline in value.

CHAPTER 2

INVESTMENT TRUSTS IN A WIDER FUND CONTEXT

"The investor who wants to make an intelligent commitment in fund shares has thus a large and somewhat bewildering variety of choices before him – not too different from those offered in direct investment."

—**Benjamin Graham,**
The Intelligent Investor

THE WIDE CHOICE of funds that Benjamin Graham observed just after the Second World War has become even more bewildering today. In this chapter I'll attempt to put this bewildering choice into context. I will delve into some more of the key features that bind, but also distinguish, different types of collective investment schemes (which we shall refer to simply as 'funds' from here on).

Fund types

Having established how the basic structures work, we can now look at the different types available (refer to Table 2A).

Table 2A: UK fund classification

UK FUND TYPES		
Open-ended	**Closed-ended**	
Mutual funds	**Investment companies**	**Limited partnerships (LPs)**
Unit trusts	Investment trusts	Private fund LPs
Open-ended investment cos (OEICS)	Other listed investment cos	
	Real estate investment trusts	
	Venture capital trusts	

Open-ended versus closed-ended

The first key distinction to note is that all funds can be categorised into open-ended (variable capital base) and closed-ended (fixed capital base). Unit trusts and OEICs are the most common examples of the former in the UK. Confusingly, although OEICs are technically companies, the 'shares' they issue behave in the same way as unit trust units (discussed shortly). In the US open-ended funds are referred to as mutual funds, a term that is increasingly also used in Europe.

Exchange traded funds (ETFs) are a type of open-ended fund that can be traded in real time via a stock exchange. Many ETFs traded on the London Stock Exchange are effectively OEICs with a real-time trading facility. As a result, they combine some of the features of mutual funds with those of individual shares. Trading on an exchange, such as the London Stock Exchange, means that ETF shares can be bought or sold at any time of the trading day at a known price. Conventional mutual funds, on the other hand, are usually priced once a day.

Open-ended funds allow capital to be invested in, or recovered from, them ('redeemed') on a regular basis via the purchase or sale of units, or shares. By way of an example, we could take the Fundsmith Equity Fund, which with

c. £23bn of assets is one of the largest of its type in the UK at the time of writing. Provided the fund manager receives an order to buy or sell units by midday, the relevant transaction takes place. Given that unit trusts and OEICs don't trade openly in the same way as, say, listed companies, the price is based on a valuation of the underlying portfolio at the same point in time. To value an investor's individual holding, the manager simply divides this valuation by the number of shares in issue. So, in very simple terms, if the total assets of the fund are £22bn and there are currently 22bn units, or shares, in issue, the price for each will be £1.

Contrast this with closed-ended funds such as investment trusts. These funds usually raise initial capital from investors and issue exchange traded shares in return. So, for example, we could compare the Fundsmith Equity Fund, introduced earlier, and 3i Group, the largest UK investment trust over the same time horizon. Whereas the number of Fundsmith shares increases and reduces as they are bought and sold to and from the fund, 3i Group has an almost constant number of shares in issue during the same period.

Figures 2A and 2B show the number of shares in issue for both Fundsmith Equity Fund and 3i Group. These figures simply measure the number of shares in issue, not the value of the shares or the performance of the shares. Simply the number. Figure 2A (Fundsmith) shows that there are 660m shares in issue at the start of the period in November 2019. The number of shares then declines to 630m by the summer of 2020 as investors take their money out. The fund then sees steady inflows from investors and rises to a peak of 700m shares by early 2022 before investors decide to take money out again and the number of shares declines to 656m.

Figure 2B (3i Group) is almost a straight line. This is because the fund started the period with 973m shares and ended the period with 973.4m shares. Fewer than a million new shares were created or redeemed.

This illustrates a key difference between open- and closed-ended funds. Fundsmith, the open-ended fund, had to sell investments when the line was falling to pay investors back their money and buy investments when the line was rising, to put the new money (from investor subscriptions) to work. 3i Group, on the other hand, was not forced to buy or sell any investments during the period. Whereas sellers of Fundsmith Equity Fund got their money back from Fundsmith when they redeemed, sellers of 3i Group got their money back by selling their shares to someone else in the market.

New shares can be issued or bought back periodically by an investment trust, but this is determined by the board rather than decided by investors.

Figure 2A: Fundsmith Equity Fund, shares outstanding (m)

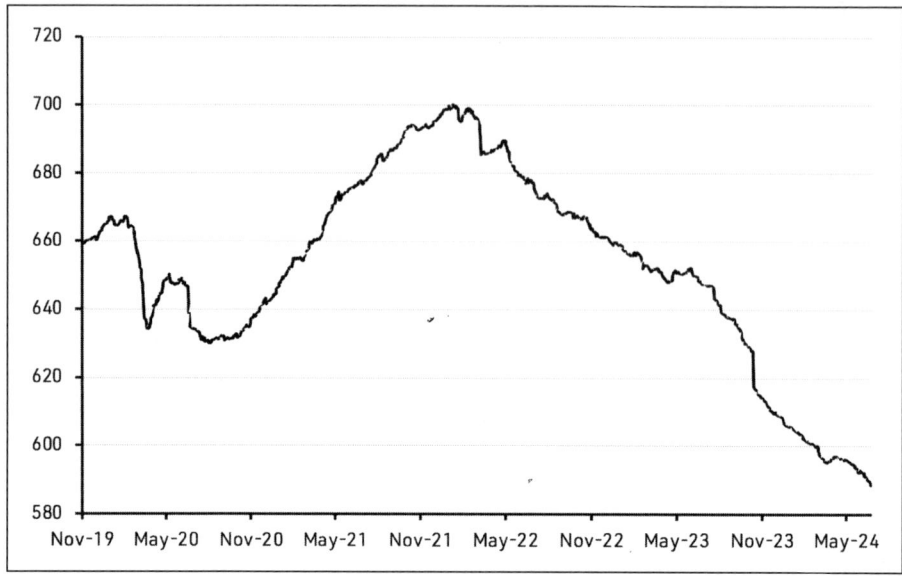

Source: Bloomberg

Figure 2B: 3i Group, shares outstanding (m)

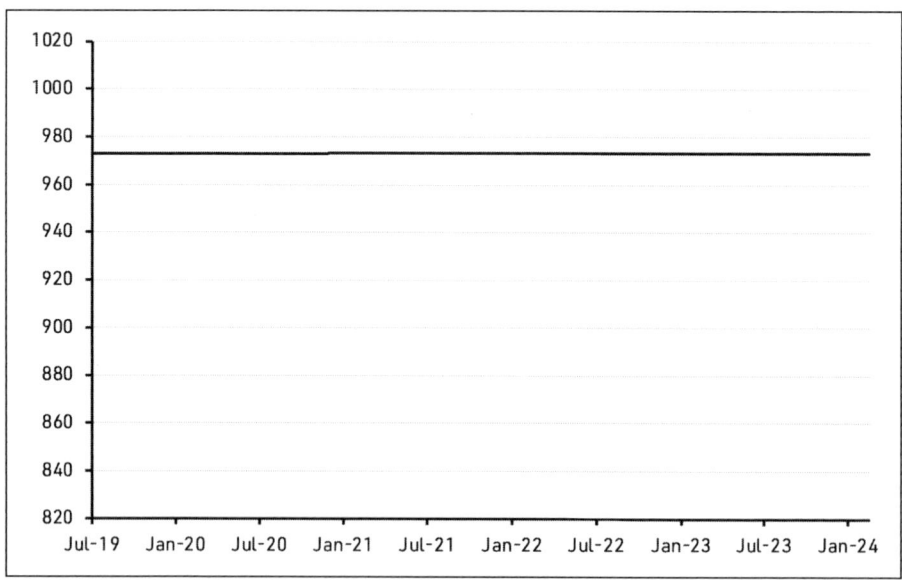

Source: Bloomberg

Now let's zoom in a bit more closely on the closed-ended fund part of Table 2A introduced earlier.

UK investment trusts

These make up the first and main closed-ended fund category. However, there are several nuances to be aware of within this broad umbrella term. Pure UK investment trust status confers some useful tax advantages, but to qualify requires formal approval from the UK tax authorities, that is His Majesty's Revenue & Customs (HMRC).

HMRC recognises UK investment trusts as a distinct type of company. As such, investment trusts are not liable to tax on gains in the value of their investments. However, a company must fulfil several conditions before HMRC can approve it. Various pieces of tax legislation (Section 842 of the Income and Corporation Taxes Act 1988, section 1158 of the Corporation Tax Act 2010 and the Investment Trust (Approved Company) Regulations 2011) outline these conditions.

> "HMRC recognises UK investment trusts as a distinct type of company. As such, investment trusts are not liable to tax on gains in the value of their investments."

Essentially, there are three principal conditions that a company must meet before HMRC can approve it as an investment trust:

1. The company must invest in shares, land or other recognised assets with the aim of spreading investment risk and giving members of the company the benefit of the results of the management of its funds.

2. Its shares should trade on a regulated market, such as the main market of the London Stock Exchange.

3. At least 85% of its net income (i.e. income received after costs) must be distributed.

The favourable tax status (i.e. no tax payable on capital gains) puts investment trusts on a level playing field with UK open-ended funds in terms of how gains are treated. However, investment trusts have greater flexibility in terms of gearing and dividend payments, amongst other things.

Other listed investment companies

It is worth noting that there are other investment companies which comply with these key requirements but do not have investment trust status. In all other respects they look and behave like a UK investment trust.

A key takeaway is that the term 'investment trust' is often used to refer to listed closed-ended investment companies, whether or not they have sought approval from HMRC. Many choose to be tax resident outside the UK. This is usually because the tax advantages in other jurisdictions may be even greater, or because the cost and administration burden is lower. There are, for example, more than 70 closed-ended investment companies listed on the London Stock Exchange which are tax resident in Guernsey and Jersey.

Since finance professionals and the media often refer to these companies as investment trusts, we will do the same and refer to all investment companies (except VCTs and REITs – discussed later), listed on one of the markets operated by the London Stock Exchange, as investment trusts.

Also, for ease of use, from this point onwards in the book, we will refer to open-ended funds, such as unit trusts and OEICs, as mutual funds.

REITS and VCTs

Two more types of closed-ended funds in Table 2A are also categorised as investment companies. These include real estate investment trusts (REITs), now a globally recognised investment vehicle. US Congress created the first REIT legislation in 1960 to facilitate investment in large-scale commercial property portfolios in a way that was as straightforward as buying conventional shares. American Realty Trust was the world's first of its type launched in 1961. Since then, governments have introduced REIT legislation in more than 30 countries including the UK, Ireland, Jamaica, Australia and Thailand.

Venture capital trusts (VCTs), on the other hand, are a specific form of investment company introduced by the UK government in 1995. In summary, VCTs encourage investment in early-stage UK companies. Investors receive several important tax breaks as an incentive to commit capital to high-risk companies. Their capital-raising success is evident in the fact that as of April 2024, VCTs had raised over £12bn and helped to finance companies such as Secret Escapes and Zoopla.

Limited partnerships

At the top level, the closed-ended fund category includes limited partnerships. The private equity and property sectors are active users of this type of structure, which is designed primarily for institutional or sophisticated investors. Capital is usually committed by investors (who become limited partners) upfront and then called upon by the general partner (usually the manager of the fund) when the right investment opportunities arise. A key advantage of this approach is that investors retain control of their cash until the manager has identified suitable investments on their behalf.

Within this sub-category we find the popular private equity limited partnership vehicles. They typically take capital from investors for a limited period, in return for giving them certain rights subject to a minimum 'lock-up' period, often of 7–10 years. This structure provides the private equity fund's managers with the flexibility to invest in illiquid assets (such as private companies). These can then be held for extended periods, which would be difficult to replicate within a conventional open-ended structure. Investors must accept that their money is not easily accessible. There may be a facility available to match buyers and sellers during the investment period but there are no guarantees.

With those parameters in place, these funds often have a two- or three-year initial investment period, during which the managers aim to identify investments and put investors' capital to work. This is followed by a 'harvesting' period during which they look to realise their underlying value. The general partner will then usually return initial capital (hopefully along with any gains) to the fund's investors. The limited shelf life mentioned earlier can ratchet up the pressure to invest quickly and realise investments early.

Just to complicate things further, several private equity investment trusts invest in limited partnership structures, as limited partners.

Under the bonnet of investment trusts

When an investment trust launches it has a clear set of objectives and parameters within which to achieve them. That said, they can be quite broad and flexible, such as, 'To maximise total return from a portfolio of long-term investments chosen on a global basis … to provide capital and dividend growth.' Or it might be very specific: 'The Company's aim is to provide investors with an annual dividend that increases in line with RPI inflation via the direct ownership of UK windfarms.'

One of the key benefits of an investment trust structure is that it allows the investment managers to make long-term decisions. This point was highlighted by Chambers and Esteves in their 2013 paper 'The First Global Emerging Markets Investor: Foreign & Colonial Investment Trust (FCIT) 1880–1913'. As they noted, during the market panics of 1890–93 and 1907:

> *FCIT continued with its careful buy-and-hold approach based on its ability to pursue a long-term investment horizon consequent upon its choice of a closed end fund structure. Unlike mutual funds which ... offered shareholders the facility to redeem units on a daily basis, this structure diverted the pressure of shareholders withdrawing their funds ... and left the managers free to hold onto their investment positions through the crisis.*

This is a distinct difference when compared to most collective investment schemes, such as mutual funds, most of which allow investors to add money and withdraw it at short notice. That, in turn, can constrain a portfolio manager's time horizon. A closed-ended structure provides the investment trust manager with the flexibility to invest in illiquid assets and to take a long-term view. Investors can, nonetheless, still buy or sell shares during the trading day should they wish to do so.

"A closed-ended structure provides the investment trust manager with the flexibility to invest in illiquid assets and to take a long-term view."

Further, buyers often get the opportunity to buy at a discount to the underlying NAV of the investments held, a point we covered in Chapter 1. This is not afforded to the holders of mutual funds. Let's take a quick look at why.

The key to understanding discounts is to realise that there is no obligation on the trust (as there is with, say, an ETF) to perfectly match supply and demand at the end of each business day. This means that the investment trust share price may not always accurately reflect the underlying value of the assets held. For example, an investment trust that issues a share at 100p with an underlying asset value of 98p (to reflect issue costs of 2p) may see its shares trade at perhaps 105p (a 'premium'), if demand is strong, or 95p (a 'discount') if it is weak. This feature can be seen as a good, or bad, one. Where it is the latter, as we will discover later, there are ways to try to address the underlying supply and demand mismatch.

SUMMARY OF KEY POINTS

- All funds can be categorised into open-ended (variable capital base) and closed-ended (fixed capital base).

- An investment trust is a type of closed-ended fund which is listed on the stock market.

- When an investment trust launches, it has a clear set of objectives.

- Investment trusts have greater flexibility than mutual funds, in terms of gearing and dividend payments, amongst other things.

- A closed-ended structure provides the investment trust manager with the flexibility to invest in illiquid assets and to take a long-term view.

CHAPTER 3

A BRIEF HISTORY OF INVESTMENT TRUSTS

"The object of the Trust is to give the investor of moderate means the same advantages as large Capitalists."

—Foreign & Colonial Government Trust prospectus

INVESTMENT TRUSTS HAVE a rich and colourful history. They have been in existence since 1868, which is a testament to both the robustness of the underlying structure and their ability to adapt to prevailing market conditions. Here are some of the highlights from the journey they have undertaken from their origins to the sector we see today.

Getting started

As previously noted in Chapter 1, the oldest example, the F&C Investment Trust (FCIT), was formed in 1868 as the Foreign & Colonial Government Trust. It became the Foreign and Colonial Investment Trust in 1891 and then, in 2018, the name was changed to the one we know it by now, F&C Investment Trust (FCIT).

In his 2017 book, *The Origins of Asset Management from 1700 to 1960*, Nigel Morecroft explains how the most common type of investment vehicle in 1868 was life assurance based. However, most life assurance companies adopted a very conservative investment approach based on holding sufficient capital to meet death claims. That left the field open to F&C to offer investors a way of committing their capital in exchange for a potentially more attractive yield, unfettered by the liability considerations that restricted life assurers.

F&C's initial target was a return of 7% (double the yield available on UK gilts at the time) over a period of 24 years. It aimed to achieve this by taking investors' money in return for its own shares and then investing the capital it received in a diversified portfolio. Although 24 years was the original investment horizon, investors could enter and exit at any time by buying or selling their interest in F&C. It also boasted further attractive features, such as strong governance, accessibility, diversification, a global reach and a cash reserve. As the prospectus put it at the time:

> *The object of the Trust is to give the investor of moderate means the same advantages as large Capitalists, in diminishing the risk of investing ... by spreading the investment over a number of different Stocks and reserving a portion of the interest as a Sinking Fund to pay off the original capital.*

These features made it a refreshing new offering and was especially true when compared to existing insurance policies and bank deposit accounts. At the time, the only alternative direct investments available were investing in land or in bonds issued by companies and governments.

Five professional trustees were responsible for overseeing the trust. These included its architect, Philip Rose, a lawyer, former adviser to Prime Minister Benjamin Disraeli, and the 'Rose' in what would become the well-known legal firm of Norton Rose.

Investing primarily in sterling-denominated assets via the London Stock Exchange, F&C adopted a 'buy and hold' investment approach. The initial portfolio comprised 18 government bonds issued by 15 countries, including Argentina, Egypt and the US. The prospectus indicated a maximum issue size of £1,000,025 (compared to FCIT's assets now of c. £5bn) and management expenses were not to exceed £2,500 per year, implying an annual management fee of about 0.25% (compared to c. 0.29% today).

Following suit

Imitation being the best form of flattery, other investment trusts followed F&C's lead. The first Scottish vehicle launched in 1873. Originally the Scottish American Investment Trust (not to be confused with the Scottish American Investment Company Limited, or SAINTS, also formed in 1873 and still trading today), it became the First Scottish American Trust and then in 1990 changed its name to Dunedin Income Growth, by which it is still known today. Scottish American improved on the F&C offering by granting its trustees the power to sell investments as well as buy them. Around 80% of its original portfolio was made up of bonds issued by US railroad companies.

The floodgates were by now well and truly open, which was both good and bad news. As *The Economist* put it in 1880 (Walker, 1940):

> *...after one or two had been placed successfully, they became the rage, and others were brought out which offered impossible returns to the buyers of their securities. To effect this end, risks were incurred which, had their subscribers been informed beforehand respecting them, would have effectually disposed of those trusts altogether. They promised great returns but hid the means whereby those results were to be attained.*

That heritage might help to explain why only 17 trusts that launched before 1900 still survive today (Table 3A).

Table 3A: The oldest investment trusts still in existence

Investment Trust	Ticker	Inception date
F&C Investment Trust	FCIT	1868-03-19
Investment Company	INV	1868-11-14
Dunedin Income Growth	DIG	1873-02-01
Scottish American	SAIN	1873-03-31
JPMorgan American	JAM	1881-06-18
Mercantile	MRC	1884-12-08
JPMorgan Global Growth & Income	JGGI	1887-04-21
Henderson Smaller Companies	HSL	1887-12-16
Bankers	BNKR	1888-04-13
Alliance Witan	ALW	1888-04-21
The Global Smaller Companies Trust	GSCT	1889-02-15
Merchants Trust	MRCH	1889-02-16
Edinburgh Investment	EDIN	1889-03-01
AVI Global Trust	AGT	1889-07-01
Law Debenture Corporation	LWDB	1889-12-12
City of London	CTY	1891-01-01
abrdn Diversified Income & Growth*	ADIG	1898-01-05

Note that some of the trust names stated here may not be the original trust names. *In managed wind-down.

Source: Morningstar, 31/12/2024

Claims to fame

Many well-known figures have been associated with investment trusts through the years, which helps to explain their longevity. John Newlands brings many of these personalities to life in his 1997 book, *Put Not Your Money In Trust*. The Scottish American Investment Trust, for example, was conceived by Robert Fleming. A man from modest beginnings in Dundee, he later went on to form Fleming's bank. He was also grandfather to Ian Fleming, the author of the James Bond novels.

Then there was John Maynard Keynes, the renowned economist and philosopher, who was involved with the Independent Investment Trust, established in 1924. One of his fellow trustees was Thomas Carlyle Gifford, a founder of Baillie Gifford, the Edinburgh-based investment management firm. Unfortunately, by deploying a market timing approach, which aimed to move capital between asset classes based on a reading of the credit cycle, the trust incurred significant losses which were compounded by leverage and the Wall Street Crash of 1929. Remarkably, given that backdrop, the Independent Investment Trust survived the Great Depression and ran until 2022, at which point it decided to wind up.

Meanwhile, Alexander Graham Bell, the inventor of the telephone, had a brother William who was a senior partner at Bell & Begg. They were stockbrokers to the Edinburgh American Land Mortgage Company (EALM), which became the subject of one of the earliest acquisitions in the investment trust sector. In 1920, British Assets Trust (now abrdn Diversified Income & Growth), acquired the share capital of EALM, renaming it in 1925 as the Second British Assets Trust Ltd.

As we sweep forward right up to the present day, the list of names associated with these vehicles includes Herbert Hoover, the 31st President of the US; Edwin Waterhouse, a founder of accountancy giant PricewaterhouseCoopers; Norman Lamont, a former Chancellor of the Exchequer; Edward Bonham Carter, the brother of actor Helena Bonham Carter; Sir John Kay, CBE, the British economist and first dean of Oxford's Saïd Business School; Sir John Templeton, the legendary investor and founder of the Templeton Growth Fund; and Anthony Bolton, who made his name at Fidelity.

Investment trusts have not been immune to controversy and some less respectable associations, however. For example, Robert Maxwell, the disgraced media tycoon, was behind several controversial predatory raids in the 1980s. Some years later, Bramdean Alternatives, an investment trust launched in 2007, was tarnished by losing 9.5% of its assets, which were held in trading accounts managed by the fraudster, Bernie Madoff.

Wrapping up

Those reputational headwinds aside, it is fair to say that investment trusts have served their original purpose well, which has been to provide investors of moderate means with a way of accessing investments that had previously only been available to the wealthiest in society. In the next chapter, we will explore this further, alongside some of the other societal benefits that investment trusts have brought to the financial world.

SUMMARY OF KEY POINTS

- The first investment trust, the F&C Investment Trust, was formed in 1868 as the Foreign & Colonial Government Trust.

- F&C adopted a 'buy and hold' investment approach, with the initial portfolio comprising 18 government bonds issued by 15 countries, including Argentina, Egypt and the US.

- The first Scottish vehicle, the Scottish American Investment Trust, launched in 1873 and improved on F&C by granting its trustees the power to sell investments as well as buy them.

- The Scottish American Investment Trust was the brainchild of Robert Fleming, the grandfather of Ian Fleming, the author of the James Bond novels.

- However, investment trusts have not been immune to controversy and some less respectable associations.

CHAPTER 4

SOCIETAL BENEFITS: DIVERSIFIED SAVINGS VEHICLES, SOURCES OF LONG-TERM CAPITAL

"Society is always taken by surprise at any new example of common sense."

—Ralph Waldo Emerson, US essayist, philosopher and abolitionist

INVESTMENT TRUSTS ARE great common-sense investments and can play a significant role in society. They do this not just through their ability to generate wealth but also by promoting financial inclusion, supporting innovation and bolstering overall economic stability. We will look at these in a bit more depth here.

Accessing markets

In 1868, the F&C Government Trust prospectus stated its purpose as, "to give the investor of moderate means the same advantages as the large capitalist ... by spreading the risk over a number of different stocks" (Scratchley, 1875). Back then stockbroking services were the preserve of the wealthiest members of society. So, the arrival of investment trusts offered smaller investors a way of participating in shares that would otherwise have been almost impossible to access. As such, investment trusts have continued to help widen financial inclusion right up until the present day.

"Investment trusts have continued to help widen financial inclusion right up until the present day."

So much so that the wealth of investment opportunities on offer today to retail investors spans biotechnology, early-stage fintech, space-related investments, hedge fund strategies, infrastructure, private equity and renewable energy. Many of these areas were once the preserve of large, sophisticated investors such as Family Offices, University Endowments, Large Pension Funds and Sovereign Wealth Funds. This is therefore a welcome trend.

Expanding knowledge

Investment trusts also provide investors with access to useful information and resources related to investing in financial markets. Most, for example, have websites where anyone can find out about market trends, as well as a trust's investment strategy and performance. This information can help investors to learn and make informed decisions. Many investment trusts also publish regular reports on their investment strategies and some of these provide insightful summaries and guidance about specific sectors.

The manager's section in the Polar Capital Technology Trust's annual report, for example, is excellent reading and covers all the topical developments in the key technology sub-sectors. As such, it is in some ways a 'must read'. Elsewhere, the equivalent section within the TR Property Investment Trust annual report is essential reading for property investors. It provides an interesting overview of how interest rates and supply / demand dynamics have influenced the market over the year and delves into the various sub-sectors such as offices, industrial and residential. It also provides the reader with a steer on the most attractive opportunities both now and further out.

The Association of Investment Companies (the trade body for investment trusts) also provides a wealth of information about investment trusts, including educational resources for investors of all levels of experience. It also offers several training courses and workshops.

"The manager's section in the Polar Capital Technology Trust's annual report ... is excellent reading and covers all the topical developments in the key technology sub-sectors."

Supporting growth

Most investment trusts invest in stock markets around the world. These, in turn, provide a means of funding ideas and, in doing so, help businesses to accelerate their growth, creating employment and prosperity. For example, there is currently around £5bn invested in investment trusts which invest in small UK listed companies. This represents material financial capital for businesses that rely on long-term investors to help them finance new projects and scale up.

Naturally, investment trust managers seek to invest in productive assets. These include shares in, or loans to, companies that produce goods and services, or direct investments in infrastructure or property. All help to support economic growth.

Some investment trusts invest in early-stage businesses. Take Augmentum Fintech (AUGM), an investment trust that specialises in fintech businesses and has a holding in Zopa, the financial services company formed in 2004. Zopa became the world's first peer-to-peer lender in 2005 and was in the initial Augmentum portfolio when it launched on the stock market in 2018. AUGM subsequently provided further funding before Zopa received a full UK banking licence in 2020. Zopa now has more than 800,000 customers and employs more than 700 people. This is just one example of how investment trusts can help businesses to scale up, create employment and contribute to the wider economy.

Turning to bonds (in effect tradeable loans issued by companies), Invesco Bond Income Plus is an example of an investment trust that holds securities issued by B&M Stores, British Airways, Gatwick Airport, Ocado and Travis Perkins. Once a bond is issued, the capital that it raises is then available to the issuing company to help it expand operations or refinance more expensive debt. Structured in the right way, this can be a win-win.

Boosting spending

The stock and bond markets also support consumer spending and investment via the 'wealth effect'. When the stock market is rising, investors tend to feel wealthier and are more likely to spend money on goods and services. This can boost economic growth. Equally, when investment trusts generate positive returns, investors may choose to spend some of their gains. Many investment trusts, particularly those focused on income generation, also provide regular dividend payments to investors. And whilst there is an argument for reinvesting them, the reality is that some are used immediately. Investors often use investment trusts as long-term vehicles for their retirement savings. As people accumulate wealth in this way, they should become more confident in their financial future, a factor that can also boost their willingness to spend.

"Investors often use investment trusts as long-term vehicles for their retirement savings."

Helping charities

Some investment trusts make regular donations to charity. Not all investors agree with this approach, preferring to independently target their own causes. However, if channelled correctly, these funds can deliver a meaningful impact over time. The Battle Against Cancer Investment Trust (BACIT) is an example of a trust that has made material charitable contributions whilst also making some great strategic investments. Launched on the London market in 2012, BACIT aimed to provide an attractive return from a portfolio of leading investment funds across multiple asset classes. BACIT was unique at the time in that the underlying funds did not charge it any management or performance fees. The management team also provided their services free of charge. The trust made an annual donation of 1% of its NAV to charity, with half of it going to the Institute of Cancer Research (ICR) and half to the BACIT Foundation, for onward distribution to other charities.

Meanwhile, in the same year that BACIT launched, the Wellcome Trust set up Syncona Partners, a venture capital division, with a long-term vision of building innovative life science businesses. Then, in December 2016, BACIT expanded its investment policy to allow it to make life science investments alongside its existing commitments. In conjunction with this change of policy, and change of fee structure, Syncona Partners took over as managers of the investment trust and BACIT changed its name to Syncona Limited, a vehicle in which Wellcome Trust became, and remains, the largest shareholder. This transaction provided the investment trust with a portfolio of life science investments, together with a highly regarded investment management team.

Dr Jeremy Farrar, Director of the Wellcome Trust, said at the time: "We launched Syncona with a long-term vision to offer backing to some of the best innovators in life sciences and to deliver impact to patients."

Since its launch in 2012, BACIT / Syncona has made charitable donations of almost £50m. The trust has also helped to seed and develop new life science companies. In essence, it creates, builds and scales portfolio companies to become standalone entities that create jobs, train employees and share knowledge with others in the sector. Over 1,200 people are now employed by Syncona and its portfolio companies, with trials in clinical development spanning 19 sites across the UK. Although the SYNC share price has declined markedly from its 2018 high, this trust holds a portfolio of promising young biotechnology companies and trades at a substantial discount to its net asset value.

> "BACIT was unique ... in that the underlying funds did not charge it any management or performance fees."

Literacy Capital, an investment trust that provides growth capital to UK businesses, also has a mission to advance the education of children in the UK. It aims to achieve this mission by promoting or supporting the development of literacy. The trust, which uses the stock market identifier BOOK, makes an annual donation to charities focused on improving UK literacy. By committing an annual percentage of its net assets, it has provided material support to its chosen charities. Since the creation of Literacy Capital in 2017, more than £11.6m has been donated to charities focused on improving UK literacy. The charitable donation is in addition to management fees.

Wrapping up

The accessibility, diversification, professional management and long-term focus of many investment trusts makes them a valuable tool for individuals and institutions looking to build and preserve wealth. Furthermore, the fact that they can offer benefits which span financial education, job creation and efficient capital allocation also makes them an important component of a healthy and prosperous economy.

SUMMARY OF KEY POINTS

- The first investment trust launched with the objective of giving the investor of moderate means the same advantages as the large capitalist.

- Investment trusts provide useful information which can help investors to learn and make informed investment decisions.

- Stock markets provide a means of funding ideas and, in doing so, help businesses to accelerate their growth, creating employment and prosperity.

- Investors often use investment trusts as long-term vehicles for their retirement savings.

- Some investment trusts make regular donations to charity. Since its launch in 2012, Syncona has made charitable donations of almost £50m.

CHAPTER 5

INVESTMENT TRUST STRUCTURES

"Simplicity is the ultimate sophistication."
**—Leonardo da Vinci,
Italian polymath**

MOST INVESTMENT TRUSTS have a simple capital structure comprising solely of ordinary shares, along with a modest amount of borrowing. However, a small number of trusts use, or have used, a variation of this capital structure, issuing different share classes with varying rights. Although these, less simple, trusts are in a minority, and although some would argue that many of these variants are a thing of the past, I think it is important to be aware of them.

The chapter also revisits two of the most important and distinctive features of investment trusts – their ability to take on gearing and trade at a discount (or premium) to their underlying NAV.

Raising money

Investment trusts raise capital from investors when they first come to market, typically in exchange for ordinary shares. As such, most have a simple structure, with a single type of 'ordinary share' in issue. Each represents a shareholder's portion of the investment trust's value and entitles them to receive their allocation of any dividends paid. They also expose the holder to any capital growth (or share price downside) and confer the right to vote on matters regarding the investment trust. However, beyond this straightforward arrangement, there are a few twists.

Voting and non-voting shares

A very small number of investment trusts have issued securities that come with varying rights. The difference between them usually lies in their voting rights. Take the Hansa Investment Company, which invests via a portfolio of underlying funds. The trust has two separate share classes, both of which are traded on the London Stock Exchange. The ordinary shareholders are entitled to one vote per ordinary share held. The 'A' non-voting ordinary shares do not entitle the holders to vote or receive notice of meetings, but in all other respects they have the same rights as the company's ordinary shares.

C shares

Investment trusts may also issue C shares. These enable different investment pools to be merged in an equitable manner. C shares usually only exist for a brief period to allow for the segregation of certain rights.

Cordiant Digital Infrastructure is a trust that invests in assets such as mobile networks and data centres. The trust initially came to market in February 2021, raising £370m via ordinary shares. Most of this capital was committed to two large investments within the first three months of the trust's life. However, the managers subsequently identified some further opportunities that needed additional capital. Raising it via another ordinary share issue could have presented a problem in so far as it would have diluted the stakes of existing shareholders. That's because raising additional capital can create 'cash drag' when the associated funds are left in cash prior to being committed. Enter 'C' shares. These were issued separately by Cordiant in June 2021 with the sole purpose of making additional acquisitions.

This class of share is subsequently converted into ordinary shares but only once the portfolio managers have invested any new capital in a way that fairly reflects the value of each equity pool (being the pre-existing ordinary shares and these newer ones), whilst being transparent with both sets of shareholders. Following conversion, everyone holds ordinary shares and has the same rights.

Dual shares

Some investors are risk averse and need income. Other investors are risk tolerant and desire capital growth. These differing needs led to the birth of the dual share class investment trust, one where the same underlying pool of assets could be used to serve two separate investor interests.

Whilst split capital trusts became very popular in the 1990s the very first dual structure share class was born as early as 1873, according to John Newlands (Adams, 2005):

> *...the 38 year-old Scots lawyer [William Menzies]*
> *knew that he had two main classes of client, who can*
> *be summarised respectively as the risk tolerant (e.g.*
> *wealthier individuals) and the risk averse ('widows and*
> *orphans'). To meet their very different investment needs,*
> *Menzies chose to ignore the legal trust structure used*
> *by F&C and its early successors. Instead his brainchild,*
> *SAINTS [The Scottish American Investment Company],*
> *was formed from day one not just as a limited liability*
> *company but one with a dual-purpose capital structure.*

The widows and orphans share class (a debenture) offered a fixed 5.5% in perpetuity, with the other share class receiving all excess returns, that is bearing the risk of failure if returns (after costs) were less than 5.5% or enjoying the rewards of any success if they were greater.

During the 1990s, this dual share structure developed a step further as other classes were issued. The market referred to the resulting vehicles as 'split capital' trusts. The capital that investors contributed was literally 'split' across distinct types of shares and security. Single trusts with more than one share class still exist today, albeit they are not very common.

Zero Dividend Preference Shares (ZDPs)

These were favoured by the split capital investment trusts that became popular in the 1990s, as trust sponsors sought to satiate investors' appetite for a triple whammy of high income, defined returns and capital gains, accessed via different share classes.

ZDPs are a type of security that entitles the holder to a predefined return ahead of ordinary shareholders. For example, the NB Private Equity Trust issued a ZDP in 2018 which entitled the holder to receive the equivalent of a 4.25% compound return up to the point it was wound up in October 2024. The price of this sort of preference share tends to reflect prevailing interest rates, as well as the likelihood that there will be sufficient assets to fund their ultimate redemption.

That important caveat was tested in the early 2000s when a combination of high debt levels and declining stock markets left several split capital trusts unable to meet their liabilities. Many split capital trusts bought shares in other split capital trusts, creating a form of pyramid scheme that would eventually collapse. In some cases, both ordinary shares and ZDPs were rendered worthless during a spell the media dubbed the 'split cap crisis'.

However, the principle behind a ZDP is a sound one. The success, though, depends on the underlying assets being sufficient in value to support the final payout to the ZDP holders. Today, the few ZDPs in issue tend to be associated with trusts that invest in illiquid assets (e.g. private equity or property). They do so to fill the gap created by a lack of economical bank funding or a desire to conserve cash flow by deferring what would otherwise be interest on conventional borrowings.

Debentures

By contrast, many large investment trusts that operate portfolios of liquid assets, such as quoted shares, borrow using debentures. As a form of 'IOU' or bond, they enable a trust to lock into attractive long-term borrowing rates. They tend to appeal to pension and life insurance funds, which often like to hold them to maturity.

Subscription shares and warrants

The presence of discounts to NAV (which we have touched on earlier and will return to shortly) presents a dilemma for a new investment trust wishing to raise capital. That's because investors may prefer to avoid buying at an IPO, knowing that they may be able to acquire shares later, at a discount. Warrants and subscription shares can offer a solution to this dilemma. Investors who commit to the initial capital raise receive these securities as part of the process and are then entitled to use them to buy further shares on attractive terms. As such, they act as an incentive to encourage participation in IPOs.

Having looked at the different types of shares that may be issued by investment trusts, we will now revisit a couple of their key distinguishing features – gearing, and the fact they can trade at premiums or discounts to their underlying value.

Gearing up

Investment trusts are permitted to 'gear', that is use borrowed money for investment purposes, and this can add significant shareholder value over time.

In a nutshell, the term 'gearing' reflects the use of borrowed money for investment purposes. Provided a trust can borrow on attractive terms and deploy the resulting capital into sensible investments, gearing can enhance investment returns. Table 5A shows how this might work using four examples.

Table 5A: Gearing examples

Example	A	B	C	D
Capital invested (Equity)	£50,000	£50,000	£300,000	£300,000
Borrowed funds / Mortgage	£300,000	£300,000	£50,000	£50,000
Total invested / Purchase price	£350,000	£350,000	£350,000	£350,000
Level of gearing (Borrowings / Total invested)	86%	86%	14%	14%
Total growth over 10 years	65%	−25%	148%	−25%
Value after 10 years	£577,500	£262,500	£868,000	£262,500
Loan / Mortgage outstanding	£300,000	£300,000	£50,000	£50,000
Investor's capital	£277,500	−£37,500	£818,000	£212,500
Return on investor's capital (Equity)	455%	−75%	173%	−29%

In the upper section, we have two scenarios A and B. In A, a house is being purchased for £350,000, with a £50,000 deposit and £300,000 of mortgage debt. That equates to a gearing level, or 'Loan To Value', of 86% (£300,000 / £350,000).

Examples C and D, on the other hand, reflect equity portfolios where the investor's initial capital is £300,000 and borrowed funds are £50,000. That means the gearing level is 14% (£50,000 / £350,000). This is typical for an investment trust that invests in the stock market, where the gearing range is usually 0% to 25%.

To keep things simple, I ignore borrowing costs and assume the debt levels remain constant over time.

Further down the table, we assume that the property in scenario A grows by 65% to reflect the rise in UK house prices over the 10-year period ended 31/08/2023 (UK Land Registry, Bloomberg). The equity portfolio in scenario C, on the other hand, grows by 173%, being the capital return on the MSCI World Index over the same timeframe. When we then deduct any debt (whether in the form of borrowing or a mortgage) from the total value after 10 years, we arrive at the amount of free capital remaining to investors.

Turning to what that means as a percentage return on an investor's original capital, we can see that the property in the first example produces a larger overall gain (+455%) than the stock market-based example C (+173%). That is even though the return achieved on property (+65%) was well below that achieved by the stock market (+148%). This is because the property investment was much more highly geared, as they often tend to be. Nonetheless, we can see that even 14% gearing has boosted the investment trust's return from 148% to 173%.

By contrast, however, scenarios B and D reveal the risk that leverage creates when used to purchase an asset that subsequently declines in value. In B, we are assuming that the property purchase was identical to example A. However, instead of rising 65% in value over 10 years, it declines by 25%. Although 25% may look like an extreme scenario, UK house prices declined as much as 17.5% between November 2007 and April 2009 (UK House Price Index. Source: UK Land Registry, Bloomberg). I use 25% as a nice round number to illustrate the negative impact of gearing in a way that most people can relate to. In example B, that leaves the overall investment in a severe 'negative equity' situation, where borrowings exceed the value of the underlying asset by 75%. Example D, meanwhile, shows an equity portfolio with the same 14% gearing level as scenario C. Here, the equity portfolio also declines by 25% over the same 10-year period to generate a painful, but less precipitous drop of –29%.

This all illustrates how gearing can work in your favour when asset values are rising but against you when they are falling. The overall level is therefore important, since high gearing combined with declining asset values can be disastrous. Little wonder, therefore, that the boards of most investment trusts keep a close eye on it. Equally, any bank which lends money to an investment trust will insist on certain covenants – conditions that must be adhered to such as the absolute level of gearing and the extent to which income covers interest payments. They may even mandate the minimum level of portfolio diversification. A breach of such terms can result in a bank taking control of the underlying assets.

> "One of the greatest case studies in how to use cheap borrowing effectively is Berkshire Hathaway, the investment vehicle managed by Warren Buffett."

In terms of real-life examples, one of the greatest case studies in how to use cheap borrowing effectively is Berkshire Hathaway, the investment vehicle managed by Warren Buffett. The investment community widely regards Buffett as one of the most successful investors since the mid-1970s. That's in part because for decades Berkshire Hathaway has used the cheap funding available from its reinsurance operations to buy and hold stocks for the long term. So much so that a paper by Frazzini et al. (2018) estimates that much of the firm's performance is attributable to the use of leverage: "In essence, we find that the secret to Buffett's success is his preference for cheap, safe, high-quality stocks combined with his consistent use of leverage to magnify returns while surviving the inevitable large absolute and relative drawdowns this entails."

By contrast, some of the biggest mistakes made by investment trusts can be ascribed to poor decisions concerning leverage. For an extreme example, we could look back at the 1920s, a period during which many US trusts took on huge levels of debt. That was to prove fatal when the Wall Street Crash came in 1929. In his book, *The Great Crash 1929*, Galbraith (1954) notes:

> *The common stock [of the highly leveraged trust] would have nothing behind it. Apart from expectations, which were by no means bright, it was now worthless. This geometrical ruthlessness was not exceptional. On the contrary, it was everywhere at work on the stock of the leveraged trusts.*

That is why gearing is one of several factors that investors must be alert to when looking at investment trusts. However, it is important to bear in mind that many trusts have zero gearing (i.e. borrowings / net assets).

Discounts and premiums

Any analysis of investment trust structures would not be complete without discussing this last area.

As a reminder, a mutual fund with adequate liquidity can match redemption requests and new subscriptions with sales and purchases of its underlying assets. Investment trusts, on the other hand, operate with a fixed number of shares in issue. This can lead to a mismatch, such that the market value of the investment trust and that of its underlying portfolio can deviate, in some cases markedly.

To help investors, most investment trusts publish a regular NAV. This is an estimate of the value of the underlying assets underpinning each of its own shares. For example, let's say that the net value (i.e. after deducting any debt or costs) of a trust's equity portfolio is £100m, based on the market prices of the underlying company shares it holds. If it also has 100m of its own shares in issue, they will have an NAV of £1 each (£100m / 100m).

In theory, these investment trust shares should trade in the market right now at £1. However, that price may then change as supply and demand for that fixed number of shares rises and falls. Where there is strong demand, perhaps because the trust is strongly in favour with investors, they will move above £1 (to trade at a 'premium' to NAV). The reverse situation, triggered by a fund's strategy drifting out of favour, can create the opposite scenario and give rise to an associated 'discount'.

"The tendency for investment trust share prices to deviate from their NAV offers an opportunity for the board of an investment trust to add additional value."

The tendency for investment trust share prices to deviate from their NAV offers an opportunity for the board of an investment trust to add additional value. That's because the trust can time the issuance of new shares and buy back existing ones when it is financially attractive to do so. For example, issuing new shares at a price above NAV should add value for existing shareholders, as should buying back shares at a discount and cancelling them. This useful ('sell high and buy low') strategy is not available to mutual funds and it can therefore give investment trusts an edge over the long term.

Wrapping up

Having covered some of the key features of investment trusts, we must now turn to some important investing principles that underpin both their historic longevity and ability to generate long-term returns. The next chapter will focus on one of the most important and powerful of these – compounding.

SUMMARY OF KEY POINTS

- Most investment trusts have a simple capital structure, with a single type of 'ordinary share' in issue.

- Some investment trusts issue securities that come with varying rights. The difference between them usually lies in their voting rights.

- Investment trusts may also issue C shares, which enable different investment pools to be merged in an equitable manner.

- Zero dividend preference shares (ZDPs) are a type of security, sometimes issued by investment trusts, that entitle the holder to a predefined return and ranking ahead of ordinary shareholders.

- Investment trusts are permitted to 'gear', that is use borrowed money for investment purposes, and this can add significant shareholder value over time.

PART 2

HOW INVESTMENT TRUSTS WORK / ADVANTAGES AND STRENGTHS OF INVESTMENT TRUSTS / COMPARING AND ANALYSING INVESTMENT TRUSTS

CHAPTER 6

THE STAKEHOLDERS

"To make progress we have to build a multi-stakeholder process, harnessing the appropriate energies."
**—Mary Robinson,
first female President of Ireland**

THOSE WORDS FROM Mary Robinson frame what follows in this chapter. So, let's start off by considering what we mean by the word 'stakeholder'. Naturally, it captures any party that has an ownership stake, via their shareholding, in an investment trust. We will be returning to shareholders in Chapter 7. We will also cover the independent board in Chapter 11 and then the fund management function in Chapter 19. However, here I want to home in on the other players who are also necessary to an investment trust's efficient functioning. Although you are unlikely to have much, if any, contact with them as an investor, or be able to directly influence their actions, an awareness of who they are and the functions they provide is useful.

From the top

What follows is not intended to be an exhaustive list, but it does contain most of the important stakeholders involved in the launch and operation of an investment trust:

- Accountants
- Administrators
- Association of Investment Companies (AIC)
- Board of directors
- Custodians
- Depositaries
- Financial Conduct Authority (FCA)
- Independent consultants
- Independent valuers
- Investment / portfolio managers
- Investment banks
- Lawyers
- London Stock Exchange
- Media
- PR companies
- Registrars
- Shareholders
- Third-party analysts.

Defining terms

Here is a summary of what each of these contributors brings to the table.

Accountants

These professionals provide a range of services to investment trusts. They include providing an opinion as to the fairness and reasonableness of asset valuations, auditing the trust's interim and year-end accounts, and providing advice on reporting procedures, alongside general tax matters. An accountant can also draft separate reports that meet specific regulatory requirements and assist the directors, or a sponsor, when it comes to fulfilling their wider obligations.

Administrators

Responsible for providing administration services, they often act as company secretary too. Their specific role normally includes maintaining the books and financial accounts, as well as overseeing the calculation of the NAV of the trust. In return, an administrator typically receives a monthly fee, either as a flat amount or based on a percentage of assets. For UK-based trusts these fees are subject to VAT.

The Association of Investment Companies (AIC)

The trade body for the investment trust sector is funded by investment trusts and carries out several very useful functions. These include marketing, press relations, governance guidance, plus lobbying HMRC and the Treasury. Their website also provides access to a wealth of information for the private investor. We will revisit this in Chapter 40.

Board of directors

The role of an investment trust board is to provide oversight and ensure that investment objectives are being met. That is why they are typically comprised of people with relevant industry experience. This could be evidenced by a background in portfolio management, knowledge of the sector or particular geography that a trust is focused on, experience in marketing investment trusts, an understanding of how their financing works, or wider skills drawn from general accounting, legal and governance roles. We will revisit this topic in Chapter 11.

Custodians

Custodians are responsible for the safekeeping of the investment trust's assets, such as shares. They look after physical and electronic custody, handling settlements and transactions, and maintaining accurate records of holdings. The custodian is usually a large, financially sound, global business – examples include JPMorgan Chase Bank and Royal Bank of Canada.

Depositaries

This role supplements the last one by going beyond safekeeping and into the monitoring of cash flows, foreign exchange, cash management, income collection and tax reclamation. Northern Trust is one of the largest global players in this space and is used by many investment trusts.

Financial Conduct Authority (FCA)

The FCA regulates the financial services industry in the UK. It aims to protect consumers, maintain market integrity and promote competition. The FCA's rules on financial promotions and disclosure govern how investment trusts can be marketed to investors. The FCA oversees the activities of investment management companies to ensure they comply with regulatory requirements.

Independent consultants

These are individuals and firms that can provide independent, that is unconflicted, advice to boards. The boards typically seek such independent advice when considering or dealing with exceptional events, such as strategic reviews or shareholder disputes.

Independent valuers

These are specialists who are normally instructed by the board to provide third-party valuations for any assets where there is no freely available market price provided on a tradeable exchange or via multiple competing counterparties. Common examples include private businesses or properties. Valuers play a vital role as their opinion is normally used by the board to determine the NAV. The basis of the valuation is therefore usually laid out in the annual report, or in the listing prospectus in the case of an IPO. We will cover valuation approaches in Chapter 18.

Investment / portfolio managers

The investment manager is the firm that has been instructed by the board to manage the trust's portfolio assets. The portfolio manager, or managers, are then the named individuals that are responsible for the day-to-day management of the portfolio. Both tend to have a higher profile than the board itself, typically because they have developed a strong reputation based on previous investment performance, or thanks to their own marketing efforts. The latter may encompass promoting certain individuals in conjunction with other funds that the manager runs. BlackRock, JPMorgan and Schroder are examples of investment management companies that manage several trusts. We will come back to this in more detail in Chapter 19.

Investment banks

These may be described as a trust's corporate financiers. That means they seek to raise finance and advise on financial matters. Although there are many such firms in the UK, a lot of which operate in niche areas, when it comes to investment trusts most corporate finance involvement comes from investment banks.

These differ from traditional banks in that their main source of income is not based on taking deposits and making loans, but rather a range of investment and trading-related activities. The list of activities is long and includes raising capital for companies, acting as their broker, making a two-way market in their shares and producing research.

For listed investment trusts the capital raising fee charged by investment banks is typically 1.0–1.5% of the amount raised, with all costs (i.e. including legal, accounting, etc.) usually capped at 2.0%. The London Stock Exchange rules demand that all companies, including investment trusts, seeking a main market listing must appoint and use a sponsor. The sponsor is usually an investment bank tasked with guiding the relevant investment trust through the application and admission process. The sponsoring bank may also advise on the FCA's legal requirements.

Further, it will often help an investment trust not only to raise sufficient capital at its initial launch through various marketing and networking activities but also maintain ongoing demand for its shares. Post launch, the bank can provide guidance on raising further capital, which may come via loans and debt securities as well as additional equity finance. It may also advise on matters such as diversifying the shareholder base, acting as a conduit between the board and shareholders, and the best way to manage any discount or premium that arises between the share price and NAV.

When a company lists on the London Stock Exchange, its broker is obliged to make a two-way market in the shares, that is provide a price at which it is willing to buy shares from sellers as well as sell shares to buyers. This is known as market making. Several banks would normally provide this service to any given investment trust, helping to facilitate good ongoing liquidity in its shares.

An investment bank usually produces research on the trust it is sponsoring. However, given the commercial relationship between such a bank and an investment trust, there is a potential conflict of interest. That is why the FCA's Rulebook distinguishes between independent research (which should be objective) and non-independent research, which must be clearly labelled as marketing.

Lawyers

Their main tasks include producing the trust's corporate 'constitution', known as the memorandum and articles of association, along with any issuing prospectus. They also advise on legal issues that might arise on admission to the stock market, including the necessary disclosure requirements and continuing obligations. Lawyers may also be instructed when a conflict requires resolution, for example between the board and the investment manager.

London Stock Exchange

UK investment trusts are usually listed on the London Stock Exchange for capital raising and subsequent trading purposes.

Media

Several newspapers and magazines make regular references to investment trusts as they are well suited to retail investors. As such, the media can play a useful role in highlighting them to anyone who may not be aware of their existence, as well as flagging trusts that may have undeservedly drifted out of favour.

> "Money Makers is an excellent weekly podcast run by the writer Jonathan Davis. It covers all the key news stories in the investment trust sector and provides interviews with key players such as analysts, investment managers and non-executive directors."

The Telegraph's Questor column, for example, is a widely read source of investment trust ideas. Positive mentions tend to move prices. Other financial publications, such as *Investors Chronicle*, also follow the sector closely, providing commentary and recommendations. *Investors Chronicle* also produces regular podcasts, many of which contain commentary on investment trusts. Elsewhere, newspapers that have regular references to investment trusts include *The Times*, the weekend edition of the *Financial Times*, and the *Daily Mail*.

Meanwhile Citywire, the media group which covers the asset management industry, provides regular news and commentary to subscribers by email. Citywire has a dedicated online channel called Investment Trust Insider which hosts news, videos and podcasts.

Money Makers is an excellent weekly podcast run by the writer Jonathan Davis. It covers all the key news stories in the investment trust sector and provides interviews with key players such as analysts, investment managers and non-executive directors.

PR companies

Public relations companies facilitate positive press coverage and assist access to investment managers amongst other things. They are often appointed by investment trusts to help promote their investment case to the wider world.

Registrars

These organisations legally register shares and other interests, as well as acting as the paying and transfer agent for an investment trust. Their duties are normally laid out in a Registrar Agreement which will cover the transfer and settlement of shares held both in certificated and uncertificated form. The registrar usually receives a fixed fee and reimbursement of any other expenses reasonably incurred on behalf of the investment trust.

Shareholders

These can include private and institutional investors. As a group, they are the most important stakeholders of all given it is their capital being invested. Shareholder interests are represented by another key stakeholder, the independent board.

Third-party analysts

Earlier we referred to investment trust research produced by investment banks. Whilst detailed and useful, it is generally only available to their clients. However, there are several other sources of third-party analysis available to the wider public.

Private client stockbrokers and wealth management firms are a prime example. They often produce investment trust research and do not usually have any commercial relationship with specific investment trusts, which minimises conflicts of interest. Clients and potential clients should be able to access this research via a firm's client portal, website or by requesting it directly from an adviser.

Some third-party firms provide separate paid research. Examples include Edison Group, Hardman & Co, Kepler Partners and Marten & Co. This is typically paid for by the investment trust in question and any recommendations should be read with that in mind. Nonetheless, these research reports can be a useful source of structured factual content which helps someone to form an opinion on a trust. Such research is typically available via the website of the investment trust in question. Details of where to find these third-party providers is available in Chapter 40.

Wrapping up

Hopefully, you now have an understanding of the roles and responsibilities of all of the main stakeholders involved in the creation and ongoing operation of an investment trust. We will return to two of the most important ones – shareholders and the non-executive board – in more detail in later chapters.

SUMMARY OF KEY POINTS

- 'Stakeholders' refers to the various parties that are necessary to an investment trust's efficient functioning.

- Shareholders are the most important stakeholders of all given it is their capital being invested.

- The role of an investment trust board is to provide oversight and ensure that investment objectives are being met.

- The investment manager is the firm that has been instructed by the board to manage the trust's portfolio assets.

- Other key stakeholders include independent valuers, investment banks, the AIC, the FCA and the London Stock Exchange.

CHAPTER 7

SUPPLY AND DEMAND

"Demand creates its own supply."

—Keynes' Law

THE PRICES OF freely tradeable securities, such as investment trust shares, are driven fundamentally by two forces – supply and demand. When demand exceeds supply, prices rise and vice versa. The extent of any rise or fall is, in turn, influenced by factors such as market trends, investor sentiment and economic conditions. In this chapter I want to take a deeper dive into both sides of the supply and demand equation, taking in a few important twists along the way.

Getting going

On the supply side, the first is the fact that new investment trust shares are supplied to the market via several different routes. The principal ones are an IPO, an institutional placing or a combination of the two. An IPO makes the shares of a new investment trust available to the public via a listed exchange. With an institutional placing, on the other hand, shares are selectively placed with institutions such as pension funds, wealth managers and fund management groups.

Shares can be made available subsequently by way of a secondary issue. In this instance, a trust that is already listed makes an application to issue further shares. This is normally done when the existing shares are trading at a premium to their NAV, for reasons we will return to very shortly.

Before that, it is worth noting that listed companies in general, particularly smaller ones, often undertake the opposite – a dilutive (or 'discounted') equity fund raise. However, these tend to be for business-critical reasons, either to see the business through a difficult trading period or to enable an acquisition. They are usually only justifiable on the grounds that, in time, they will enhance shareholder value. Investment trusts are different. They are not trading companies. Equity-based investment trusts do not usually provide ad hoc capital to the underlying trading companies whose shares they hold. For the most part they are simply holding the shares. Dilutive issues are therefore somewhat frowned upon and are much rarer as a result.

Once investment trust shares are listed on the stock market the main source of supply is from sellers. The shares of larger trusts can be sold by placing orders directly on the stock exchange order book. Very large orders of these trusts tend to go via an investment bank as these firms are well placed to source likely buyers of larger positions.

The shares of smaller investment trusts are usually sold via an investment bank's market makers, based around prices they quote to the market.

The dilution dilemma

Issuing shares at a discount dilutes NAV per share. To illustrate why, let's take an investment trust that has 100m shares in issue and an NAV of £1 each. Its shares trade at 80p, being a 20% discount to NAV. Suppose the board then issues a further 10m shares at the same 80p, raising £8m. The net assets are now £108m (£100m + £8m). However, with 110m shares in issue, the NAV per share falls to 98.2p (£108m/110m), a decline of 1.8%. Unsurprisingly, dilutive investment trust issues like this are usually viewed pretty dimly by shareholders.

They nonetheless happen from time to time. Oakley Capital is a private equity investment trust that carried out a dilutive equity raise in 2015. Shares representing 40% of the enlarged trust were issued at a 17% discount to NAV. Although supported by some shareholders, the capital raise diluted the NAV per share, negatively impacting small private investors and received mixed reviews from the market. Although the share price increased by a few percentage points in the month that followed, it declined to more than 25% below its placing price not long thereafter. The Oakley Capital share price has recovered well since these lows, with a vow to avoid further dilutive equity raises no doubt helping.

Dilutive share issues are rare in the world of investment trusts and justifying them is tough. Conceivably, a new investment opportunity might arise at a time when it is not possible to sell any of the existing portfolio in order to take advantage, but that scenario is unlikely in most cases.

The other justification might be as a last resort to prevent investors losing even more money than they are already destined to, even after they have been diluted. For example, a trust may have made an irreversible financial commitment to invest in a project and find itself unable to raise the necessary funds in any way. However, such instances are extremely rare.

Exploring warrants

Investment trusts occasionally raise additional equity via what are known as warrants. These are instruments that confer the right on the holder to buy newly issued shares on favourable terms.

Historically, some trusts have issued warrants at their IPO as a sweetener for investors who may worry about the share price falling post issue. The possibility of a discount arising can lead investors to shun certain new issues in the hope that they can purchase the same shares more cheaply later. Clearly, if all investors take this same view, then the IPO cannot go ahead. An offer of warrants may help to ease this problem.

These instruments typically entitle the holder to buy ordinary shares at a predetermined (exercise) price within a fixed period. For example, the warrants may entitle the holder to buy ordinary shares, which are issued at IPO at 100p, at 105p in the first year, 110p in the second year and 115p in year three, at which point the warrants expire. Although there is no implicit cost to an IPO investor, there is an economic cost to any new shareholders that buy ordinary shares post IPO. Since they are not entitled to any warrants, they will get diluted on exercise. This dilution is reflected in the trusts' NAV per share once the ordinary shares rise above the warrant exercise price.

As such, warrants serve two primary purposes. Firstly, they encourage investors to participate in the IPO, rather than wait. Secondly, they offer the trust another way of raising more capital via the issue of new shares as and when they are exercised. There have also been a few instances of investment managers being awarded private warrants as an incentive. In any scenario, as a rule of thumb, the higher the expected volatility of the shares in question post IPO, the higher the value of any warrants related to them.

Selling subscription shares

Although warrants have been quite popular at various points in time, they started to be replaced by subscription shares once Personal Equity Plans (the precursor to the ISA) started to gain popularity during the 1980s, because warrants could not be held inside them. The reason rested on a technical point – warrants were not deemed to be part of a company's capital structure, but rather as a separate contractual agreement between warrant holders and the company. Subscription shares were designed to solve this problem whilst carrying similar characteristics and achieved a degree of popularity up until about 2015 before almost dying out.

Some trusts have also issued bonus subscription shares. For example, a trust may announce that shareholders will receive an extra free share for every five ordinary shares they currently own. This has been viewed as a controversial route, however, as quite often these subscription shares could be converted even if the trust's ordinary shares were trading at a discount to NAV, thereby diluting NAV per share.

Tapping investors

Trusts can also make regular share issues via 'tap issues'. This is where the company seeks permission to 'tap' the market on an ad hoc basis over a set period (typically its financial year) by issuing new shares.

Tap issues enable the sponsoring bank to size any equity issue to the level of demand at a particular point in time. They also reduce the time and administrative burden of producing a fresh prospectus every time some new capital is issued.

Understanding incentives

Beyond these technical methods of getting shares into the market, supply is also strongly driven by financial incentives. Fund management groups that manage investment trust portfolios tend to be remunerated on the level of assets they have under management. This provides them with a motive to not only grow these assets through positive performance but also via the issue of new investment trust shares. Investment banks are also incentivised to launch new investment trusts via the financial compensation they can earn as advisers and sponsors. This has typically been around 1.5% of the amount raised, with all costs (including legal, accounting, etc.) usually capped at 2.0%.

Buybacks and fresh equity issues

Investment trusts can also help to satisfy supply and demand for their own shares directly. They can buy back shares when supply is outstripping demand, thereby helping to bring supply and demand towards an equilibrium. With a share buyback the trust instructs its broker to buy its shares in the market and pays for them using the trust's own capital. These shares can then either be cancelled or they can be held by the trust for future reissue. This action helps to soak up some supply, improve liquidity in addition to any narrowing in the trust's discount, as well as any enhancement to dividend per share or NAV per share.

> "In the short term, any share repurchases or fresh equity issue will enhance liquidity because it creates a new source of demand, or supply, for the shares."

When demand is outstripping supply, this often results in the share price trading at a premium to NAV. In such instances the trust, via its broker, can issue new shares, helping to satisfy that demand, which tends to have the effect of limiting the premium to NAV.

Issuing shares at a premium to NAV (or buying back at a discount) may also reduce price volatility, by issuing before the premium gets too high and buying back before the discount gets too wide. It may also increase trading volumes sufficiently that it opens up new investors that have minimum liquidity criteria.

In the short term, any share repurchases or fresh equity issue will enhance liquidity because it creates a new source of demand, or supply, for the shares.

Shifting demand

On the other side of our equation, demand for investment trust shares comes from a wide variety of parties. These include wealth managers, pension funds, institutional fund managers, index funds and private investors. We will return to many of these in later chapters, as here I want to highlight some of the key forces shaping demand within my industry – wealth management.

Starting with the basics, a wealth manager's primary purpose is to manage the wealth of private individuals. Killik & Co, the firm I work for, is one example of an organisation operating within this space. Across the sector, I can point to two distinct trends that have had a strong effect on the investment trust market.

Killik & Co is an increasingly rare beast, being an independent firm, which is owned by its partners and is likely to remain so. Beyond my firm, the wider wealth management sector has seen a lot of consolidation. Many of its biggest players have grown by acquisition and their assets under management have swelled by a corresponding amount.

The challenge is this – all wealth management firms typically run buy lists of preferred stocks, bonds and funds, including investment trusts. This helps to channel client money into the firm's preferred ideas. Where wealth management firms have become very large – running more than, say, £25bn in assets – it becomes more difficult for them to recommend small investment trusts. This is a pity in my opinion.

Another important shift in the wealth management world has been a move away from advisory to discretionary services. In the case of the former, the final investment decision rests with the client but is typically taken after consultation with an adviser. With a discretionary account, on the other hand, decisions are taken solely by an adviser, within agreed parameters. Greater compliance hurdles for advisory accounts and the inherent lack of scalability have led to a shift towards discretionary management. As a result, firms tend to funnel more money towards the ideas on their buy lists. These ideas tend to be larger, more liquid investments, further compounding the problem of low investor interest in smaller trusts.

Buying big

This trend is accentuated by the fact that many wealth management groups offer investment management services to smaller independent financial advisers (IFAs), who do not have the scale and budget to manage large amounts of money efficiently. Much of this IFA-directed capital is invested via what are often labelled Managed Portfolio Services (MPSs). This is the generic term for a (usually) fund-based investment management service where the wealth manager has discretion over the underlying assets on a day-to-day basis in a way that is scalable and cost effective.

As IFAs have consolidated more assets with wealth management firms, the latter have seen their assets under management swell and that has put a brighter spotlight on investment trust size and liquidity.

Wealth managers that are managing tens of billions of pounds must think very carefully about liquidity. They also need to consider scalability. Investment trusts have more 'moving parts' than mutual funds, in the form of market liquidity considerations and discounts or premiums to NAV. For these reasons they don't fit neatly into MPSs, with most wealth management firms showing a preference for mutual funds in these services.

It is impractical, in most cases, to invest in small investment trusts. That's because it creates the headache of becoming a large party on the shareholder register very quickly, thereby finding it more difficult to exit on attractive terms. These investment trusts have been referred to as 'lobster pots' – relatively easy to get into but a nightmare to get out of.

Missing out

This strong demand for liquidity has bifurcated the investment trust market. Smaller, somewhat overlooked funds tend to trade at a discount to NAV and struggle to grow their asset base. Despite trying to market themselves, they generally don't get onto the larger wealth management buy lists. This is a shame as I think some very interesting niche trusts do not get sufficient representation in client portfolios as a result. The added irony for many of them is they need to stay relatively small and nimble in order to maintain their exposure to the asset classes they specialise in, many of which are themselves relatively small. Examples of such trusts include River UK Micro Cap and Rockwood Strategic, both of which invest in very small UK companies.

The larger investment trusts, on the other hand, often trade at premiums and can create a virtuous circle whereby their premium rating allows them to issue more shares, thereby increasing their scale and the commensurate demand from investors.

> "This strong demand for liquidity has bifurcated the investment trust market. Smaller, somewhat overlooked funds tend to trade at a discount to NAV and struggle to grow their asset base."

Wrapping up

A further tailwind for the investment trust sector was the low interest rate environment that persisted until quite recently. It triggered a rush to alternative sources of income that the industry was happy to respond to. It did so by creating new trusts that generated income from diverse sources including infrastructure, renewable energy assets, music royalties and property. The dramatic rise in market interest rates in 2022 provided competition for high-income alternative investment trusts. This came in the form of lower-risk government and corporate bonds with equally attractive yields. Demand for alternative income investment trusts waned as a result.

It is yet another reminder that the supply and demand dynamics within this sector don't stand still for long.

SUMMARY OF KEY POINTS

- The prices of freely tradeable securities, such as investment trust shares, are driven fundamentally by two forces – supply and demand.

- Once investment trust shares are listed on the stock market the main source of supply is from sellers.

- New investment trust shares are supplied to the market principally via an IPO or an institutional placing.

- Issuing new shares at a discount dilutes the NAV per share.

- Investment trusts that trade at a premium can create a virtuous circle whereby their premium rating allows them to issue more shares, thereby increasing their scale.

CHAPTER 8

DISCOUNTS AND PREMIUMS

"I will always choose the dollar bill carrying a wildly fluctuating discount rather than the dollar bill selling for a quite stable premium."

—**Michael Burry, American investor, portrayed in the movie *The Big Short***

As we noted in an earlier chapter, an investment trust 'discount' arises when the market price of a trust's share is lower than its NAV. Conversely, a 'premium' reflects the exact opposite scenario. In this chapter, I want to explore the factors that influence them in more depth.

The mechanics

First some basics. If we take a trust with £100m of net assets (all of its investment assets minus liabilities, such as debt) and 100m of shares in issue, it will have an NAV per share of £1. But, given that these shares trade freely in the open market, when demand is weak, they may trade below £1, perhaps at 90p, 80p or lower. However, if demand increases, they might trade above NAV, at 105p, 110p or higher.

Although supply and demand play their part, these discounts and premiums can exist for other reasons. Enter a host of explanatory academic studies, amongst which one stands out for me. In their paper, 'Yes, discounts on closed-end funds are a sentiment index', Chopra et al. (1993) conclude that discounts, in particular, can be attributed to investor sentiment. This, in turn, is influenced by a number of factors, prime amongst which is interest rates.

Understanding interest rates

During the ultra-low interest environment that persisted during the decade up to 2021, many trusts traded at premiums thanks to the market valuing their ability to generate income above their underlying NAV. This was also effectively happening in the bond market, and the parallel is useful as an explainer. As such, please forgive a small detour.

The UK government issues bonds (known as 'gilts') to supplement its spending requirements. It typically issues them at £100, pays income (known as coupons) on them twice yearly and redeems them (i.e. pays back the holder) £100 at the stated redemption (or 'maturity') date. In the meantime, these bonds are freely tradeable.

Now let's consider the '4.75% 2030 gilt'. It was issued in 2007 at £100, offering a 4.75% yield (i.e. the annual coupons equated to £4.75 per £100), with a promise to redeem it at £100 in 2030. When the gilt was issued, the Bank of England 'base' interest rate was 5.75%. This subsequently dropped to below 1.0% in 2009, where it remained until 2022. At the same time, the 4.75% 2030 gilt rose in price to a peak of £153. A simplistic way of looking at that is that it was trading at a 53% premium to its face value of £100.

But why? The short answer is that with prevailing interest rates so low, a 4.75% income stream was highly attractive. Demand duly pushed up the price of the gilt. A more technical explanation would say something like 'investors were discounting future coupons and any principal repayment at a very low rate, resulting in a very high present value for the bond'. However, that takes us into an area of maths that I will leave to one side for now. The main takeaway is that interest rates impact discount rates used to value all assets. Those asset values in turn affect the value of an investment trust. Often they affect the value more quickly than the trust's regular valuation update is able to recognise.

Challenging NAVs

Big discounts can also suggest that the NAV of a trust is artificially high, or that the underlying assets themselves are less attractive than some investors realise. This may occur in sectors where an NAV is derived from an independent valuation, rather than market prices. This is usually the case with illiquid assets. Investors should take note of trusts where the board is actively buying back stock. This suggests that the existing portfolio, which is available to buy on a discount, is more attractive than any alternative use of the trust's cash.

Be warned, however, that discounts can turn out to be value traps, especially where trusts hold hard-to-value assets, extreme examples being overseas property or emerging-market private equity.

Outside of those instances, poor NAV performance may be due to overall market direction or to a specific investment style drifting out of favour. However, individual performance rarely remains poor for extended periods as markets and styles tend to be mean reverting. Should it persist, the board can make changes, or activists can buy large stakes and agitate to wind up the trust. For anyone taking a long-term view, these pivotal moments are often good opportunities to buy.

Focusing on fees

All else equal, the higher the running costs associated with a trust, the bigger I would expect the discount to NAV to be. After all, the share price should reasonably discount all known information, and that includes costs. Consider two hypothetical trusts (A and B) with identical portfolios, and identical in all other respects apart from one aspect – Trust A has ongoing costs of 1.0% and Trust B has ongoing costs of 2.0%. Trust B should logically trade at a wider discount (or smaller premium) to NAV than Trust A, to reflect the higher running costs.

However, all else is not equal. It is extremely difficult to keep all other things (liquidity, gearing, etc.) constant to isolate the impact of costs on a trust's rating. That said, logic suggests that costs have a bearing on trust discounts.

Looking at liquidity

Small trusts, with assets below (say) £100m, tend to suffer higher fixed costs, when expressed as a percentage of NAV. They also tend to have wider bid to offer share price spreads. This puts them off-limits for many investors and can result in wide discounts.

Taking action

Another important influence is the board's policy on discount management. Many boards look to ensure that any discount does not widen materially beyond that of the immediate peer group. One of the best discount control policies is to have consistently strong NAV performance that sets a trust apart from peers or via a strategy, style or set of assets that are highly differentiated.

Introducing 'Z-scores'

There is a more objective way of gauging the extent to which a discount is out of kilter with its long-term trend – the Z-score. This version is not to be confused with Altman's Z-score, which measures the likelihood of a corporate default. The investment trust Z-score is calculated as:

[Current discount – average discount] / Volatility of the discount

Low Z-scores are generated by trusts where the current discount is below its long-term average. Equally, higher ones reflect a discount (or premium) that is above its long-term average.

So, let's say we have two trusts that are both trading at 20% discounts to NAV compared to an average discount of 5%. Trust A has a volatile discount that has ranged between 0% and 30%, compared to Trust B which has consistently seen its discount at single-digit percentages, but with a recent move out to 20%. Without bashing the numbers, it should be obvious that Trust B will have a lower Z-score. That, in turn, indicates a potentially attractive discount level for a buyer, albeit there are many other factors to be considered first.

An adviser should be able to provide you with investment trust Z-scores.

Weighing up premiums

There may be instances, such as the low interest rate environment mentioned earlier, where a premium to NAV is justified. However, investors should be wary of overpaying. There are no fixed rules here. Given that a lot of fresh equity is issued at around a 2% premium to NAV, for trusts which have persistent scarcity value, paying up to that level might be deemed reasonable. Anything significantly above may be unwise.

Investors who are nonetheless determined to pay a high premium should view it in the context of their expected return and intended holding period. Over, say, a 25-year period, an initial 5–10% premium is not a huge risk. However, someone buying a trust that is expected to return 7% a year on a five-year view has an expected return of 40% over those five years [$(1.07 \wedge 5) -1 = 40\%$]. In NAV per share terms, this equates to a value of 100 growing to 140. So what if this trust trades at a 10% premium to its NAV and that premium evaporates over the five years, as the share price converges to the same value as the NAV per share? The share price of 110 (because it is trading at a 10% premium to the NAV per share of 100), normalises to the year five NAV per share of 140. By buying at a 10% premium you are effectively reducing the expected 40% gain to 27% (140-110)/110 = 27%. In this comparison the premium has reduced the annual return of 7.0% per annum to 4.9% per annum.

Very high premiums can be unhelpful. If any bad news emerges, the price can fall significantly more than if the premium was modest. This can result in unhappy shareholders who bought high and could subsequently be nursing a loss for a long time.

By way of a real-world example, Impax Environmental Markets (IEM) is an equity trust which traded at a 15% premium to NAV in late 2021. Environmental stocks were in vogue and the manager had said it wanted to limit capacity and not issue any new shares for the foreseeable future. This helped to drive the price to a large premium. However, investor enthusiasm subsequently waned in 2022 and by December 2023 the shares traded at a 10% discount. For anyone unfortunate enough to buy in late 2021, this represented a 25% drop in value, before considering any change in the NAV.

Wrapping up

Discounts and premiums are a fascinating aspect of this whole sector and reflect the interplay of sentiment, market conditions and trust-specific factors. By monitoring them, investors can make better decisions, for example avoiding hyped-up trusts on large premiums. A historic perspective can also help investors to choose attractive opportunities to buy their favourites at sensible prices.

SUMMARY OF KEY POINTS

- Investment trust discounts and premiums are primarily due to supply and demand.

- Interest rates can have a material impact on the supply and demand of income-producing investment trusts.

- Investment trusts that hold illiquid assets often trade at a discount to the stated NAV.

- All else equal, the higher the running costs of an investment trust, the bigger the discount (lower the premium) it should trade at.

- The policies of the investment trust board can have a meaningful impact on the level of the discount.

CHAPTER 9

INDEX INCLUSION

"Don't look for the needle in the haystack. Just buy the haystack."

—John Bogle, American investor and founder of the Vanguard Group

INVESTMENT TRUSTS ARE listed companies. As such, they are eligible for inclusion in stock market indices. In this chapter I want to discuss some of the features of indices, the benefits of being included within them and offer a few pointers to investors.

Following the FTSE

The FTSE 100 Index is probably the best-known UK index. It measures the change in the combined market value of the largest 100 companies listed on the London Stock Exchange. However, its prominence should not obscure the fact that the FTSE UK Index Series covers several other indices, including the FTSE 250, FTSE Small Cap and FTSE All Share.

Trusts listed on the London Stock Exchange's Specialist Fund Segment (SFS) are excluded from the FTSE UK Index Series. The SFS is a dedicated segment for specialist, closed-ended investment funds. It targets institutional, professional and generally more knowledgeable investors. Trusts listed here tend to be more niche or offer concentrated portfolios (sometimes containing a single asset) than trusts listed on the main market. Trusts can choose to migrate from the SFS to the main market once their portfolios become more diversified.

The London Stock Exchange also operates the Alternative Investment Market (AIM), designed for small and medium-sized growth companies. Some trusts such as the Weiss Korea Opportunity Fund are listed here. AIM tends to have lower costs and regulatory obligations. Trusts listed on AIM do not qualify for inclusion on the main FTSE UK indices, although they may qualify for inclusion in the FTSE AIM Index, an index that is not widely tracked.

Joining the club

Beyond those specific and somewhat niche listing categories, why do many investment trusts worry about whether or not they can be a constituent member of an index? The short answer is that it creates an additional source of demand for their shares via index trackers.

Index tracking is an investment strategy that aims to replicate the performance of a given stock market index. Index providers, such as FTSE Russell, MSCI, S&P and Dow Jones, construct their own indices and maintain their values. Each has a set of rules that need to be followed along with a committee that arbitrates on any disputes arising around grey areas within the rules. These cover issues such as the treatment of dividends, how periodic reviews operate and, of course, the criteria for inclusion.

"With this amount of capital focused on these reference benchmarks, many companies and their advisers are very conscious of the benefits of being included as a constituent. Investment trusts are no different."

Most institutional asset managers use one or more of the indices published by these groups. According to FTSE Russell, at the time of writing more than $20 trillion is benchmarked against their index series. With this amount of capital focused on these reference benchmarks, many companies and their advisers are very conscious of the benefits of being included as a constituent. Investment trusts are no different.

Opening the lid

Because an index-tracking approach requires less research than a conventional actively managed strategy, the cost of running it tends to be correspondingly low. This is a plus for investors, as evidenced by the fact that broad market indices tend to outperform the average managed fund (Sharpe, 1991). The simple reason for this is mathematical. You can think of the US market (or most developed equity markets for that matter) as being comprised of tens of millions of investors, each expressing a view on which stocks to hold and in what proportion. The index effectively represents the average position of all these investors. Further, an index does not incur management costs, but funds do. So, if we compare the net-of-costs performance of the average fund, which is effectively the index performance with costs deducted, with the performance of the index itself, the average fund is *mathematically* likely to underperform over time. This isn't the case in every single year, but over longer time periods it is more or less a given.

That said there are several investment strategies and styles which have historically outperformed the broader market over time, and we cover these in a later chapter. For now, suffice to say that an index-tracking approach is a credible investment strategy. However, the real skill is in determining which indices to track and in which proportion.

Growing in popularity

The broad appeal of simple index-tracking approaches is clear from the volume of money these strategies have attracted in recent years. Taking the US as an example, in 2012, index funds represented 13% of all US mutual fund assets under management. By 2022 that number had grown to 28%. The relevant dollar amount is an eye-popping $4.8 trillion (Statista, n.d.). We have seen a similar picture across the developed world, including the UK. Table 9A shows the 10 largest mutual funds domiciled in the UK and ranked by assets under management. Only three, Fundsmith Equity, Blackrock ACS North America ESG Insights Equity and ACS Climate Transition Screened and Optimised World Equity are actively managed funds. The rest are either index funds or are comprised of index funds.

Table 9A: Largest UK-domiciled mutual funds

Fund	Fund size (£m) as at 31/12/2024
Blackrock ACS US Equity Tracker X1	22,974,007,668
Fundsmith Equity I Acc	22,621,049,528
Vanguard FTSE Dev Wld ex-UK Eq Idx £ Acc	17,897,771,938
Vanguard U.S. Eq Idx £ Acc	16,740,928,555
HSBC American Index Retail Acc	16,608,214,557
Vanguard LifeStrategy 60% Equity A Acc	16,042,407,209
iShares North American Eq Idx (UK) L Acc	15,507,839,740
Vanguard FTSE UK All Shr Idx Unit Tr£Acc	14,799,879,284
Blackrock ACS NA ESG Insgts Eq X1 P Acc	14,596,911,416
ACS Clmt Transition Scrn & Optd Eq X1	13,605,890,005

Source: Morningstar, 31/12/2024

At some point, this rapid growth in index investing, at the expense of active investing, could present a structural problem for markets. Indeed, some would argue that we are already there. Most index trackers don't discern between one stock and another, apart from based on their size. Taken to an extreme by current growth rates, this could lead to market distortions.

Returning to our main theme, the most widely tracked UK equity index is the FTSE All Share, which is generally favoured over the more visible FTSE 100. That's because it is broader and provides greater choice of sub-sectors and companies – it aims to represent at least 98% of the full market capitalisation, of all companies which are eligible for inclusion in the FTSE UK Index Series. As such, it is an amalgam of the FTSE 100 (representing the 100 largest companies in the market), the FTSE 250 Index (the next largest 250 companies) and the FTSE Small Cap Index (the remaining stocks that make up that 98%). As for the missing 2%, that is explained by the existence of the FTSE Fledgling Index, which picks up stocks that are even smaller than the small caps!

There are two main ways that an investment trust can find itself included in the FTSE All Share Index. The first is mechanical. Newly launched trusts that qualify are included at the next quarterly review. The second is of more interest here – a move up from the FTSE Fledgling Index. As a result, investors should keep an eye on the larger investment trusts in that index.

> "There are two main ways that an investment trust can find itself included in the FTSE All Share Index."

India Capital Growth (IGC) is an investment trust that entered the FTSE All Share Index on 19/6/2023. Figure 9B shows the share price and Figure 9C shows the daily market volume in the shares. We can clearly see the spike when the trust enters the index as new buyers, most likely index trackers, piled into the shares. We can also see how the daily volume traded increased noticeably after index inclusion.

Figure 9B: India Capital Growth, closing daily price, 6 months before index inclusion 19/6/23 to 31/12/2024

Source: Bloomberg

Figure 9C: India Capital Growth, daily volume, 6 months before index inclusion 19/6/23 to 31/12/2025

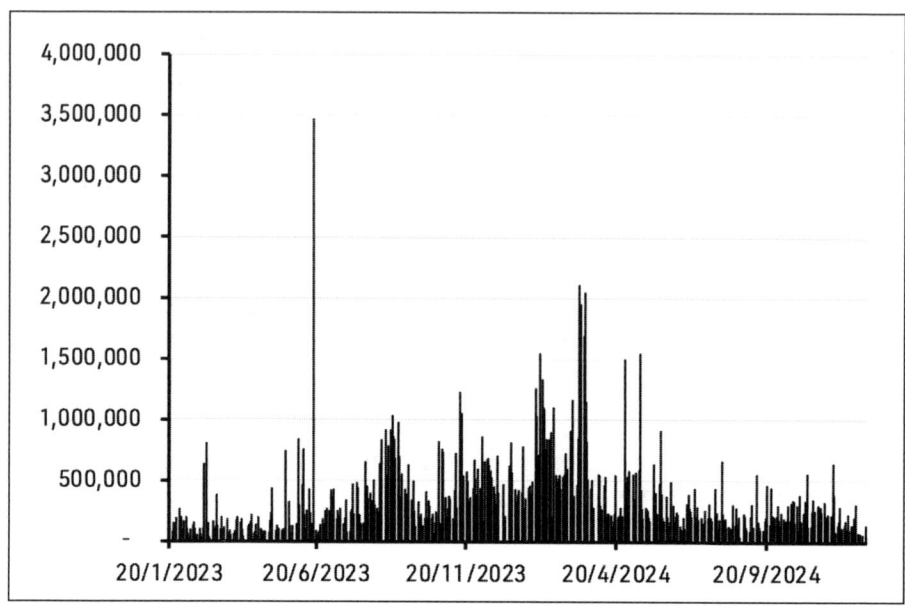

Source: Bloomberg

That said, an increase in volume may not always trigger an increase in price. There may be sellers around, for example, who wait for the moment of index inclusion to offload their holding. As such, potential index inclusion is not sufficient reason alone to justify buying a specific investment trust. However, all other things being equal it can make an attractive entry point (or exit opportunity, if a demotion looms).

Wrapping up

As for where the average investor can obtain information about index constituents, their best bet will usually be their wealth manager, stockbroker or financial adviser. Constituent data is also accessible via the LSE website, or investors can download the constituents of an index fund or ETF that tracks the relevant index (assuming a 'full replication' approach, which buys everything in it). The AIC website contains sufficient data to establish the latest market capitalisation of all listed investment trusts.

SUMMARY OF KEY POINTS

- Investment trusts are eligible for inclusion in stock market indices.

- Index inclusion creates an additional source of demand for investment trust shares from index trackers.

- Trusts can qualify for inclusion in the FTSE All Share Index if they outgrow the FTSE Fledgling Index.

CHAPTER 10

COSTS

*"Price is what you pay,
value is what you get."*

—Warren Buffett

W E COULD PARAPHRASE Buffett's quote to "Fees are what you pay. Performance is what you get." However, there is a problem with building an investment strategy on that maxim. Fees are discernible in advance. Performance is not. We can easily estimate what the running costs of an investment trust are. However, we have limited insight into what future performance will be. This means that fees and other costs become an important part of the investment decision-making process.

Adding it all up

So, what are the costs involved in buying, holding and selling an investment trust?

There are several costs that you incur when buying and holding an investment trust. The primary ones are:

- Bid-offer spread
- Broker / financial adviser commissions / fees

- Stamp duty.

Costs that are incurred by the investment trust itself and are reflected in the NAV, include:

- Administrative fees
- Custody fees
- Director's fees
- Interest expense
- Investment manager's annual management fee
- Marketing costs
- Performance fees
- Portfolio transaction costs
- Professional fees – legal, accounting, etc.
- Regulatory fees
- Tax.

Most investment trusts are externally managed. This means that they have an investment management contract with an investment manager that is external (separate) to the investment trust. A small number of investment trusts are internally managed. In this case their cost base is more akin to a normal trading company, covering items such as staff, offices, etc.

There may be other costs depending on how you purchase the investment trust shares and how you hold them, but these represent the bulk of the costs involved in operating the investment trust as well as buying and selling the shares.

Anyone thinking that list looks daunting should remember that larger trusts, in particular, enjoy economies of scale that help to offset the cost burden. Later, we will also look at a summary number that helps investors to weigh up different trusts without wading through all of these line by line.

When I compare a wide range of equity-based investment trusts with equivalent mutual funds, from a cost perspective I find a noticeable difference in management fees but no difference in overall operating costs (refer to Table 10A).

The management fee, which is usually the largest single cost item, is somewhat lower for investment trusts (average 0.69%, median 0.70%) than for mutual funds (average 0.87%, median 0.75%). I think this is primarily due to the efforts of independent boards in negotiating better terms for shareholders and, partly because of those efforts, the economies of scale enjoyed by several larger trusts.

Table 10A: Cost comparison of equity-based investment trusts and mutual funds

	Investment trust	Mutual fund
Average management fee	0.69%	0.87%
Median management fee	0.70%	0.75%
Average ongoing charge	0.98%	0.98%
Median ongoing charge	0.90%	0.90%
Sample size	131	2,455

Based on all available equity investment trusts and a large representative sample of actively managed mutual funds. Full methodology is in the appendix. Management fee is the actual percentage deducted from an investment's average net assets to pay for the investment's management, based on numbers from the latest annual report. The ongoing charge is the total ongoing operating expenses, including the management fee, expressed as a percentage of the average net assets based on numbers from the latest annual report.

Source: Morningstar, 31/12/2024

When we include other running costs in the total ongoing charges figure, both investment trusts and mutual funds show the same average ongoing charge (0.98%) and the same median ongoing charge (0.90%). The full methodology is laid out in the appendix to this chapter.

The main other costs, in addition to the management fee, are examined in the pages that follow. To illustrate how the detail works in practice first, Table 10B is a comparison of Fundsmith, which is a mutual fund, and the Smithson Investment Trust (SSON).

Table 10B: Cost comparison of Fundsmith Equity Fund (OEIC) vs Smithson (Investment Trust)

Cost item	Fundsmith	As % of NAV	Smithson	As % of NAV
Net assets	£18,831,421,402		£1,437,305,000	
Management fee	£167,548,637	0.89%	£12,509,000	0.87%
Depositary	£3,836,697	0.02%	£212,000	0.01%
Transfer agent	£2,912,320	0.02%		0.00%
Safe custody	£2,182,272	0.01%	£72,000	0.01%
Admin	£599,473	0.00%	£336,000	0.02%
Directors		0.00%	£109,000	0.01%
Company secretarial		0.00%	£137,000	0.01%
Other		0.00%	£333,000	0.02%
Total as % of NAV		0.94%		0.97%

Sources: 2019 Full Year Report & Accounts for each. Only short form annual reports are available for Fundsmith Equity Fund since 2019.

Diving deeper

From here, we can start to analyse what an investor is paying for in each case.

Management fees

It should be noted that the respective portfolios of the Fundsmith Equity Fund and the Smithson Investment Trust are markedly different. The Fundsmith Equity Fund invests in very large companies, whilst the Smithson Investment Trust invests in medium and smaller sized companies. That said, the detailed cost disclosures, albeit from 2019, allow for a helpful comparison of the costs associated to each fund structure. We can see that the management fees are similar on both funds (0.89% and 0.87%). The investment trust has marginally higher running costs due to directors' fees and other administration costs which, although a lower absolute amount, are a higher percentage of net assets. However, one way of looking at this is that investors are only paying an additional 0.03% per annum (i.e. 0.97% minus 0.94%), for an independent board and the oversight that goes with that.

Administrative fees

These are fees that are incurred in the day-to-day running of the trust. The administrator often acts as company secretary to the investment trust. Their services normally include responsibility for maintaining the books and financial accounts, as well as the calculation of NAV. The administrator's fee is often paid monthly by the investment trust and may either be based on a percentage of the trust's assets or a flat amount.

Bid-offer spread

When trading investment trust shares in the market you will encounter a price difference between the buying and selling prices. Firms that are members of the exchange can place the relevant buy and sell orders on the Stock Exchange Electronic Trading Service (SETS) order book for trusts over a certain size. As the London Stock Exchange's flagship electronic order book, it allows trading in a wide range of securities, including constituents of the FTSE 100, FTSE 250 and FTSE Small Cap Indices.

Stocks, including investment trusts, that are not large enough or liquid enough for SETS trade on the Stock Exchange Electronic Trading Service: Quotes and Crosses (SETSqx). This is where the majority of non-FTSE All Share constituents are traded. If the trust shares being traded have registered market makers providing non-electronic quotes, then the market makers are the only parties that can make prices in the trust.

Investors that buy SETSqx shares electronically, or via an automated platform, are likely to suffer the full bid to offer spread. As such, for investors that are likely to be active in a trust's shares which are this illiquid, it may be worth instructing a broker. They can call market makers and often negotiate improved prices, although this is not always guaranteed.

As such, although there are some great smaller investment trusts around, it is important to take a long-term view when buying them. A bid to offer spread of (say) 5% is a big hurdle if you are buying the trust in the hope of exiting it in just a year or two. For trusts with this level of entry and exit costs I advise taking a long-term view (5 years minimum, but ideally 10 years plus). That way you are effectively amortising the entry cost over a longer period and thereby reducing its impact on your overall investment returns.

Custody fees

These cover the cost of safekeeping the trust's assets. One of the directors' many responsibilities is to ensure that custody costs are competitive and to renegotiate them or move the service to another provider if they are not.

Director's fees

These are the fees paid to the non-executive directors to compensate them for their time and effort in overseeing the trust. They tend to be reviewed regularly. Some trusts are internally managed, meaning they have executive directors, who usually receive a base salary, a pension and a performance-related element as part of their package.

Interest expense

This is the cost incurred in borrowing money to invest. It mainly comprises the interest payable on any loan or bond that has been issued. There may also be arrangement fees levied by a bank for arranging debt facilities.

Investment manager's annual management fee

This tends to be the largest element of the overall running costs. It is the fee payable to the investment manager for managing the portfolio. This fee typically ranges from 0.30% to 1.5%, although it can be higher for private equity trusts and other specialist vehicles. There are a small number of trusts that do not levy any management fee, preferring to be rewarded purely on performance. We will cover these at a later stage. The board monitors the management fees, both in absolute terms and relative to peers, and often renegotiates them.

A positive feature of these management fees is scaling. Many investment trusts operate a sliding scale. For example, the investment management fees on the JP Morgan Emerging Markets Trust are charged on a tiered basis of 0.75% pa on the first £500m of NAV, 0.65% between £500m and £1bn, and 0.60% over £1bn. This makes sense as there are clear economies of scale achievable as a trust gets bigger – it is unlikely to be twice as costly to manage £2bn as it is £1bn, in terms of the number of analysts and portfolio managers involved. This is a key advantage of larger equity investment trusts when compared to large equity mutual funds, where sliding fee scales of this kind are rare indeed.

We have established that there can be a material difference between a trust's market value and its NAV. This differential is particularly important when it comes to the investment management fees that investment trusts incur.

The established norm in the investment trust world is that the investment manager is remunerated based on the value of the assets that they manage.

However, should trusts use NAV, or should they use the trust's share price (i.e. market value) as the basis for fees? A justifiable reason for using NAV is that this is something the investment manager has more control over. Investment managers might reasonably argue that the trust's share price is outside of their control.

However, the investor doesn't buy and sell the NAV, they buy and sell the share price of the trust. The value of the investor's holding goes up or down based on the fortunes of the share price. When they decide to realise some value, they do so by selling shares at the prevailing share price. In this respect, basing fees on the market value of a trust represents a better alignment of interest between the investment trust and the shareholder.

Clearly there can be instances where the shares trade at a premium to NAV. In these instances, isn't it better for the shareholder to have the management fees levied on NAV? Maybe it is in the short term, but I don't think it is in the long term. I say this for two primary reasons. Firstly, a premium rating is usually a reward for a job well done. It is normally a reflection of strong portfolio performance, confidence in management, an attractive income relative to interest rates, or a combination of these and other positive attributes.

> "Basing fees on the market value of a trust represents a better alignment of interest between the investment trust and the shareholder."

In these instances, I would be happy to pay a slightly higher fee (than if it were based on NAV) and I suspect other investors would too. The second reason refers to share issuance. When trust shares trade at a premium to NAV for a prolonged period, a typical response from the investment manager is to push the board to issue more equity. This is unsurprising given the commercial incentive to increase the total NAV and thereby increase management fees.

However, if the management fee incentive is linked to market value (rather than asset value) I think the board and manager must give greater consideration to the impact of any additional equity issuance. Yes, there is a commercial incentive to issue more equity, whether fees are levied on market value or asset value. However, I think where the fee is based on market value there will be slightly greater consideration given to the impact that further issuance will have on the trust's rating (i.e. the level of premium to NAV).

It may also be that the premium to NAV needs to be much higher to justify fresh equity issuance. Issuing 10% more shares, when trading at a 10% premium, increases NAV per share by 0.9% (a figure that goes a long way to offset a year's worth of fees), compared to increasing the share count by 10% at a 2% premium, which increases NAV per share by a mere 0.2%. So, waiting for a much higher rating, rather than issuing at the first signs of a premium, can be a useful way of enhancing value for existing shareholders.

Several trusts now compensate their investment managers based on market value, rather than asset value. Examples include Alliance Witan, FCIT, Mercantile and Smithson. These are all traditional investment trusts with portfolios that are mainly invested in easy-to-value assets and so the difference between the NAV and the market value should not be too extreme. Cordiant Digital Infrastructure is a trust that invests in hard-to-value assets, and it also levies its management fees based on the trust's market value.* This demonstrates that it is possible for alternative investment trusts to also have an investment management fee based on the market value of the trust.

A problem arises when an investment manager receives fees based on an NAV which is higher than the trust's market valuation. Investors can become understandably unhappy, especially if this situation persists. So, how widespread is this issue?

To help answer this question, I carried out an exercise comparing management fees if they were based on asset value versus the comparable fees if they had been based on market capitalisation. The full methodology is in the appendix.

Table 10C shows the five trusts where the fees' differential (expressed as a % of the fee based on asset value) was the greatest.

We can see that, over this five-year period, shareholders have paid (based on estimates) between 40% and 70% more in management fees because of an asset value basis, compared to what the situation would have been on a market value basis.

Some might argue that it would be difficult to attract good-quality managers to work on a fee basis where their income is tied to the stock market performance of the trust rather than the portfolio value. However, isn't it normal for operating companies, such as traditional UK REITS, to link the success of their management long-term incentive plans to shareholder returns?

---

* Since 31/12/2024 several trusts holding hard-to-value assets have adjusted their fee basis from one based solely on NAV to one based on market value, or a combination of NAV and market value.

Table 10C: Comparison of (estimated) investment management fees based on asset value vs scenario where investment management fees are based on market capitalisation

Investment	Estimated fees on NAV – 5 years	Estimated fees on GAV* – 5 years	Estimated fees on mkt cap – 5 years	Differential as % of fee based on NAV (or GAV in case of JZ Capital Partners)
JZ Capital Partners*		£20,049,024	£8,653,696	70%
Riverstone Energy	£35,128,778		£19,351,206	45%
EPE Special Opportunities	£9,380,504		£5,379,677	43%
Ground Rents Income Fund	£4,533,666		£2,590,374	43%
Phoenix Spree Deutschland	£24,022,438		£14,492,001	40%

Data covers five years to 12/12/2024. Estimates are based on actual management fee rate, as published by Morningstar, pro-rated on monthly NAV or GAV and market cap. Calculations are based on calendar years, rather than financial years. * JZ Capital Partners levies management fees based on gross asset value (GAV). Full methodology is in the appendix.

Source: Morningstar.

Some trusts, such as Fidelity China Special Situations, charge a variable management fee based on performance. In the case of this trust, the fee is based on the NAV per share performance relative to its benchmark, the MSCI China Index over rolling three-year periods. Net assets up to £1.5bn attract a management fee of 0.85%. This 0.85% can be increased by 0.033% for every 1% of outperformance over the prior three years, to a maximum of 1.05%. Conversely, it can be reduced by 0.033% for every 1% of underperformance over the prior three years, to a minimum of 0.65%. For net assets over £1.5bn, the fee ranges between 0.45% and 0.85% in a similar manner, based on performance. This is one way of helping to better align fees with investor outcomes.

> "A small number of trusts have a structure which levies fees based on the lower of NAV and market capitalisation."

A small number of trusts have a structure which levies fees based on the lower of NAV and market capitalisation. This is the gold standard, in my view, of ensuring a better management fee alignment between the interests of investors and the trust's managers. Polar Capital Global Healthcare is a good example, albeit it also levies a performance fee. As we have seen, there are several ways to value an investment trust's underlying assets. This, in turn, drives its own valuation and the size of any discount (or premium) to NAV it may attract.

Finally, be wary of management fees that are linked to gross asset value. This provides the investment manager with an incentive to maximise leverage.

Performance fees

These are levied on returns over and above a certain pre-agreed level. For example, Worldwide Healthcare Trust, a trust that invests in healthcare businesses around the world, levies a fee of 15% of any outperformance of the MSCI World Health Care Index. Investment trust performance fees like this have reduced in number over the years as investors and boards have negotiated against them. Where they still exist, they often (but not always) supplement lower management fees.

At a small number of trusts, the investment manager has eschewed management fees in return for higher-than-average performance fees. Although I am not a huge fan of performance fees, I think this 'no-win no-fee' approach is worth a look. Trusts in this category include Aurora UK Alpha (ARR), which charges no management fee but takes up to a third of any outperformance of the FTSE All Share Index as a fee. This is paid in ARR shares and is subject to clawback for three years from issue if there is sufficient subsequent underperformance.

This stands in contrast to the performance fees levied by Third Point Investors. This trust invests all of its capital in Third Point Offshore, a US managed hedge fund, which levies a 1.25% management fee and a performance fee with no hurdle. As such, 20% of all gains are taken in the form of a performance fee.

Performance fee conditions require careful attention. You should familiarise yourself with terms such as hurdle rate (the level of return required to generate a performance fee), performance measurement period (the time frame over which the performance fee is calculated), high water mark (the level the share price, including income, must exceed before future performance fees can be generated), claw back (whether performance fees that have been generated can be clawed back if future performance is poor). Given their complexity, we will revisit performance fees in Chapter 31.

Tax

Investment trusts themselves do not incur capital gains tax on the disposal of UK shares, or other assets. They are also not liable for any additional tax on UK dividend income or interest received. However, they may incur capital gains tax in certain overseas jurisdictions, as well as withholding tax on overseas dividend income. If so, they are disclosed in the income statement.

Portfolio transaction costs

Portfolio transaction costs include stamp duty (see next), bid to offer spreads and any broker commission. When an equity investment trust buys and sells shares, it normally incurs a bid to offer spread. If a broker has been instructed to achieve a specific price, they would normally take a transaction commission, although this is usually less than 0.05% of the deal value.

Stamp duty

Stamp duty is a tax paid on the purchase of shares. It is normally 0.5% of the transaction value, based on the share price at which a transaction takes place. It is payable by a buyer on both existing shares in a company incorporated in the UK and shares in a foreign company that has a share register here. You do not have to pay the tax if you are given shares for free or subscribe to a new issue.

The UK stock market is one of the few global markets that still incurs stamp duty on purchases of domestic company shares. Investment trusts are no exception. However, the rule does not apply to non-UK investment companies that are traded on the London market, provided they do not have a share register in the UK.

For instance, 3i Infrastructure, which is domiciled in Jersey, is the largest investment trust listed on the London Stock Exchange that does not attract stamp duty on purchases by UK investors. Here is an extract from its prospectus:

> *Stamp Duty and Stamp Duty Reserve Tax ('SDRT').*
> *The following comments are intended as a guide to*
> *the general stamp duty and SDRT position and do*
> *not relate to persons such as market makers, brokers,*
> *dealers, intermediaries, and persons connected with*
> *depository arrangements or clearance services, to whom*
> *special rules apply. No UK stamp duty or SDRT will*
> *be payable on the issue of the ordinary shares or the*
> *warrants. Transfers of ordinary shares or warrants will*
> *not be liable to stamp duty unless the instrument of*
> *transfer is executed within the United Kingdom, or,*
> *wherever executed, relates to any matter or thing done*
> *or to be done within the United Kingdom. In such a*
> *case, ad valorem UK stamp duty is charged at the rate*
> *of 0.5% of the amount of the value of the consideration*
> *for the transfer rounded up where necessary to the*
> *nearest £5. Provided that neither the Ordinary Shares*
> *nor the Warrants are registered in a register kept in*
> *the UK by or on behalf of the company and transfer*
> *is settled electronically via CREST, any agreement*
> *to transfer Ordinary Shares or Warrants will not be*
> *subject to UK SDRT.*

Ongoing charges

So far in this chapter, we have delved into what may seem like a bewildering array of costs incurred by investment trusts. However, the good news is there is a standardised number, known as an ongoing charges figure (OCF) or ongoing charges ratio (OCR), which is designed to capture them and make life easier for investors.

The AIC provides the following guidance to its member trusts:

Ongoing Charges (previously Total Expense Ratios or TERs) is a figure published annually by an investment trust which shows the drag on performance caused by operational expenses. More specifically, it is the annual percentage reduction in shareholder returns because of recurring operational expenses assuming markets remain static, and the portfolio is not traded. Although the OCF is based on historical information, it provides shareholders with an indication of the likely level of costs that will be incurred in managing the fund in the future.

The AIC's recommended methodology for calculating an OCF requires the identification of all relevant expense items. Broadly speaking, ongoing charges are the costs that the investment company would have to pay in the absence of any purchases or sales of investments and if markets remained static through the period. Ongoing charges are therefore different from total expenses as not all expenses are operational and recurring.

The AIC's recommended methodology is based on the formula:

$$\text{Ongoing charges (\%)} = \frac{\text{Annualised ongoing charges}}{\text{Average undiluted net asset value in the period}}$$

Items to be included in ongoing charges are "those expenses of a type which are likely to recur in the foreseeable future, whether charged to capital or revenue, and which relate to the operation of the investment company as a collective fund, excluding the costs of acquisition/disposal of investments, financing charges and gains/losses arising on investments. Ongoing charges are based on costs incurred in the year as being the best estimate of future costs."*

The Key Information Document (KID) is a pre-contractual disclosure document that is intended to inform retail investors of the main features of

---

* The full AIC ongoing charges methodology can be found at www.theaic.co.uk.

a packaged retail product, as well as the risks, costs, potential gains and losses associated with investment in that product, in a clear and accessible manner in advance of any potential investment.

There has been a lot of controversy around KIDs and serious lobbying efforts to address the negative impact they have been having on investment trusts. At the time of writing, the FCA has published a consultation paper, "A new product information framework for Consumer Composite Investments". This consultation paper considers the replacement of the UK regime for packaged retail and insurance-based investment products (PRIIPs), a category which investment trusts currently fall within.

The new regime is intended to introduce "a more flexible and proportionate product information framework". It will replace PRIIPs KIDs with a 'Product Summary' which must be provided to consumers.

Wrapping up

In summary then, independent boards play a pivotal role in safeguarding investor interests by negotiating fair fee structures. Although fees are inevitable, understanding the key components and how they work can help an investor to minimise their impact and maximise their investment returns.

SUMMARY OF KEY POINTS

- Fees are an important part of the investment decision-making process.

- A comparison of equity-based investment trusts with equity-based mutual funds showed a noticeable difference in management fees but little difference in overall operating costs.

- Larger investment trusts trade on an order-driven market and smaller trusts on a quote-driven market.

- Basing investment management fees on the market value, rather than the NAV, of a trust represents a better alignment of interests between the investment manager and the shareholder.

- One of the board's responsibilities is to keep a lid on costs and negotiate better terms for shareholders.

CHAPTER 11

THE INDEPENDENT INVESTMENT TRUST BOARD

"The job is very simple, ensure the fund is managed in the interests of shareholders. No more, no less."

—Alan Brierley, Head of Investment Companies Research at Investec Securities

Setting the scene

IN THIS CHAPTER I want to consider the role of an investment trust board. The board is one thing that differentiates this type of vehicle. One of the board's key responsibilities is to ensure that the investment objectives of the trust are being met by its managers. As such, boards are typically comprised of people that have relevant experience. This might include a background in portfolio management, marketing, finance, general accounting, legal or corporate governance roles. In most cases, trust board members are non-executive. In other words, they do not have a hands-on day-to-day involvement with the trust.

Occasionally, a member of the separate, external fund management group may sit on the board, in which case they will be referred to as non-independent. This presents a conflict of interest, particularly when that external fund manager is not performing well and/or when investor sentiment towards the trust is deteriorating. In such cases, the board may wish to review the underlying fund management contract and appoint a new manager.

The AIC produces a Code of Corporate Governance to help guide boards of investment trusts. Last updated in August 2024, it is endorsed by the Financial Reporting Council (FRC), the body that monitors the development of international accounting and auditing standards. It means that investment trusts that report in line with the AIC Code meet their obligations in relation to the FRC's UK Corporate Governance Code (only AIC members may state that they report in line with the AIC Code).

Remunerating directors

Non-executive directors are typically remunerated for their time via directors' fees (effectively a salary). There is a wide range across the investment trust sector. For example, the total cost of directors' fees was 0.10% of NAV in the case of Riverstone Energy (RSE) and the highest-paid director received $159,000 in the 2023 financial year. At the other end of the spectrum, at Smithson (SSON) directors' fees totalled less than 0.01% for the equivalent period and the highest-paid director received £45,000.

The very fact that investment trust directors are paid in this manner can sometimes present another conflict. This could arise where, for example, an investment trust is no longer commercially viable. Although the best outcome for the shareholders might be to wind it up, or merge it with another trust, the directors may be reluctant to 'make themselves redundant'. That is one possible reason why small, lower-profile investment trusts sometimes limp along for longer than they should.

It is worth noting that a small number of investment trusts do not have a management contract with an external fund manager. In this instance, the board of directors have executive roles and are responsible for overseeing all day-to-day operations including portfolio management responsibilities.

Improving diversity

In 2022, the FCA finalised rules requiring listed companies to report on the representation of women and ethnic minorities on their boards, making it easier for investors to gauge the diversity of senior leadership teams. The rules also cover investment trusts. Given their size, certain disclosures may not be applicable to investment trusts, but in such cases the trust must disclose why. For example, the FCA sets positive diversity targets – if listed companies cannot meet them, they need to explain why not. These rules are due to be reviewed in 2025, but in the meantime, here is a snapshot of the current requirements, assuming they are fully applicable:

- At least 40% of the board should be women.

- At least one of the senior board positions (Chair, Chief Executive Officer (CEO), Senior Independent Director (SID) or Chief Financial Officer (CFO)) should be held by a woman.

- At least one member of the board should be from a minority ethnic background (as advised by the Office for National Statistics).

I have heard critics of such rules claim that this push for diversity has weakened some investment trust boards by forcing them to appoint directors who have insufficient experience of the investment trust sector, simply to hit a target. This view may have some substance in the short term. However, if the longer-term objective is to achieve diversity of thought, business skills and perspective then it is important that we start to make changes today to achieve that objective tomorrow.

Hitting targets

Once set up, a key responsibility of a non-executive board is to hold the trust's investment managers to account. Typically, a set of key performance indicators (KPIs) will be used as a gauge of the trust's effectiveness. These usually focus on a mixture of:

- NAV performance relative to a benchmark

- Dividends

- Any discount or premium to NAV

- Ongoing charges.

The board has a degree of control over most of these KPIs except the trust's NAV. In my view, a strong board will want to see a clearly stated investment philosophy, process and style in evidence. Here is a summary of the investment approach employed by the Smithson Investment Trust, based on comments in its 2022 annual report:

> *The manager selects companies that have an established track record of success, such as a dominant market share in their niche product or service or having brands or patents which others would find difficult to replicate. Small and mid (SMID) sized companies tend to out-perform large companies. The manager seeks to invest in SMID sized companies that exhibit strong profitability that is sustainable and generate substantial cash flow. The manager avoids companies that are heavily leveraged or rely on debt to provide an adequate return, as well as sectors and industries that innovate very quickly and are rapidly changing. It instead focuses on companies that continue outperforming competitors and rely heavily on intangible assets in industries such as information technology, health care and consumer goods.*

This clarity of purpose is helpful because it can be measured and benchmarked. For example, the size of the underlying companies chosen, the level and persistency of their profitability, their cash flow generation and leverage are all things that can be objectively verified.

Failing to deliver

If the board feels that the investment manager is not sticking to the investment process or style, then this is a clear case for reviewing the manager and appointing an alternative. This is something that the board can help to establish with attribution reports which look at outperformance or underperformance relative to key factors such as sector allocation, gearing, investment style or stock selection. Visibility over a trust's investment philosophy and process is important. In too many instances, investors place undue emphasis on the investment manager themselves rather than their process. An opaque investment process makes it difficult to establish the conditions under which a trust's NAV should perform well or perform poorly.

Let's take the example of the Schroder UK Growth investment trust, managed by Schroder Unit Trusts until April 2018. The portfolio was value-biased (despite the name!) and focused on UK equities. As a result, it targeted the cheaper stocks in the UK market, when measured using traditional valuation metrics. This approach performed poorly during the five-year period ended 30/4/2018 and the board subsequently changed the manager to Baillie Gifford, a firm with a high-growth investment style. Value and growth investment approaches involve hunting for stocks in different parts of the market. The timing of this change was unfortunate to say the least.

The MSCI UK Value and UK Growth index series data clearly shows that UK value stocks performed relatively badly over the five-year period I just referenced. However, the Schroder UK Growth strategy still outperformed the MSCI UK Value benchmark, implying that its managers had done reasonably well, given their stated investment approach.

Following the change of investment manager, the portfolio (of the newly named Baillie Gifford UK Growth Trust) performed in line with the market for about 18 months, then rallied strongly as high-growth stocks responded to the pandemic-induced stimulus measures. However, in 2022, many high-growth stocks de-rated sharply against a backdrop of rising long-term interest rates. At the time of writing the portfolio (NAV) of the Baillie Gifford UK Growth Trust has materially underperformed both the MSCI UK Value Index and the MSCI UK Growth Index as well as the broader UK stock market as measured by the FTSE All Share Index. The change the trust made may look like a simple switch from one UK equity manager to another, but it turned out to be a call on investment style. It is a call that has yet to justify the change.

Temple Bar is another trust that was faced with a similar case of underperformance but experienced a rather different outcome. The board reviewed its management arrangements in early 2020. As with Schroder UK Growth, the incumbent manager also had a value bias. In this instance the board elected to maintain the investment style but appoint a new manager with experience of value investing. This change proved to be rather more successful – an improvement in the fortunes of value stocks, from their 2020 lows, has helped Temple Bar to subsequently deliver strong returns.

Another key board responsibility is to put a lid on costs. Since they eat into returns, keeping them low helps investors. Encouragingly, many trust boards have succeeded in reducing management and other fees in recent years.

If things aren't working

If the trust is failing to achieve its objectives the board may undertake various corporate actions to help improve shareholder returns. Where the trust's shares trade at a wide discount to NAV, for example as a result of low demand, it may weigh various options, including:

1. Changing the investment mandate. Although large shareholders may no longer wish a trust to continue with its existing investment mandate, they may be reluctant to exit the shares for tax reasons, or they may have identified an alternative investment mandate they wish to pursue.

2. Merging with another trust. This is one way that a small, illiquid trust can help to broaden its appeal to a wider range of investors, including those that have size and liquidity minimums to worry about. However, this route usually only makes sense when both trusts have a similar mandate such that investor preferences can be maintained.

"If the trust is failing to achieve its objectives the board may undertake various corporate actions to help improve shareholder returns."

3. Providing a rollover option into a mutual fund. This might make sense where some shareholders wish to retain exposure to the investment manager and their investment style. The investment manager may help subsidise any costs involved in the rollover.

4. Winding up the trust. This is a last resort but may be the only viable option.

Protecting smaller shareholders

For minority private shareholders, I'm afraid the bad news is that they may not be consulted on such matters. However, they will usually be given an opportunity to at least vote on the chosen route. In that context, they are entitled to attend the annual general meeting, either in-person or online, and ask questions on any matter related to the trust, including board member re-election. Where the relevant shares are registered in their name, voting is very straightforward via letter or email. However, most are held in a nominee account these days. In that instance, a wealth manager or platform should notify them about any forthcoming corporate action, often with a recommendation on voting.

Wrapping up

An independent board is one of the differentiating features of investment trusts and having a strong one in place is important when it comes to looking after the interests of investors. As such, investors should not hesitate to use their voting rights to express satisfaction, or dissatisfaction, with the direction of travel.

SUMMARY OF KEY POINTS

- The role of an investment trust board is to provide oversight and ensure that the investment objectives are being met.

- The AIC produces a Code of Corporate Governance to help guide boards of investment trusts.

- The FCA requires listed companies to disclose the representation of women and ethnic minorities on their boards.

- The board usually has a set of KPIs that are used as a gauge of the trust's effectiveness.

- An independent board is one of the differentiating features of investment trusts and sets them apart from mutual funds.

CHAPTER 12

GEARING UP

"I think over any period of time, especially if you don't use leverage, it is difficult to continually beat the S&P 500."

**—Eli Broad, US businessman
and philanthropist**

IN CHAPTER 5 I introduced the concept of 'gearing' or 'leverage', which means borrowing money to invest. I cited Berkshire Hathaway, managed by Warren Buffett, as an example of an investment vehicle which has employed this technique to very good effect. So, in this chapter I want to build on the ground covered there by diving deeper into the mechanics of leverage and how it relates to investment trusts.

The bare bones

At its heart, gearing is all about using debt to increase the amount of overall exposure taken to equities, or other assets. The principle is very simple. If we can borrow money, for illustration, at an annual cost of 5% and use it to buy an asset that grows at an annual rate of 10% this relatively cheap form of financing will enhance our overall return.

However, leverage is a double-edged sword. That is because, although it can amplify returns when asset prices rise, it can also magnify losses when they drop. In that context, it is worth noting that whilst investment trusts often employ leverage successfully to underpin a diversified portfolio of assets, it can sometimes work against them. They can, however, seek to mitigate that risk by only deploying modest amounts of borrowed money and negotiating attractive terms by using their portfolios as collateral.

Digging deeper

In doing so, they have two choices – they can take on short-term, flexible (i.e. easy to repay) debt or longer-term structural borrowing. The latter refers to IOUs which usually come with a fixed rate of interest over a predetermined period. If we look at the example of Scottish Mortgage, we note from its March 2024 financial statements (Table 12A) that it has borrowed several tranches of capital, with interest rates ranging from 1.65% to 12.0%.

Table 12A: Extract from page 84 of the Scottish Mortgage annual report and financial statements 2024

12 Creditors – amounts falling due after more than one year

	Nominal rate %	Effective rate %	2024 £000	2023 £000
Debenture stocks:				
£50 million 6-12% stepped interest debenture stock 2026	12.0	10.8	51,118	51,537
£675,000 4½% irredeemable debenture stock			675	675
Unsecured loan notes:				
£30 million 2.91% 2038	2.91	2.91	29,971	29,969
£150 million 2.30% 2040	2.30	2.30	149,842	149,831
£50 million 2.94% 2041	2.94	2.94	49,949	49,945
£45 million 3.05% 2042	3.05	3.05	44,918	44,913
£30 million 3.30% 2044	3.30	3.30	29,943	29,941
£20 million 3.65% 2044	3.65	3.65	19,973	19,972
€18 million 1.65% 2045	1.65	1.65	15,372	15,797
£30 million 3.12% 2047	3.12	3.12	29,942	29,939
£90 million 2.96% 2048	2.96	2.96	89,899	89,896

€27 million 1.77% 2050	1.77	1.77	23,057	23,695
£100 million 2.03% 2036	2.03	2.03	99,932	99,927
£100 million 2.30% 2046	2.30	2.30	99,927	99,923
US$175 million 2.99% 2052	2.99	2.99	138,368	141,361
US$110 million 3.04% 2057	3.04	3.04	86,973	88,855
US$115 million 3.09% 2062	3.09	3.09	90,925	92,893
Long-term bank loans:				
US$180 million RBSI 2.60% fixed rate loan 2026	2.60	2.60	142,940	145,579
US$300 million Scotiabank 2.23% fixed rate loan 2026	2.23	2.23	237,447	242,570
Provision for deferred tax liability			7,259	3,225
			1,437,980	**1,450,443**

Other trusts will take on flexible shorter-term debt. Worldwide Healthcare Trust is an investment trust that invests in quoted equities in the healthcare sector globally. The managers prefer to run an overdraft, rather than tie the trust into any long-term debt arrangements. Table 12B is an extract from the 2023 financial statements, showing that its only real borrowing is via an overdraft with JP Morgan Securities LLC at 0.45% above the prime lending rate.

Table 12B: Extract from page 88 of the Worldwide Healthcare Trust annual report for the year ended 31 March 2024

12 Creditors amounts falling due within one year

	2024	2023
	£'000	£'000
Amounts due to brokers	23,973	9,432
Overdraft drawn*	68,942	55,928
Other creditors and accruals	7,458	6,745
	100,373	72,105

* The Company's borrowing requirements are met through the utilisation of an overdraft facility provided by J.P. Morgan Securities LLC. The overdraft is drawn down in U.S. dollars. Interest on the drawn overdraft is charged at the United States Overnight Bank Funding Rate plus 45 basis points. As described on page 96 of the annual report, J.P. Morgan Securities LLC may take investments up to 140% of the value of the overdrawn balance as collateral and has been granted a first-priority security interest or lien over the Company's assets.

Long-term fixed rate debt is, nonetheless, a core feature of numerous investment trusts. Table 12C shows long-term fixed rate debt issued by investment trusts between 2020 and early 2022. The table shows the amount of money borrowed, what it represents as a percentage of net assets, the term and the relevant interest rate.

Table 12C: Investment trusts that have issued long-term fixed rate debt between 2020 and early 2022

Fund	Date	Value	% of net assets	Maturity	Interest rate
Scottish Mortgage	Jan-22	$400m	1.8%	30yrs / 35yrs / 40yrs	2.99% / 3.04% / 3.09%
Greencoat UK Wind	Jan-22	£200m	6.6%	8yrs	-
Impact Healthcare REIT	Dec-21	£37m / £38m	19.1%	14yrs	3.00% / 2.92%
F&C IT	Dec-21	£50m / £45m / £45m	2.7%	15yrs / 34yrs / 39yrs	2.06% / 1.96% / 1.87%
Home REIT	Dec-21	£130m	21.8%	15yrs	2.53%
Tritax Eurobox	Dec-21	€100m / €50m / €50m	21.8%	7yrs / 10yrs / 12yrs	1.22% / 1.45% / 1.59%
Law Debenture	Nov-21	£20m / £30m	5.2%	20yrs / 29yrs	2.54% / 2.53%
Pershing Square	Sep-21	$700m	6.6%	10yrs	3.25%
Pershing Square	Sep-21	€500m	5.4%	6yrs	1.38%
Blackrock Smaller Companies	Sep-21	£25m	2.3%	25yrs	2.47%
Mercantile	Sep-21	£150m	6.1%	20yrs / 30yrs / 40yrs	1.98% / 2.05% / 1.77%
Scottish Mortgage	Aug-21	£100m	0.5%	15yrs	2.03%
Scottish Mortgage	Aug-21	£100m	0.5%	25yrs	2.30%
Bankers IT	Jul-21	£37m	2.39%	24yrs	2.28%
Bankers IT	Jul-21	€44m	2.55%	10yrs	1.67%
Baillie Gifford European Growth	Jun-21	€30m	4.4%	15yrs	1.55%
Murray International	Apr-21	£50m	3.2%	10yrs	2.24%
Baillie Gifford European Growth	Nov-20	€30m	5.6%	20yrs	1.57%

Fund	Date	Value	% of net assets	Maturity	Interest rate
North American Income Trust	Nov-20	$50m	9.9%	10 / 15yrs	2.70% / 2.96%
Aberdeen Standard Asia Focus	Oct-20	£30m	7.8%	15yrs	3.05%
Pershing Square	Aug-20	$200m	2.6%	12yrs	3.00%
Monks	Aug-20	£100m	4.2%	25 / 34yrs	1.77% / 1.86%
JPMorgan American	Feb-20	$65m	4.8%	11yrs	2.55%
Scottish Mortgage	Jan-20	£188m	2.2%	20 / 25 / 30yrs	2.3% / 1.65% / 1.77%

Source: Numis Securities

From this data, we can see that some of these trusts, such as Baillie Gifford European Growth, have obtained very attractive rates when it comes to their financing. However, I suspect that is often down to luck as much as judgement. That's because trusts that use long-term gearing will tend to renew their debt facility around the time that it expires or matures. As such, the prevailing interest rate will often dictate the ongoing cost of debt. For example, many trusts either took on, or renewed, existing borrowing during the 1980s and 1990s at a time when interest rates were relatively high. That is why Scottish Mortgage is still paying 12% on one tranche of its debt, the £50m 6-12% Stepped Interest Debenture issued in 1986 and due to mature in 2026.

Sources of debt

In terms of obtaining debt, most short-term or flexible varieties are arranged via a bank. Longer-term borrowing, on the other hand, can be secured via a debt issue. Being companies, investment trusts can issue debt securities in the form of bonds or debenture stock (a loan agreement giving the lender security over the borrower's assets). These are often purchased by long-term investors such as pension funds.

"Being companies, investment trusts can issue debt securities in the form of bonds or debenture stock (a loan agreement giving the lender security over the borrower's assets)."

By way of an example, we could look at the FCIT 4.25% perpetual (i.e. non-redeemable) debenture stock. Investors, such as pension funds, provided capital to F&C and in return were issued with this fixed income debenture. It entitles the holder to receive 4.25% per annum in perpetuity. This debenture was issued in 1960 (F&C, 2023, p. 94, note 15), a year in which the 2.5% Consol (an undated gilt) was yielding 5.25% (St. Louis Fed, n.d.), so it represents an incredibly competitive cost of capital.

It is worth noting that this ability to issue debt securities is a key feature that sets investment trusts apart from mutual funds.

Although many investment trusts incur their debt at the trust level, some do so via subsidiaries. This is often the case where a subsidiary, such as a special purpose vehicle, holds debt which is specific to the asset, or assets, which it holds. Some trusts use derivatives, such as Contracts For Difference (CFDs) and Swaps to achieve their leverage. BlackRock Throgmorton Trust (THRG) is an example of a trust that leverages its portfolio via derivatives. The THRG 2024 annual report states: "*The Company can be leveraged up to 30% of net assets, which it does through the use of CFDs and total return swaps (instead of through conventional bank borrowings). This enables it to increase or reduce market exposure flexibly and at more competitive margins.*"

Assessing indebtedness

So, how can we compare two similar trusts, when one might enjoy cheap debt whilst the other is saddled with much more expensive borrowing? Most of the legwork here is done by the market, which takes the relative debt positions into account in determining how to price each trust. However, there is an additional adjustment that the trusts themselves often make when it comes to disclosing their NAVs.

To illustrate, let's return to the idea of a pension fund that has bought £100,000 of an investment trust perpetual debenture at 4.25%. Let's also assume that this was issued when prevailing interest rates were 4%, but they are now only 2%. That means the pension fund is enjoying annual coupons of 4.25% of its original investment, which is above the market rate of 2%. This begs a question: what should the value of that £100,000 of debt be to a new buyer? If it were to change hands now, it would likely do so at a higher amount than £100,000 via a process known as 'marking to market'. This effectively values a bond by reference to the market price of similar instruments, given prevailing interest rates. Stay with me!

That implies that the mark to market valuation in the issuer's books, for £100,000 nominal value of debenture issued, might be £120,000. By extension, the trust that has issued the debenture will need to reduce its overall asset value by £120,000, rather than £100,000 of nominal value, to arrive at a mark to market net asset (i.e. after debt) valuation.

That explains why most trusts that issue fixed rate debt disclose several NAV figures. These should include the standard calculation, alongside one where any debt is valued at its par value and a further one where it is valued at its market value. In situations where debt bears an interest rate below the prevailing market rate, the market value figure will be higher than the standard NAV, and vice versa where the interest rate being borne is above prevailing rates.

The preferred AIC standard is for debt to be measured at fair value in calculating NAV per share and, therefore, in calculating discounts and premiums.

Hunting down data

Let's turn to F&C once again. We can see from Table 12D that when debt is valued at its par value – being the value at which it was issued, or £100,000 in the previous example – we get an NAV per share of £9.716. However, if F&C marks the debt to market, we get an NAV per share of £10.0614.

Table 12D: Extract from NAV announcment (on 04/01/2024) of FCIT as at close of business on 04/01/2024

RNS Number: 8312Y

F&C Investment Trust PLC		
05 January 2024		
	05/01/2024	

Net Asset Values per share as at close of business on	04/01/2024	

The unaudited net asset values (NAVs) of the Company are noted below (where applicable) in pence per share. NAVs are calculated in accordance with stated policies. Applicable accounting standards and AIC recommendations are followed.

	Pence per share	Pence per share
	Cum Income	Ex Income
F&C Investment Trust PLC		
LEI: 213800W6B18ZHTNG7371		
Financial liabilities at fair value	1,006.14	1,003.09
Financial liabilities at par value	971.6	968.55

Source: RNS, the news service of the London Stock Exchange

So, where can investors find information regarding leverage? As usual, the financial statements should contain most of what they need. Table 12E is an extract from the balance sheet for the Alliance Trust,* another large global trust investing primarily in equities. We can see that short-term debt under 'current liabilities' is primarily comprised of a £63.5m bank loan. Meanwhile, long-term debt is almost entirely comprised of £143.1m of unsecured fixed rate loan notes. The numbers next to these values indicate notes to the accounts which contain further information. Note 12 for example reveals the interest rate payable on each tranche of borrowing along with information about outstanding terms and other relevant details.

---

* Now Alliance Witan.

Table 12E: Extract from page 79 of the Alliance Trust annual report for the year ended 31/12/2023

BALANCE SHEET AS AT 31 DECEMBER 2023

£000	Note	2023	2022
Non-current assets			
Investments held at fair value	9	3,482,329	3,012,492
Right of use asset			54
		3,482,329	3,012,546
Current assets			
Outstanding settlements and other receivables	10	9,321	9,648
Cash and cash equivalents	17	84,974	88,864
		94,295	98,512
Total assets		3,576,624	3,111,058
Current liabilities			
Outstanding settlements and other payables	11	−9,792	−9,344
Bank loans	12	-	−63,500
Lease liability	19	-	−38
		−9,792	−72,882
Total assets less current liabilities		3,566,832	3,038,176
Non-current liabilities			
Unsecured fixed rate loan notes held at fair value	12	−215,144	−143,141
Bank loans	12	-15,000	-
Lease liability			−16
		−230,144	−143,157
Net assets		3,336,668	2,895,019
Equity			
Share capital	13	7,106	7,314
Capital redemption reserve		11,892	11,684
Capital reserve		3,233,372	2,773,687
Revenue reserve		84,318	102,334
Total Equity		3,336,688	2,895,019

There are also normally covenants attached to debt arrangements, such as debentures or bank loans. These are conditions that a lender (a bank or bond investor) builds into the agreement. Examples may include a requirement that the trust's assets must always exceed £100m, or that total debt must not exceed 25% of total assets.

I accept that trawling through multiple annual reports at this level of depth might seem quite onerous to many investors. Fortunately, headline information can be obtained from the AIC website. There, for example, investors can rank trusts by their gearing level, or identify those that carry none at all.

Wrapping up

In terms of practical applications, this sort of analysis and data can help investors to identify trusts with very high levels of gearing. As to how much that is, the answer requires a bit of judgement. For me, a ratio of debt to total asset over 25% is very high in the context of an equity portfolio. That is because even a large cap equity index such as the FTSE 100 can experience drops of 40% or more, peak to trough, and it has done so on at least two occasions since the mid-1990s. That could put a highly geared trust in trouble.

"Gearing of 10%, in this scenario, would add around 0.4% per annum, whilst at 20% we'd be looking at more like 1.0%."

Taking a slightly more scientific approach to justifying this ceiling, if we agree that the long-term (100 years+) return from UK equities is around 9% (Meli and Rajadhyaksha, 2024; iamkate.com, n.d.), during a period when interest rates have averaged about 5% (Bloomberg UKBRBASE Index), then the average differential is roughly 4%. Gearing of 10%, in this scenario, would add around 0.4% per annum, whilst at 20% we'd be looking at more like 1.0% (refer to Table 12F). Over the long term, that feels like a very healthy additional level of return, without taking crazy additional amounts of risk.

Table 12F: Impact of gearing on equity portfolio return

	£m	%
Equity portfolio return		9
Debt cost		5
Equity (£m, as % of net assets)	80	75
Debt (£m, as % of net assets)	20	25
Total assets	100	100
Gross return (Equity return × Total assets, 9% x £100m)	9	
Less cost of debt (Debt cost × Debt, 5% × £20m)	1	
Net return (Gross return less cost of debt)	8	
Return on equity (Net return / Equity, £8m / £80m)		10
Enhancement from gearing (Return on equity less Equity portfolio return, 10% - 9%)		1
Gearing, debt as % gross assets (Debt / Total assets, £20m / £100m)		20
Gearing, debt as % net assets (Debt / Equity, £20m / £80m)		25

I do accept, however, that there is a case for taking on greater leverage in trusts that hold real assets which themselves generate high levels of income. However, even in that scenario, I would be wary of investing in any trust where leverage exceeds 50%. By way of a cautionary note, during the Great Financial Crisis of 2008–09, several trusts that had very high levels of debt (>50%) were forced to rapidly dispose of assets at 'fire sale' prices as debt covenants kicked in and values dropped.

To sum up, we can conclude that the strategic use of financial leverage by investment trusts adds a layer of complexity but also opportunity. The trick is to be selective, so that buying geared funds becomes a reliable way to enhance portfolio returns rather than a gateway to value destruction.

SUMMARY OF KEY POINTS

- Berkshire Hathaway, managed by Warren Buffett, has employed gearing, or leverage, to very good effect.

- Gearing is about borrowing monies to increase the amount of overall investment exposure.

- Gearing can amplify returns when asset prices rise, but it can also magnify losses when they drop.

- Investment trusts can take on short-term, flexible (i.e. easy to repay) debt or longer-term structural borrowing.

- The long-term (100 years+) return from UK equities is around 9%, whilst interest rates have averaged about 5%, underlying the case for gearing up an equity portfolio.

CHAPTER 13

LONG-TERM CAPITAL

"Investing should be more like watching paint dry or watching grass grow. If you want excitement, take $800 and go to Las Vegas."

—Paul Samuelson,
Nobel Prize-winning US economist

SAMUELSON IS MAKING the point that proper investing should be for the long term. But how long is that?

Staying invested

To help answer this important question, Figure 13A, from the Barclays Capital Gilt Equity study, illustrates the range of possible 12-month outcomes for investors in the UK stock market since 1899. The numbers are calculated over different time periods (calibrated on the vertical column) ranging from just one year up to 23 years. The conclusion it draws is stark. The worst one-year investment would have lost close to 60% in real terms (i.e. after inflation). Meanwhile, the best would have led to a gain of almost 100%. This vast range of possible outcomes reveals that investing in equities on only a one-year view is something of a lottery.

Figure 13A: Maximum and minimum real returns over various periods

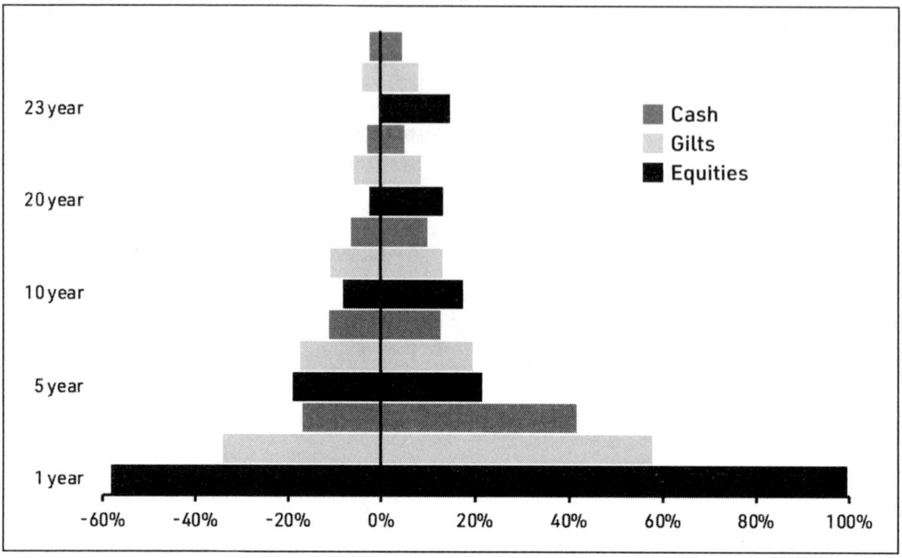

Source: Barclays Capital Gilt Equity Study

The obvious conclusion from this is that one year is a short timeframe during which major events, such as pandemics, wars, major corporate bankruptcies and profit warnings can have a profound effect on the stock market. Anyone unfortunate enough to invest just before such an event is likely to take heavy losses, in the short term. So, if a year is too short as an investment outlook, what about five years? As we can see from the figure, even this may not be an adequate time horizon over which to generate inflation-beating returns from equities if you are unlucky with your initial timing.

It is only once we get to a minimum investment period of 10 years that the odds really tip in our favour when it comes to making money in real terms. As such, I think that is a more reasonable timeframe. Figure 13A then shows that with a very long-term horizon of say 20 years plus, you stand an excellent chance of making money in real terms. Importantly, the 'variance' of returns (i.e. the range of likely outcomes) also falls significantly as the holding period is extended. So much so, that historically when equities have been held for as long as 20 years, the worst recorded outcome (i.e. the minimum inflation-adjusted return) has been greater than that for either (theoretically safer) government bonds (gilts) or cash deposits.

Bailing out

So why do so many investors fail to take a 20-year view? The simple truth is that life often gets in the way. Circumstances change – you may need to buy a house, move to a bigger one, pay school fees or support a family member. Without some careful planning, all of these things may make an unexpected dent in a long-term investment portfolio.

Unfortunately, many professional managers are also unable to take a truly long-term view because they are measured on short-term performance. As such, if they stick with a poorly performing investment strategy, they risk investors withdrawing their capital. In such a scenario, managers of mutual funds may find themselves caught in a tricky situation as redemption requests come in. Under pressure to meet them, they may resort to damage limitation at the expense of longer-term gains.

Taking the long view

Investing for the long term requires a strategic approach. It requires an approach that considers factors such as stability of the capital base, growth potential of the portfolio holdings and risk management to avoid outsized losses.

Fortunately, short-term performance pressures don't usually impinge as much on investment trust managers. Although unhappy investors may sell shares, thereby increasing the risk of a wide discount emerging, this should not trigger the mass outflows seen by an equivalent mutual fund. That's because the trust board is likely to be more patient than the average investor and allow the portfolio manager time to run with a chosen strategy. And even when a manager is removed, an incoming one will expect to discuss not just the existing portfolio but also the investment horizon and minimising transaction costs. Further, the way that investment trusts are structured makes them ideal in other ways for long-term investors.

Take their ability to invest in illiquid assets, which should provide investors with a higher return than an identical liquid asset. This additional compensation, for the risk of not being able to sell an asset easily, is so prevalent that it has a name – the 'illiquidity premium'. As such, we will be devoting the whole of Chapter 25 to it. For now, the point is that provided investors can take a very long-term perspective, they gain an advantage through their ability to bag this type of premium. The closed-ended structure of investment trusts facilitates the kind of buy and hold approach that is needed and can result in lower portfolio turnover and reduced transaction costs.

"The problem for investors in mutual funds and publicly quoted stocks is that they miss the opportunity to gain exposure to the best of these fast-growing private businesses."

In that context, investment trusts often venture beyond the traditional realm of publicly traded stocks, and into unlisted companies. By opting to stay private, an unlisted company can avoid the scrutiny and short termism that comes with the public company quarterly results circuit, reduce costs by maintaining a concentrated investor base and enjoy a lower regulatory burden. The problem for investors in mutual funds and publicly quoted stocks is that they miss the opportunity to gain exposure to the best of these fast-growing private businesses. As Figure 13B shows, this means they may miss out on some of their best years. The figure shows the timeline of funding rounds for Airbnb up until its IPO in 2020. We can see that its value rose exponentially in the 10-year period prior to the firm going public.

Chart 13B: Airbnb: Timeline of cumulative private funding and post money valuations from inception to IPO

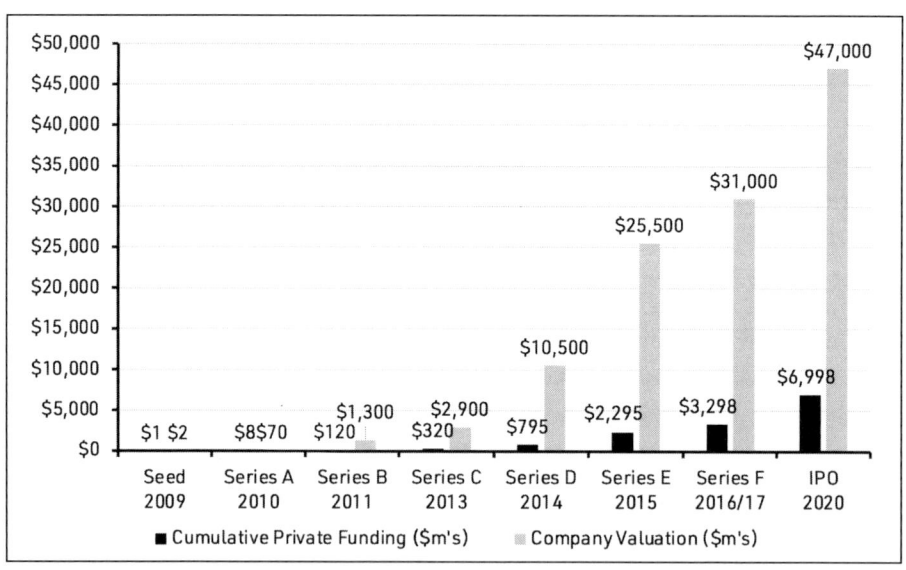

Source: Stanford Venture Capital Initiative; Sharespost, Techcrunch

Many investment trusts invest in early-stage growth companies. Unlike conventional venture funds, investment trusts can often hold these investments indefinitely.

The fact that many investment trusts employ 'gearing' (borrowing money to enhance returns) allows them to further capitalise on promising opportunities and boost long-term performance. It is worth noting that the power of gearing increases over time. At, say, 10% it boosts a 10% portfolio return to 11% (before interest costs). Let's say that this translates into an additional 0.5% after interest costs. Compounded over 25 years, that would generate an additional 13% return.

Another structural advantage of closed-ended investment trusts is the requirement to provide investors with a diversified portfolio. Diversification is a crucial aspect of managing risk, especially over the long term.

As for the trusts which focus on generating dividend income, a closed-ended structure gives them a high degree of control over dividend payments. This stability and income visibility can be particularly appealing to investors who may rely on a consistent income stream during their retirement years.

Wrapping up

Investment trusts are a compelling vehicle when it comes to long-term wealth accumulation. A closed-ended structure, combined with a focus on the long term, make them ideal for patient investors seeking to capitalise on a wide range of investment opportunities.

SUMMARY OF KEY POINTS

- One year is a very short timeframe to invest in equities.

- Being able to take a long-term view is a huge advantage in the investment world.

- The closed-ended structure allows fund managers to buy and hold investments without the need to sell assets to meet redemption requests.

- Investment trusts often venture beyond the traditional realm of publicly traded stocks, providing access to illiquid assets that can enhance long-term returns.

- Many investment trusts invest in alternative assets like infrastructure, private equity and real estate, offering exposure to assets that can improve portfolio diversification and mitigate risk.

CHAPTER 14

SMOOTHING INCOME: DIVIDEND HEROES AND RESERVES

"Do you know the only thing that gives me pleasure? It's to see my dividends coming in."

—John D. Rockefeller,
US business magnate

ONE DISTINCTIVE FEATURE of investment trusts is their ability to control the level of dividend income that they distribute to investors. In this chapter, I want to explore the benefits of this for investors in a bit more detail.

Creating flexibility

Unlike mutual funds, which must distribute all the income they receive (net of costs) during the accounting period in which it is received, investment trusts can retain some of it to build reserves for future distribution. Specifically, although they must ensure that *at least* 85% of their net income is distributed to shareholders to enjoy the tax benefits associated with investment trust status (primarily the ability to sell assets free of capital gains and corporation tax), the remaining undistributed income (i.e. *up to* 15% of the total income) can be set aside for future years.

This retained income can then be applied to smooth dividend payments to shareholders during periods of market volatility, or when specific assets in a trust's portfolio may experience income fluctuations.

Further, in 2012, HMRC amended the rules so that investment trusts could also make distributions from capital profits. This has added another level of flexibility when it comes to paying consistently high dividends which may even grow over time to take account of the impact of inflation.

Delving into the detail

So, what are these 'reserves' from which dividends can be drawn? Despite the volume of material available on this topic, I still think there is some misunderstanding here. There is nothing untoward happening, in so far as these reserves are not invested in a separate pot to the main portfolio. They are the product of a simple accounting convention, but a very important one for investors seeking income.

By way of an illustration, let's say that an investment trust has £25m of previously undistributed income (being the maximum 15% of prior years' income that has not been paid out to shareholders) and has generated £100m of gains on investments that have been sold. The result is that it now has an additional £125m available, over and above the current year's net income, which can be distributed in the form of dividends. Some critics frown at the idea of distributing capital reserves as income in this way. However, I am not one of them.

To explain why, we'll start with two trusts. Both invest in global equities and are the same size. One has been around for 50 years and has diligently tucked away 15% of its annual net income, such that it now has a distributable pot of £50m. The second has been around for 10 years. It doesn't have any revenue reserves, but it does have £50m of capital reserves generated by profitable asset sales.

Despite these different origins, to me there is no practical difference between the two. Neither trust will be holding specific investments that can be tied to their respective £50m of reserves. Neither will you find a special holding account at either, with £50m sitting in it generating interest. In both cases the £50m is a function of an accounting convention. In order to realise this £50m and distribute it to shareholders, both trusts will need to find the relevant cash, perhaps by liquidating £50m of investments. As such, there is no reason why the first trust's distribution (based on £50m of revenue reserves) is any different from the second's (based on £50m of capital reserves).

There is an argument that the distribution of capital reserves could lead to overdistributions that might be more than the trust's long-term annualised total return. However, this does not mean that all distributions from capital reserves are a bad thing. Ultimately, both revenue and capital reserves represent monies that *do not have to be* distributed. They are presumably being distributed because the board has determined that this is what shareholders want.

What matters far more than the nuances of this ongoing debate is the sustainability of the overall dividend policy, given the need to maintain long-term capital growth. In that context, the use of capital reserves could trigger overdistributions above a trust's long-term annualised total return. But ultimately, both revenue and capital reserves represent monies that could either be prudently held back, or be paid out, according to what the board deems most advantageous to a trust's shareholders. As such, a portfolio manager should be guided as to the proposed size of any distribution, so that they ensure they can meet it out of income reserves, capital reserves, or both.

This flexibility is valuable. An exclusive focus on trusts that pay their distributions from current year receipts and revenue reserves could skew a portfolio towards certain markets, such as the UK, and away from certain investment styles, such as growth. Trusts that distribute from capital reserves, on the other hand, can divorce their distribution policy from their overall investment policy. In short, including 'capital distributors' in a portfolio helps achieve greater balance.

Focusing on returns

So, what is the best portfolio strategy for an investment trust that wishes to grow its income over the long term? My answer is it should aim for an attractive and sustainable total return. Once the board has decided what the dividend policy should be, the portfolio manager should try to maximise the trust's total return, unconstrained by whether, or not, an attractive area of the market is income producing.

There are several ways this can be done. The cornerstone of any equity investment strategy should be to focus on companies run by management teams with willingness, and ability, to grow profits over time. It helps if the business model is robust, such that profits are not overly sensitive to the gyrations of the economic cycle.

Then there are fixed income securities such as high yield bonds. Although the income from these does not increase over time, a high cash yield can help to take away the pressure to generate income from the rest of the portfolio, which in turn offers more scope for capital growth. For example, Murray International combines global equities and high yield bonds in its portfolio. The result has been a high yield from a trust that consistently increases its dividend.

A small number of trusts also employ income enhancing options strategies. This is quite a complex area so we will only take a brief tour of it here. Let's say a trust holds a share priced at 100p. The portfolio manager thinks that, whilst the long-term upside is attractive, the near term is less certain. They could choose to sell a 'call' option with an exercise price of 110p. This effectively hands the buyer of such an option the benefit of any share price upside above 110p, usually over a period of three months. In return the trust receives some income (by way of a 'premium') from the buyer. The overall impact of this deal is to turn an uncertain capital gain into a known level of income for the trust. Whilst some investment trusts sell these 'covered calls', this is not a common practice.

Weighing up strategies

So far, so good. However, what is to stop investors selling investments to meet their own income requirements, rather than relying on an investment trust to do it for them? After all, if investments are held within an ISA, all gains are free of income and capital gains tax. Meanwhile, as say a higher rate taxpayer operating outside of a tax wrapper, you could opt to sell investments to trigger a capital gains tax liability instead of income tax. This may reduce the rate at which you are taxed as the two regimes are different.

"Investment trusts with sound dividend policies ultimately offer greater visibility over the income stream that lands in your bank account each month and come with less monitoring and lower transaction costs."

The truth for most investors, however, is that liquidating ISA holdings is often a bad idea (given the tax shelter effect is subsequently lost), whilst outside of this realising capital is fiddly and only tax free to a decreasing extent thanks to progressive reductions in the annual capital gains tax-free allowance.

Investment trusts with sound dividend policies ultimately offer greater visibility over the income stream that lands in your bank account each month and come with less monitoring and lower transaction costs.

Searching for heroes

With that in mind, one subset of the investment trust community has used past reserves to such good effect that they have managed to increase their dividends for at least 20 consecutive years. These are known as the 'dividend heroes', a term coined by the AIC. An up-to-date list can be found at https://www.theaic.co.uk/income-finder/dividend-heroes.

The most impressive record belongs to the City of London Investment Trust. If you bought this trust as England were winning the World Cup in 1966 and held it until 2024, you would have enjoyed an unbroken 58-year record of dividend increases. That is no mean feat given that most of this income stream was generated prior to the rule change that allowed the use of capital reserves to supplement dividends. Indeed, it is a doubly impressive result given that the trust weathered the 1970s oil shock, 1987 stock market crash, 2000 dot-com boom and bust, and the Great Financial Crisis of 2008–09.

That said, although most trusts that achieve dividend hero status tend to keep it, some don't. Take Temple Bar, a UK equity income trust, which was a dividend hero until it came unstuck in 2020. Having entered that pandemic year with very high leverage during a sharply declining market, the board chose to cut the dividend and rebase it at a lower level for the future.

We will return to this theme in more detail in Chapter 33.

Wrapping up

In summary, income smoothing plays a key role in the financial management of investment trusts, offering a mechanism by which they can create a consistent income stream for investors. As such, the associated investment strategies may deploy reserve accumulation, derivatives (e.g. covered calls) and diversification in a bid to mitigate the impact of market volatility on income distribution. However, in doing so, they must always strike a balance between maintaining both income and transparency for their underlying investors if they are to retain their loyalty.

SUMMARY OF KEY POINTS

- Investment trusts can retain income (in a revenue reserve) in the current year to supplement income in future years.

- Since 2012, investment trusts can also make distributions from capital profits (capital reserves).

- Both revenue and capital reserves are simply bookkeeping conventions. These monies are not separate to the investment portfolio in any real sense.

- AIC dividend heroes are investment trusts that managed to increase their dividends for at least 20 consecutive years.

- Some dividend heroes have increased their dividend every year for more than 50 consecutive years.

CHAPTER 15

DIVERSIFICATION EXPLAINED

"I think the secret is if you have a lot of stocks, some will do mediocre, some will do okay, and if one or two of 'em go up big time, you produce a fabulous result."

—Peter Lynch, manager of the Magellan Fund at Fidelity Investments (1977–1990)

IN THIS CHAPTER, we will explore the key concept of portfolio diversification, unravel the mysteries of the efficient frontier and discuss the implications for investment trusts.

Why diversify?

The principle that underpins this crucial concept is simple – instead of putting all your hard-earned money into a single investment, you spread it across a mixture instead. Eggs and baskets! The aim is to reduce the impact of a single poor investment decision. If one asset in your portfolio takes a tumble, others should help cushion the impact. Naturally, if the whole market is collapsing, then most equity-based investments are likely to fall, but in normal conditions diversification is a powerful ally.

So much so that Harry Markowitz, a Nobel laureate in economics, and the creator of the modern portfolio theory, or MPT (discussed shortly), is credited with saying, "Diversification is the only free lunch in finance." That is because by diversifying, you can potentially increase overall returns without increasing risk, or reduce overall risk without reducing returns. In other words, it is a strategy that can provide benefits at no extra cost.

"Diversification is the only free lunch in finance" (Harry Markowitz).

I once had the pleasure of sitting next to Mr Markowitz at a lunch meeting in London. During our conversation I asked him how he invested his own money. He paused before saying, "I just pick a point on the curve and invest." That curve is what economists call the 'efficient frontier', which we will return to shortly.

How much is enough?

So, how many investments do you need to properly diversify? I have often heard other people in the investment game claim that a 30-stock portfolio provides adequate diversification. In their 1970 study 'Some studies of variability of returns on investments in common stocks', Lawrence Fisher and James Lorie found that a randomly created portfolio of 32 stocks, with no more than one stock from any single industrial group, could reduce the range of returns by 95–100%, compared to a single-stock portfolio. In other words, a portfolio of 32 stocks, diversified by industrial sector, showed a very similar range of outcomes as the entire US equity market, which showed a 100% reduction in the range of returns of a single-stock portfolio. This study could be the source of the widely expressed view that a 30-stock portfolio provides most of the diversification that you need.

Is this a reasonable view? I'm not convinced. Firstly, this study only examined the distribution of returns within one asset class, equities. Furthermore, it only examined US equities. I suspect that the main source of diversification was due to the restriction that no more than one stock could be drawn from the same industrial group. Most concentrated portfolios (in investment trusts) that I have come across tend to focus on stocks with similar characteristics, rather than being broadly diversified. I posit that many people managing a 30-stock portfolio have seen that portfolio deviate markedly from the overall equity market. Also, the Fisher and Lorie study focused on the *range* of returns rather than on the investment returns themselves.

A subsequent study by Eric Crittenden and Cole Wilcox (2008) examined the lifetime returns of 8,000 US stocks between 1983 and 2006. Their conclusions pointed to the very wide range of outcomes for individual stocks. Key findings included:

- 39% of stocks had a negative lifetime total return.

- 18.5% of stocks lost at least 75% of their value.

- 64% of stocks underperformed the Russell 3000 Index during their lifetime.

- 25% of stocks were responsible for all the market's gains.

Given that (approximately) two in every five stocks in the study either lost 75% or gained more than 300% it is very difficult to see how a 30-stock portfolio can provide adequate diversification over very long timeframes.

And, if 30 holdings are not enough, how many stocks are? I'm not sure there is a correct answer to this question. However, the two studies cited and a dose of common sense lead me to say three things with a degree of confidence.

Firstly, a stock-only portfolio should have sensible industrial sector diversification. Secondly, a stock-only portfolio should have a lot more than 30 holdings to stand the best chance of capturing some of the big winners and ensuring the big losers do not 'carry you out'. Thirdly, a single holding in an equity investment trust should provide significantly better diversification than a single stock, or even a handful of stocks.

Mastering modern portfolio theory (MPT)

First, some context. The MPT mentioned earlier is fundamental to the fields of finance and investment. Developed in the 1950s, it revolutionised the way investors approach risk and return by introducing the concept of diversification. Although MPT has been heavily criticised since the 1950s, it offers a framework for optimising the risk–return trade-off for a collection of investments. Its foundations lie in the basic premise that investors face a fundamental choice when constructing portfolios – increasing investment returns generally comes with higher risk and vice versa. However, getting the mix of assets right can improve this trade-off.

Central to MPT is the idea that diversification can reduce risk. That, in turn, rests on a key insight, that different types of assets (e.g. shares, bonds and property) do not all move in the same direction at the same time. When one group performs well, others may not. This observation can be harnessed to lower overall portfolio risk.

Digging deeper

Now for a quick detour into some rocket science. Any reader who would rather stick to the pure basics may want to skip this section. For everyone else, it is time to introduce the 'efficient frontier', or what Markowitz referred to as 'the curve'. Its job, in simple terms, is to reveal the best theoretical risk–reward trade-offs and it does so as shown in Figure 15A.

On the horizontal axis, we calibrate price risk (aka 'volatility'), and on the vertical axis, the corresponding return (or 'profit'). The efficient frontier then represents the combination of investments that offers the highest overall returns for a given level of risk, or the lowest overall risk for a given level of return.

Figure 15A: Hypothetical efficient frontier – equities and bonds

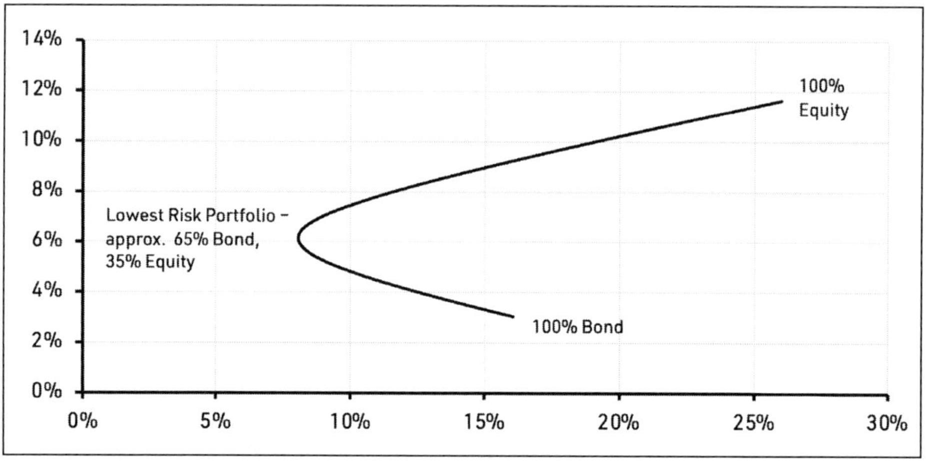

X = risk, Y = return

So, what are we looking at here? Let's start with the point on the curve top right – this represents the risk and return trade-off for a hypothetical portfolio that is 100% equity based. Move left and the equity proportion reduces whilst the bond proportion increases. Eventually you get to the point at the other end of the curve, representing a portfolio that is 100% invested in bonds. Now we can better understand what Markowitz meant when he said he just picked a point on the curve and invested. In effect, he was assessing the level of risk he felt was most appropriate for him and opting for a mixture of equities and bonds in the relevant proportion.

Diversification is then the secret sauce that helps you to move along this curve. Let us say you are weighing up two classic asset classes – stocks and bonds. When you combine them in your portfolio, their returns and risks interact in a way that reduces overall risk. Like two people on different ends of a seesaw – if one goes up, the other goes down, creating a predictably smoother ride for them than if they were both sitting on the same end.

But why is the line curved? The reason is that the prices for equities and bonds do not tend to move in the same direction at the same time. To understand why this matters, let's assume a portfolio only holds two oil stocks, Shell and BP. In that scenario, the efficient frontier, which ranges from 100% Shell / 0% BP to 0% Shell / 100% BP, would be a relatively straight line, rather than a curve. This is because these two stocks respond in a similar way to external factors such as the oil price and the sterling / US dollar exchange rate.

As such, there is limited diversification benefit from holding them. An obvious exception would be a large shock specific to one of them, such as BP's Deepwater Horizon disaster in the Gulf of Mexico in 2010. However, most of the time they will behave in a very similar manner. But as different assets such as bonds are added into the mix, this line starts to bend to reflect the fact that bonds and shares do not generally behave in the same way under similar market conditions. This fact can be exploited to reduce risk without sacrificing returns.

Benefits and risks

That said, diversification isn't just about spreading your money across different asset classes. It is also about diversifying within them. For example, it can be achieved from shares by investing across different sectors like technology, healthcare and energy. Once again, the idea is to reduce the risk associated with any single stock or sector taking a nosedive.

Meanwhile, although the efficient frontier provides a useful framework for understanding the trade-off between risk and return, investors should be aware of its limitations. One is that just because an asset or a portfolio has behaved a certain way in the past, does not guarantee similar performance in the future. There can also be downsides to very broad diversification if it means a portfolio contains a lot of underperformers.

In that context, a research paper by Hendrick Bessembinder (2018) contained some illuminating findings. The paper explored the long-term performance of a broad selection of listed US stocks compared to bonds, from 1926 to

2016. Its top-line conclusion – that stocks generally yield better returns in aggregate than US Treasury Bills (government 'IOUs') over prolonged periods – is unsurprising. The eye-opening finding, however, was that most individual stocks did not. Around 57% of those chosen *underperformed* Treasuries. Indeed, the entire gain in the US stock market since 1926 could be attributed to only the best-performing 4% of companies!

There are two ways these results can be interpreted in terms of formulating an investment approach. One is to focus on identifying the relatively small number of stocks that can deliver outsized returns. Effectively, this is the approach adopted by the investment managers of Scottish Mortgage Investment Trust. The alternative conclusion is that the only way to ensure that you have exposure to the market's winners is to get exposure to all of it.

The critics

This finding, and a desire to outperform the market rather than simply track it, may help to explain why not all investors fully embrace diversification. Andrew Carnegie, the Scottish American industrialist, led the expansion of the US steel industry in the late 19th century and is often regarded as one of history's wealthiest people. He is reported to have said to an audience of students in Pittsburgh in 1885: "Put all your eggs in one basket, and then watch that basket" (Brands, 2010).

US investing giant Warren Buffett also emphasises the importance of understanding your investments as an alternative to extensive diversification. He has always backed his own knowledge and expertise. As he puts it, "Wide diversification is only required when investors do not understand what they are doing."

"Wide diversification is only required when investors do not understand what they are doing" (Warren Buffett).

Indeed, the stronger your stomach for risk and the longer your time horizon, the less your need for overly broad diversification. In the paper, 'Keynes the Stock Market Investor: A Quantitative Analysis*' Chambers, Dimson, and Foo chronicle how John Maynard Keynes adapted his investment approach following the Great Depression by trading less frequently, becoming more patient and focusing on the long term. This approach led to very impressive investment returns. Table 15A shows Keynes' portfolio turnover (i.e. the percentage of the portfolio that changed due to trading) by decade.

Table 15A: Portfolio turnover – Keynes' discretionary portfolio, part of King's College Cambridge endowment

1921–29	55%
1930–39	30%
1940–46	14%

Source: Chambers et al. (2015)

Keynes' discretionary portfolio generated an annual return of +16.0%, from the financial year ended August 1922 to August 1946, compared to a +10.4% return for the equal-weighted UK equity market index.

The rest of us

Yet, despite the views of some high-profile fans of portfolio concentration, my personal preference has always been for diversification. The reason was perhaps best summed up by UK investing guru Sir John Templeton: "The only investors that don't need to diversify are those that are right 100% of the time" (Garner and Pratt, 2024). Yes, some highly skilled individuals may be able to outperform the market by running a narrow portfolio of stocks, but they are usually blessed with a rare combination of deep knowledge, longstanding experience and in a few cases, luck.

Which brings me back to investment trusts, an investment vehicle that can offer radically different strategies to suit a range of investors. To illustrate this point, we can look at two trusts. The first is City of London, which holds UK equities with the aim of generating an attractive, rising income. The second is Fidelity Special Values, which also invests in UK equities but with more of a growth objective. We can see from the efficient frontier graph generated by both over the last 10 years (refer to Figure 15B) that there is limited diversification benefit to be gained from holding them. We can see this from the fact that although Fidelity Special Values (9.4% pa return) has outperformed City of London (6.9% pa return) over the period there is limited diversification benefit from holding both trusts. Both trusts display similar share price volatility of around 15.3%–15.7% per annum. The 'curve' shows a very slight reduction in risk, to about 15.0% per annum – so not a very efficient portfolio when these two are combined. I'm not saying there is no point in holding both trusts. There is. They have different investment styles which will should lead to different, but profitable, long term outcomes. However, holding both does not offer much diversification benefit.

Figure 15B: Efficient frontier, based on share price total return of City of London (CTY) and Fidelity Special Values (FSV), over 10 years to 31/12/2024

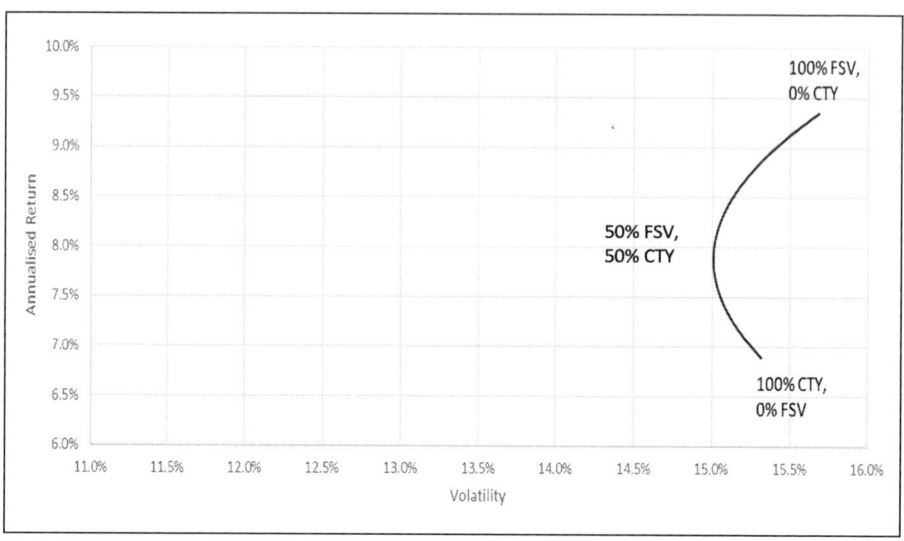

Next, we put City of London alongside BH Macro, a trust that provides exposure to several hedge fund strategies with the aim of generating steady long-term returns coupled with low volatility. As we can see from Figure 15C, this pairing has offered excellent diversification over this period (10 years to 31/12/2024). What this means is that a portfolio made up of these two trusts in equal proportions displayed markedly lower volatility than if we had simply held one or the other. Figure 15C, which shares the same volatility range as Figure 15B on the horizontal axis, clearly shows the diversification via the 50:50 portfolio, which is right over on the left, illustrating much lower overall volatility.

Figure 15C: Efficient frontier, based on share price total return of City of London (CTY) and BH Macro (BHMG), over 10 years to 31/12/2024

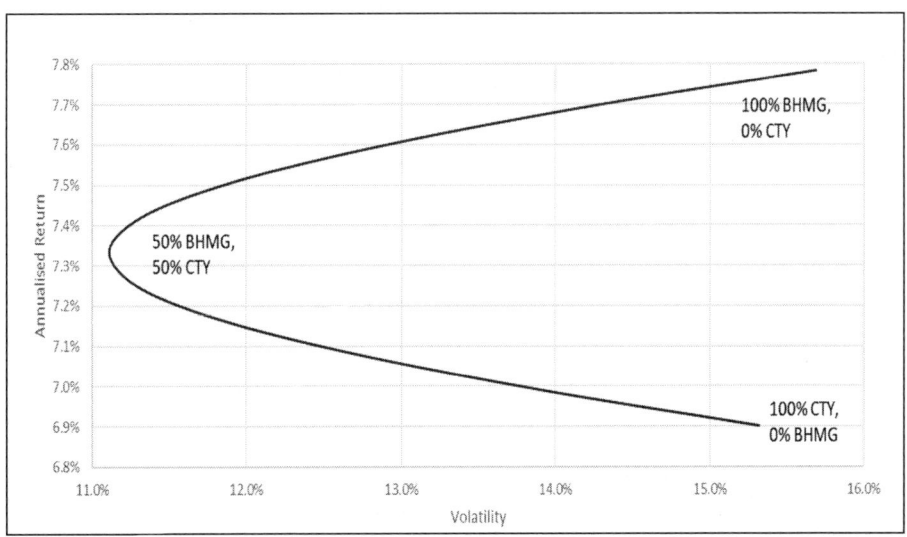

Volatility is annualised standard deviation.

A word of warning on BH Macro, however. Its ability to control its discount is another matter. BH Macro's share price dropped from a premium (to NAV) of 18% to a discount of 14% during 2022 and 2023. Much of the problem with BH Macro's discount control lies with its investment management agreement, which contains a clause whereby, if the trust makes repurchases of shares of more than 5%, it is required to pay the investment manager an additional fee equal to 2% of the value repurchased. This does detract from its diversification potential, but the key is to only buy it at a sizeable discount whilst the management agreement contains this clause.

Harnessing 'beta'

For anyone wondering whether there is a quick way to gauge the relationship between different asset classes when compared to either each other or the stock market, it is time to wrap up this chapter with a short tour of the beta measure. Without delving into the maths here, this captures in a single number, which can be positive or negative, the extent to which an asset moves in the same direction (positive beta) or different direction (negative beta) to the stock market.

Let's say that an asset has a beta of 0.9 when compared to the UK stock market. This means that based on historic observation, for every 10% movement up or down in the broader market the asset in question tends to move up or down by 9%. If, on the other hand, it had a beta of −0.9 then it tends to move down by 9% when the market moves up by 10%, and up by 9% when the market moves down by 10%.

Since betas are calculated by reference to the previous relationship between two assets, they can change over time. However, they can be helpful when comparing different assets to each other and the wider market and when it comes to measuring portfolio risk.

Given that economies and markets tend to go up for more years than they go down, most investors aim to be invested in assets with positive betas overall. However, assets with low or negative betas can provide powerful diversification benefits. The question is then how to best harness them.

Table 15B shows a sample of investment trusts with various betas compared to that of the UK stock market over the last five years. We can see that the top five trusts have betas ranging from 1.2 to 1.4, meaning that they have tended to move up or down by 12–14% for every 10% move in the market. This is partly explained by their high growth strategies or by leverage, which we covered in Chapter 12. We can see that City of London has the closest beta to the UK market over this period, which is unsurprising given it holds a broad portfolio of UK equities. The trusts at the bottom of Table 15B, on the other hand, have shown virtually no sensitivity to stock market movements (a beta of zero). This is primarily because their main objective is not to generate returns from stock markets. Instead, they build strategies around investments that are not correlated with general stock market movements.

"City of London has the closest beta to the UK market over this period, which is unsurprising given it holds a broad portfolio of UK equities."

Table 15B: Investment trust betas

Investment trust	Ticker	Beta
3i Group Ord	III	1.4
Molten Ventures Ord	GROW	1.4
Mercantile Ord	MRC	1.3
Allianz Technology Trust Ord	ATT	1.2
BlackRock Smaller Companies Ord	BRSC	1.2
City of London Ord	CTY	1.0
Ruffer Investment Company Ord	RICA	0.2
BH Macro GBP Ord	BHMG	0.0
BioPharma Credit Ord	BPCR	0.0
Chenavari Toro Income Fund Ord	TORO	0.0
US Solar Fund Ord	USF	−0.1

Beta versus the FTSE All Share Index, over a five-year period ended 31/12/2024. Daily data points.

Source: Morningstar

It is worth noting that although a textbook might suggest investors should seek some exposure to trusts which are *negatively* correlated with equities, these are difficult to find in practice. This is primarily because investment trusts are themselves quoted on the stock market and are therefore bound to mimic at least some of its gyrations.

Wrapping up

I will close out this chapter by cautioning readers that whilst diversification can help to reduce volatility, it cannot render any investment trust strategy entirely risk free. Further, the effectiveness of diversification can vary based on market conditions. Fortunately, investors can also help themselves when it comes to weathering market cycles through something called 'pound cost averaging'. This is a topic we will return to in Chapter 22.

SUMMARY OF KEY POINTS

- Harry Markowitz, a Nobel laureate in economics, and the creator of modern portfolio theory, is credited with saying, "Diversification is the only free lunch in finance."

- Different types of investments move in different ways and by different magnitudes. This tendency can be harnessed to lower overall portfolio risk.

- The efficient frontier represents the combination of investments that offers the highest overall returns for a given level of risk, or the lowest overall risk for a given level of return.

- The stronger your stomach for risk and the longer your time horizon, the less your need for overly broad diversification.

- Several investment trusts aim for low volatility. They do this via different strategies such as multi-asset diversification, fixed income or hedging strategies.

CHAPTER 16

THE ANNUAL REPORT

*"Other guys read Playboy.
I read annual reports."*
—**Warren Buffett**

WHILST PERHAPS NOT the most exciting read for a layperson, the annual report is nonetheless an essential one and should be readily available from a trust's website. The AIC also stores the annual reports of most trusts on its website (https://www.theaic.co.uk). All listed companies are required to produce this document and investment trusts are no different.

In overview, it provides a summary of market conditions and portfolio performance over the course of the last financial year. More specifically, it includes an overview from the Chair, a report from the investment manager and usually an outlook statement from both parties. It also gives useful information about the portfolio, including key holdings that have added, or lost, value over the period under review. For those investors who have the inclination and the time, other interesting areas include the statement of a trust's investment objectives as well as some useful insight into dividend policy, how the portfolio is valued and the level of co-investment by the board of directors.

The annual report contains a lot of useful numbers, including a breakdown of the costs that the trust has had to bear during the year. There are several other things that the board (as overseers of the portfolio) and the investment manager (as its manager) have control over. These include risks, time horizon and investment process. However, it is worth noting that they can never fully control investment returns, which are subject to many unpredictable, external influences. With that caveat in mind, here is a short tour of some of the key sections of the annual report.

Drilling down

Chair's statement

This is where you will find an overview of market conditions across the course of the financial year along with an assessment of how the portfolio has performed. It should also provide some insight into what the board might be thinking about dividends, any discount or premium to NAV, and costs.

Key developments are usually highlighted here too. These might include changes to the investment policy, dividend policy, management arrangements or the announcement or conclusion of a strategic review. Since it is difficult to draw any firm conclusions from a single year of investment performance, the Chair should always keep investors focused on the long term.

Many of these statements follow a relatively predictable pattern and use similar, sometimes dense, language. However, a few are refreshingly direct. A good example comes from the 2023 annual report of Pantheon International (PIN), a private equity investment trust. The Chair, John Singer CBE, gets right to the heart of the discount problem and how best to take advantage of it. Here are a few extracts:

> *I believe that the listed private equity (LPE) sector has not kept up with the changing needs of its stakeholders and that there is a real opportunity now to do more to put shareholders' interests first.*

One recurrent theme, both for the Board and investors, has been the persistent discount to net asset value (NAV) at which the Company's shares trade. Whilst this is typical of the whole LPE sector, it presents a challenge, implying that the market does not believe the integrity of our NAVs, despite our long history of delivering significant uplifts to NAV when we realise our investments.

The current discount, however, also represents an exciting opportunity that we intend to seize on behalf of shareholders.

Working with Pantheon [PIP], we are revising our capital allocation policy, which in the past has not taken sufficient account of the returns to be generated by reinvesting in PIP's portfolio when the discount is high. By using buybacks, we are effectively committing capital to a portfolio that we know well, and in whose asset value we have faith. At high discount levels, most obviously the current 40% for example, the resulting improvement to NAV per share is significant and immediate.

Insights like this make the effort of finding and reading the annual report well worth it in my view.

Investment manager's report

These tend to be longer and more in-depth. They usually talk at length about market conditions and how the portfolio has weathered them. In that context, several investment trusts are sector specialists. Examples include Polar Capital Technology Trust (PCT), TR Property Trust (TRY), Worldwide Healthcare Trust (WWH) and BlackRock World Mining (BRWM). The investment managers' statements in these instances merit particular attention as they offer detailed insights into the dynamics of their respective niches and, sometimes, an early warning of any important structural shifts.

It is also worth reading the portfolio manager statements from multi-asset trusts such as Capital Gearing (CGT) and Personal Assets (PNL). These pay close attention to the relative valuations and prospects of different asset classes and are a useful source of asset allocation information for investors.

I always find references to asset valuation useful too. They can help put the portfolio's performance into context and facilitate comparisons with any benchmark and previous periods. This, in turn, can help to reveal whether the portfolio is becoming more or less attractive than it has been historically. Below is an extract from the 2007 annual report for Personal Assets, an investment trust that seeks to preserve capital first and foremost and employs a multi-asset approach (it invests across equities, bonds and other asset classes). The investment manager at that time, Ian Rushbrook, warned on valuation levels, using a proprietary valuation model. To put this extract into context, global equities peaked in September 2007, ahead of the Global Financial Crisis. The annual report was released just four months earlier and contained this warning from the investment manager:

Over the last 40 years, there have been seven periods where the [equity valuation] model has shown the FTSE as being overvalued by more than 30%. The table below presents the outcomes.

Maximum overvaluation	Jan 1970	Mar 1972	Jan 1976	Jul 1987	Mar 1998	Jul 1999	May 2007
Overvaluation per model	40%	52%	30%	35%	55%	71%	45%
Month of subsequent low	Jul 1970	Dec 1974	Oct 1976	Oct 1987	Oct 1998	Mar 2003	When?
FTSE All Share fall to low	−28%	−70%	−32%	−33%	−25%	−45%	Awaited!

In summary, UK equities according to our model are now overvalued by 45%, long-dated gilts by 34% and long index-linked gilts by 70%. Given such an overvaluation of all three classes of financial assets, our largest investment is liquidity [i.e. cash and short-term government bonds], at 51% of shareholders' funds (up from 41% last year).

Those were wise words as it subsequently turned out.

The investment portfolio

The annual report usually provides a lot of detail on the investment portfolio. Where a portfolio contains quoted shares, it often discloses the entire portfolio position at the year end. Then there is usually a more detailed insight into the top holdings. The level of disclosure may be limited where some are particularly illiquid, or if publication could compromise the portfolio manager's efforts.

The better versions also provide attribution data. In other words, they attribute any over or underperformance of the portfolio (versus benchmark) to components of portfolio positioning. For example, it might reveal how much value was added (or lost) thanks to gearing. It may also put returns in the context of sector positioning (whether the portfolio was, say, underweight financials or overweight technology) or stock selection. Table 16A is an extract from the Smithson 2022 annual report and shows the sector performance of global medium and smaller equities along with the relevant Smithson allocation. It helps to explain this investment trust's underperformance in 2022 (when the trust's NAV was down 28% compared to a 9% decline in the MSCI World SMID Cap Index). The trust's focus on high-quality companies with below average levels of capital expenditure means that it tends to avoid companies in the Energy and Utilities sectors, whilst its largest exposure that year was to Information Technology. The strong performance of the former sectors and weak performance of the latter helps to explain the trust's underperformance.

This sort of attribution information can help investors to establish whether the managers are underperforming at their core competency or whether market conditions have not suited their investment approach. Equally, in years of strong performance, it can help to establish whether the managers are adding genuine value or simply riding a strong market in their preferred sectors.

Table 16A: Extract from page 10 of the Smithson Investment Trust 2022 Annual Report

Twelve months to 31 December 2022
Sector Performance

Sectors	MSCI W SMID (%)	SMITHSON WEIGHT (%)
Energy	64%	–
Utilities	12%	–
Consumer Staples	0%	4%
Financials	–2%	3%
Materials	–3%	–
Industrials	–8%	23%
Health Care	–15%	15%
Real Estate	–16%	–
Consumer Discretionary	–18%	13%
Information Technology	–20%	38%
Communication Services	–23%	3%

The report should also provide some commentary on the portfolio itself, including a reminder of the managers' investment process, an in-depth description of some of the larger positions and the pillars of the investment case. Charts / figures which compare the latest situation with the prior year can add an objective indication of how the portfolio has moved and should be read in conjunction with any portfolio manager comments about changes they have made during the latest period.

Trusts that hold investments other than quoted equities, such as private equity, infrastructure and royalties, will often provide additional information about some of the key underlying investments. This can shed helpful light on the more complex ones.

Sustainability / ESG

This section outlines the steps that the trust has taken, and is taking, to improve its sustainability credentials. Be warned – they are often long on text but short on concrete measures. Metrics that might be disclosed include the portfolio's MSCI ESG (environmental, social and governance) rating versus the benchmark.

These ratings aim to identify the ESG risks and opportunities that are most material to a sub-industry or industrial sector. They categorise companies as Leaders (AAA or AA), Average (A, BBB or BB) or Laggards (B or CC). For equity investment trusts, the ratings are applied to companies held within its portfolio. As such, an ESG rating is an aggregate score. This can be helpful for trusts that invest in larger companies; however, smaller ones are much less likely to be assessed.

Carbon intensity is another ESG disclosure that trusts may make. This refers to the level of emissions associated with the underlying portfolio holdings. This is usually compared to the carbon intensity of the trust's benchmark index.

Voting policy is also an important element of governance, being part of the 'G' in ESG. Many trusts will provide a summary of their voting patterns during the year and may indicate the number of times they have voted against the management of the companies they are invested in.

Key performance indicators (KPIs)

KPIs are an objective and measurable way of gauging progress towards a set of stated objectives – as such, they help to make the board more accountable. Typical investment trust examples include NAV performance against a stated benchmark, the level of discount to NAV, the amount and growth in dividends and the overall level of costs.

Whilst the share price discount is primarily driven by investment performance, there are things the board can do to influence it. These include the introduction of continuation votes (which provide shareholders with an opportunity to vote on the continuation of the trust) and performance-related tender offers (where shareholders can get part of or all their cash back if investment performance is poor) above and beyond the usual share buybacks.

So far, so good. But the problem is that many of these KPIs are out of the board's direct control. The NAV performance, for example, is something that even the investment manager has limited control over in the short term as they are, to some degree at least, a hostage to market movements.

That means it is imperative that the board sets reasonable timeframes – of five years or more – when it comes to measuring performance. Most credible investment strategies take time to bear fruit, and market conditions can sometimes challenge even the best of them on a shorter view.

Understanding financial statements

Next, I want to take you through a roundup of the main components of this important document. The audited financial statements provide a crucial snapshot of the trust's health.

Income statement

Often referred to as the statement of comprehensive income, this page discloses the income received from investments (such as dividends and interest), as well as any unrealised gains or losses on investments. There should also be information about currency gains or losses and some useful insights into costs and tax.

Balance sheet

Also called the statement of financial position, this summarises the trust's assets and liabilities at the financial year end.

Amongst other things, the balance sheet can shed light on the level of debt that a trust is carrying as well as any reserves that may be used to supplement future dividends and fund buybacks. It also reveals the NAV, or total equity value, of the trust as well as the NAV per share.

Cash flow statement

This is an important source of information for trusts that hold assets that are not 'marked-to-market'. In other words, they are difficult to value, which makes the level of cash generation more important.

Notes to the accounts

These can be many and varied and they appear after the income statement, balance sheet and cash flow statement. Several are worth reading. Costs, for example, are usually broken out into more detail, showing how much has been spent on things like directors' fees, marketing and custody. The notes on balance sheet valuation are also useful as they reveal how much of the portfolio is valued by reference to market prices, third-party inputs or via another method. This is a particularly important section to check, so we will revisit this in Chapter 18. Finally, those relating to borrowings help indicate what form they take and the relevant terms.

Annual report checklist

Given the sheer volume of information contained within these reports, here is a quick aide memoire of the key sections and what to look for:

> "The annual report is an invaluable, if sizeable, resource that provides a comprehensive summary of a fund's performance, strategy and governance."

- Chair's statement – analyse fundamental changes to investment, dividend or discount control policies, as well as costs.

- Investment manager's statement – look for guidance on current valuations and growth outlook versus prior reports.

- Investment portfolio – focus on consistency between the investment portfolio and the stated investment style.

- Ongoing charges – the report should contain a single number which represents all the ongoing costs of running the trust, expressed as a percentage of net assets, along with a definition of how it is calculated.

- Shareholder register – review who the major shareholders are and the extent to which the board is personally invested in the trust's shares.

- Income statement – monitor the level of portfolio income versus prior year as well as expenses.

- Balance sheet – look at the level of debt and its structure (flexible, fixed, etc.), as well as the level of reserves available to supplement future dividends.

- Notes to the accounts – note how the portfolio is valued, the terms associated with any debt and the breakdown of costs.

Wrapping up

The annual report is an invaluable, if sizeable, resource that provides a comprehensive summary of a fund's performance, strategy and governance. Investors who are not intimidated by it, and take the time to dissect it, often gain a competitive edge by making better-informed decisions.

SUMMARY OF KEY POINTS

- The annual report provides a summary of the market conditions and portfolio performance over the course of the last financial year along with year-end financial statements.

- The annual report, and those relating to prior financial periods, should be readily available from an investment trust's website or from the AIC website (https://www.theaic.co.uk).

- The Chair's statement covers performance as well as insights into what the board might be thinking about dividends and the discount or premium to NAV.

- Specialist investment trusts such as Polar Capital Technology Trust and TR Property Trust provide detailed insights into their respective niches in the annual report.

- The notes to the accounts are very important for gleaning further information. These come after the income statement, balance sheet and cash flow statement.

- My annual report checklist covers the key items that investors should pay attention to.

CHAPTER 17

THE AIC SECTORS: CLASSIFYING INVESTMENT TRUSTS

*"Good order is the foundation
of all good things."*
—**Edmund Burke, Anglo-Irish statesman,
abolitionist and philosopher**

WHEN IT COMES to categorising and comparing investment trusts, a great reference point is the AIC. Its various 'sectors' provide a useful framework and offer investors a way to navigate a diverse landscape of options and make better like-for-like comparisons.

One of the principles of the AIC sectors is that they mirror, where possible, the sector classification of the Investment Association (the trade body for UK investment managers), which categorises mutual funds. This makes for easier comparison of investment trust sectors against mutual fund sectors.

Sector-wide data is also useful for comparison purposes. Here is a quick tour.

AIC sectors

Quoted equity

Equity sub-sectors, being those that contain trusts which invest in listed equities, make up around half of the total investment trust sector when measured by market capitalisation. This is unsurprising given that most of the longest established trusts belong here. The oldest were set up to provide a way for people of modest means to invest at a time when even quoted equities were the preserve of the very wealthy. Most of them have maintained that exposure, albeit some have deployed their investment trust structure to good effect in order to hold unquoted stocks.

When it comes to classification, equity trusts are typically split according to:

- Geography (e.g. North America)

- Industrial sector (e.g. Technology & Technology Innovation)

- Market capitalisation (e.g. Smaller Companies)

- Income objective (e.g. UK Equity Income)

The biggest sub-sector by number of constituents is the UK smaller companies' sector with 24 trusts. This wide range originates from a time when many institutions did not have their own in-house smaller company expertise and used investment trusts as a way of getting exposure to this end of the market. Today, several UK pension funds, such as those representing members of West Yorkshire, Derbyshire and East Riding Yorkshire Councils, remain shareholders in UK smaller company trusts.

Table 17A shows all of the quoted equity sub-sectors, ranked by market capitalisation, and lists the number of constituents alongside their respective market capitalisations, NAVs and resultant discounts.

Table 17A: AIC Quoted equity sectors

AIC sector	Number of constituents	Market capitalisation
Global	12	£28,954,260,356
UK Equity Income	18	£10,437,081,995
Flexible Investment	21	£9,771,352,002
Global Equity Income	7	£6,205,492,845
Technology & Technology Innovation	4	£5,722,865,991
UK Smaller Companies	24	£5,145,154,977
Global Smaller Companies	5	£5,121,951,393
Global Emerging Markets	11	£4,802,541,217
Europe	6	£3,736,161,525
UK All Companies	6	£3,630,906,666
Biotechnology & Healthcare	7	£3,556,018,176
North America	5	£3,499,827,533
Asia Pacific	5	£2,841,158,944
Japan	5	£2,266,262,311
Country Specialist	4	£1,991,957,942
Asia Pacific Equity Income	5	£1,853,432,116
India/Indian Subcontinent	4	£1,762,182,498
European Smaller Companies	4	£1,754,304,918
Commodities & Natural Resources	9	£1,532,231,192
China / Greater China	3	£1,443,557,012
Asia Pacific Smaller Companies	4	£1,181,347,658
Environmental	3	£1,087,684,175
Property Securities	1	£991,721,813
Japanese Smaller Companies	3	£879,395,755
Financials & Financial Innovation	2	£759,454,108
North American Smaller Companies	2	£453,018,535
UK Equity & Bond Income	1	£279,730,263
Infrastructure Securities	2	£206,195,472
Latin America	1	£81,867,222

Source: Morningstar, 31/12/2024

Flexible investment

This sector has over 20 constituents and £10bn of net assets. It sits somewhere between the quoted and non-quoted equity sectors. Those in this sub-sector have the flexibility to invest in quoted equities, fixed income securities, private equity and other asset groups.

Non-quoted private equity

This is the largest cohort after quoted equity. Private equity refers to share-based ownership in private businesses. Dedicated trusts of this type have been around since 3i Group first made its stock market debut in 1994. It was formed as part of a government drive to provide capital to small and medium-sized businesses that would struggle to borrow capital from a bank and were too small to raise money via the stock market.

At this point, we should recap how most investments work in the private equity world. A partnership is usually created first. This has a finite life and is tasked with entering and exiting several investments over a period of, typically, 7–10 years. It is structured as a limited liability vehicle, so any partners are protected from further liabilities beyond their capital contributions. As with most Limited Liability Partnerships (LLPs), a general partner will source and manage the investments, whilst limited partners provide the funding in the form of an upfront commitment for the duration of the partnership. The money is called upon by the general partner as and when funds are required for investment or working capital purposes. It is important to understand this structure because investment trusts can make investments in private equity LLPs. Within private equity there are therefore some trusts that primarily invest in private equity LLPs, some that invest directly and some that do a combination of both. One of the disadvantages of investing via underlying LLPs is that this adds a further layer of fees and reduces overall control.

Private equity investment comes in different shapes and sizes, but it can broadly be categorised into:

- Early- to mid-stage businesses in need of capital to finance growth.

- More mature, typically larger businesses which may not need further equity capital but offer opportunities to increase value through improved financial or operational management.

It is worth noting that the AIC classifies trusts that *primarily* invest in the first category as growth capital and in the second category as private equity.

In recent years, many large businesses, which historically would have sought a public listing via an IPO, have instead chosen to stay private for longer. There are several reasons for this. They include lower regulatory scrutiny and costs, a shorter list of investors to answer to, and avoiding the public spotlight with its short-term focus on quarterly earnings. This has meant that public equity investors seeking an exposure to themes such as the gig economy, via the likes of Uber and Airbnb, have missed much of

"In recent years, many large businesses, which historically would have sought a public listing via an IPO, have instead chosen to stay private for longer."

the strongest growth phase in such firms' life cycles. Some investment trusts are well positioned to counter this problem for retail investors and, in many cases, maintain an exposure once they have listed.

Infrastructure

The next largest non-quoted equity cohort is made up of infrastructure investment trusts. These focus on assets that governments want built and managed, such as schools and hospitals, as well as essential services (e.g. transportation, energy and utilities). As long-term, stable investments these can all provide a steady income stream.

The first infrastructure trust, HICL Infrastructure, launched on the stock market in 2006 and was followed by a number of others. Later, the first renewable infrastructure investment trust, Greencoat UK Wind, was launched in 2013 and was supported by the UK government with an initial investment of £50m. The renewable infrastructure sub-sector targets investment trusts that focus on renewable energy assets. With a growing emphasis on sustainability, the underlying companies specialise in projects related to wind, solar and other renewable energy sources. At the time of writing, there are 29 infrastructure investment trusts, with the bulk in the renewable energy infrastructure space.

Property

Then come the sub-sectors that focus on real estate. These trusts mainly invest directly in physical properties, primarily within the UK, but also in continental Europe and farther afield. Commercial, residential or industrial properties may all be part of the underlying offering.

At the time of writing, there are 35 trusts in this cohort, sub-divided into UK Commercial, Logistics, Residential and Healthcare, then Europe and Rest of World. The investment trusts compete for capital with established UK REITs such as British Land, Land Securities and LondonMetric Property. The rules that govern UK REITs are slightly different from those of investment trusts. Leaving the detail to one side for now, a key difference that investors need to know is whether the managers are internal or external. Investment trusts tend to have an external manager when it comes to property assets. They are usually remunerated based on the NAV of the trust, with a non-executive independent board of directors providing oversight. Traditional UK REITs, on the other hand, tend to be internally managed. The managers also form the executive board and are usually incentivised in relation to total shareholder return, amongst other measures.

The latter structure offers much better alignment between the trust and the interests of its shareholders. One reason is because it avoids a situation where a property investment trust with, say, a management fee of 1% and an asset value of £400m, but which trades in the market at £300m, pays its managers £4m a year for their services. This £4m may be 1% of the NAV, but from the shareholders' perspective it is 1.33% of their value, that is the £300m market cap.

An internally managed vehicle may not always be lower cost than an externally managed equivalent. There may be less transparency and control over costs. However, in my experience with property companies, internal is better.

Other sub-sectors

Several smaller sub-sectors are worth a quick mention here.

Hedge funds: This sub-sector contains a few trusts that typically invest capital into a specific hedge fund. These aim to provide smaller investors with access to strategies that can be difficult to gain an exposure to directly. They also aim to offer a liquid way of accessing funds that normally require long notice periods. Investing directly in hedge funds can be punitive for UK taxpayers, whereas the investment trust structure enables greater tax efficiency and comes with ISA eligibility, unlike most direct hedge fund investments. As a result, this was quite a large sector at one point. However, mixed performance, high fees and poor discount control policies have led to many of the sector's constituents being wound up.

Debt: There are three debt sub-sectors, being Structured Finance, Direct Lending and Loans & Bonds. The trusts in these niches invest in debt securities, which means those that are issued by companies that pay a predetermined return. These sub-sectors tend to have fewer constituents than the equity equivalents. In summary:

- Structured Finance refers to entities which have been specially created to assist with the financing of certain activities. For example, a bank may wish to sell part, or all, of its mortgage book and recycle the capital into more attractive areas, via the issuance of residential mortgage-backed securities. Structured finance trusts are then natural buyers.

- Direct Lending is where the investment trust can make loans directly to businesses or buy loans from other lenders.

- Loans & Bonds refers to conventional fixed income securities, including high yield bonds.

- Leasing: Constituents of this sector typically acquire and then lease assets such as aircraft and ships.

Table 17B shows all the non-quoted equity sub-sectors, ranked by market capitalisation and the number of constituents in each cohort.

Table 17B: AIC non-equity sectors

AIC sector	Number of constituents	Market capitalisation
Private Equity	19	£45,446,708,788
Infrastructure	9	£11,592,984,681
Renewable Energy Infrastructure	20	£8,965,490,152
Growth Capital	7	£4,149,391,120
Property – UK Logistics	3	£4,102,050,357
Property – UK Commercial	10	£2,081,113,434
Hedge Funds	5	£1,389,378,674
Property – UK Residential	6	£1,257,708,012
Debt – Loans & Bonds	6	£1,182,435,702
Debt – Structured Finance	5	£881,037,831
Property – UK Healthcare	2	£857,880,692
Property – Debt	6	£620,859,225
Leasing	6	£485,466,764
Property – Europe	4	£482,831,594
Debt – Direct Lending	5	£313,359,269
Property – Rest of World	4	£92,826,827

Note that traditional REITs, referred to in the text above, are not included in the AIC Property sectors.

Source: Morningstar, 31/12/2024.

Wrapping up

As we have seen, the investment trust sector is dynamic. Its composition has changed over the years, such that sectors which existed 10 years ago no longer do. Equally, as new trusts emerge and are joined by competitors, new sub-sectors will entice fresh capital. That is what keeps this space so interesting for investors.

SUMMARY OF KEY POINTS

- The AIC's investment trust sector classification serves as a framework for categorising and understanding investment trusts, enabling better like-for-like comparisons.

- Equity sub-sectors, those that contain trusts which invest in liquid equities, make up around half of the total investment trust sector when measured by market capitalisation.

- The flexible investment sector sits somewhere between the quoted equity sectors and the non-equity sectors with many of its constituents investing across both groups of assets.

- The next largest cohort after quoted equity is private equity.

- The next largest sectors after private equity are infrastructure and property.

CHAPTER 18

VALUATION

"Managers and investors alike must understand that accounting numbers is the beginning, not the end, of business valuation."

—**Warren Buffett**

NOT ALL OF the holdings in an investment trust portfolio are valued in the same way. Some asset valuations are clear and independently verifiable. Other are not. This can lead to material differences between NAV and price. The fact that investment trust shares themselves are listed on a stock exchange provides an element of 'price discovery'. We will cover this in some detail in Chapter 28. Here though we will look 'under the bonnet' as understanding some of the nuances around valuation regarding a trust's assets is important when it comes to choosing which ones to buy.

Diving in

In many cases, where a trust holds shares, the approach needed is straightforward. That's because the holdings are usually quoted on a stock market and will therefore have an objective, and widely agreed, price. Other holdings, however, such as certain bonds, may not be quoted on a recognised exchange in the same way. Typically, to buy and sell these assets, investors need a price from a dealer. This makes the process less visible and not subject to the same level of market scrutiny. It is, nonetheless, a reasonably reliable valuation method.

The remaining problem is that some investments are neither listed on a stock market, nor do they have an alternative observable means of independent valuation. Examples include holdings in private companies, as well as less conventional assets such as distribution warehouses and windfarms. That is where we will be focusing our attention next, because holdings that do not have any sort of market price require a completely different method of valuation.

Before we get to that, let's go back to the NAV of an investment trust for a moment. Remember that it represents the value of all assets less liabilities. We can then divide this number by the total number of shares to determine the NAV per share. But how we arrive at the overall value of those assets matters. That's because if an investment trust's shares trade at a significant discount to NAV for a prolonged period, it may be because the market does not 'believe' the NAV. That is, it thinks it is overstated and that the true value is lower. In some cases, the market does a better job of valuing these assets than any formal, subjective valuation methodology. Investors nonetheless usually suffer fees that are based on this more subjective NAV number rather than on the market value of their investment, derived from the share price. I have always found this anomalous and have explained why in Chapter 10. So, how are NAV numbers derived?

Getting technical

To understand this, we need to take a quick detour into what are called International Financial Reporting Standards (IFRS Accounting Standards). These are issued by the IFRS Foundation and the International Accounting Standards Board and try to impose a standardised way of describing a company's financial performance and position. Their objective is to make financial statements in general, and asset valuations specifically, understandable and comparable across different jurisdictions.

One particular reporting standard, called IFRS 13 *Fair Value Measurement*, outlines the principles that help to establish 'fair value' for an asset (or liability). That is essentially the estimated price that would be received for the sale of an asset (or paid to transfer a liability) in a theoretical transaction between market participants. IFRS 13 is used by most investment trusts to help determine the appropriate valuation level for their assets, via the application of its three-tier framework. These are known as Level 1, Level 2 and Level 3 valuations, and they are based on different degrees of market observability and reliability.

Looking into 'levels'

The methodology applied at Level 1 is called 'marking to market'. It uses unadjusted quoted prices for identical instruments which are traded in an active market. That is, because these are transparent and easily observable. In the context of UK investment trusts, Level 1 valuations are most applicable to portfolio holdings, such as quoted equities, which are traded on recognised stock exchanges and therefore have a widely agreed, visible price. An example of a Level 1 investment would be shares in a company like Unilever which are freely available on multiple stock markets.

That, in turn, means that there should be a relatively close relationship between the trust's NAV and its own share price. A marked deviation should only happen in limited circumstances. One such circumstance is where the underlying shares are relatively illiquid, perhaps because they are in smaller companies. Another is when the shares of the investment trust itself are illiquid, or the shareholder structure means it is difficult to encourage a reduction in any discount via the usual mechanisms, such as buybacks or continuation votes. If neither of these circumstances exist, and there is a big difference between the share price and the NAV, it is likely to attract investors that can exploit the anomaly.

So, Level 1 valuation is straightforward. However, investment trusts, often hold a diverse range of assets which are not traded in active markets. Enter 'Level 2'.

Going down to Level 2

This uses inputs, other than quoted prices, that are directly or indirectly observable, based on market data. As such, valuations may rely on recent transaction prices for similar assets, or other valuation techniques that incorporate market-derived data. In the context of UK investment trusts, this methodology is particularly relevant for assets that are not actively traded but may attract prices from a third-party pricing vendor such as Bloomberg. Those, in turn, are often based on a variety of sources, including broker quotes, and chosen benchmarks. Naturally, Level 2 valuations are more complex and subjective than Level 1 as a result.

Three sectors that are likely to have most of their assets classified on this basis are 'Direct lending', 'Loans and bonds' and 'Structured finance'. An example of such an asset would be the Unilever 1.5% 2039 bond. This is not freely tradeable in the same way as Unilever shares but does attract competitive quotes from specialist market makers.

That leaves assets for which there is no observable price and where market data is not available in any form. Which means it is time to enter Level 3.

Hitting Level 3

These valuations sit at the least transparent and most subjective level of the hierarchy. They rely on prices being derived using assumptions about market conditions and risks. In the UK investment trust arena, such valuations are typically applied to assets for which market data is scarce or non-existent.

Private equity and certain alternative investments typically fall under Level 3. Estimating their fair value requires significant judgement and demands the use of internal models, alongside independent third-party valuations. Unsurprisingly, investment trusts are required to disclose the methodologies and assumptions used in Level 3 valuations in their financial statements.

Boards often engage an independent valuer to assist with Level 3 holdings which cannot be marked-to-market. They have a significant role to play, as their opinion is used to determine NAV. The basis of that valuation is laid out in the annual report or, in the case of an IPO, in the listing prospectus. The most common approach applies a discounted cash flow (DCF) methodology – for more on this, refer to Chapter 23.

Assets that would typically be valued in this way include unquoted company shares, physical property, royalty income streams and infrastructure contracts. Essentially Level 3 therefore applies to any asset that cannot be valued using a Level 1 or 2 approach. An example would be shares in Mars Inc. Like Unilever, Mars is a fast-moving consumer goods company but it is privately held and so there is no active market in its shares.

Making notes

So, with three levels potentially in play, how can investors work out an investment trust's asset valuation approach? The answer lies in the notes to the financial statements.

Table 18A is an extract from the 2022 annual report for the Invesco Bond Income Plus trust. We can see it held a small amount of quoted equity (£1,080m) valued on a Level 1 basis. It also held bonds (valued at £1,165m) issued by Frigoglass, a manufacturing business, which were acquired as part of a restructuring. These are valued on a Level 3 basis, due to the lack of an open market price. The bulk of the portfolio, however, is in conventional bonds (fixed interest securities) which are treated as Level 2 securities.

Table 18A: Extract from 2022 Invesco Bond Income Plus annual report

Note 20 to the financial statements. Classification Under Fair Value Hierarchy

	Level 1	Level 2	Level 3	Total
	£000	£000	£000	£000
2022				
Financial assets designated at fair value				
through profit or loss:				
Quoted Investments:				
– Fixed Interest Securities	–	294,154	1,165	295,319
– Convertibles	–	18,614	–	18,614
– Government	–	216	–	216
– Preference	2,641	–	–	2,641
– Equities	1,080	–	–	1,080
Derivative financial instruments:				
– Currency hedges		1,440		1,440
Total for financial assets	3,721	314,424	1,165	319,310

Treading with care

The reason for covering all this rather technical ground is that where investment trust portfolios are valued on a Level 3 basis, the difference between the share price and NAV can be extreme. In my experience, most investment trusts where things have gone horribly wrong, and investors have lost substantial amounts of money, fall into this valuation category.

"In my experience, most investment trusts where things have gone horribly wrong, and investors have lost substantial amounts of money, fall into this valuation category."

The odds are against you making money with trusts which hold hard-to-value assets. That's not to say you can't make money in such trusts. In fact, several of these alternative trusts have delivered very strong returns indeed. However, they appear to be the minority.

To get a sense of how well, or badly, these trusts have fared, I analysed data from Morningstar. The findings supported my suspicions. I identified 211 trusts that are valued less frequently than monthly, which I use as a proxy for a Level 3 valuation basis (the full methodology is in the appendix). Of these 211 trusts, only 78 (37%) generated a positive return between launch and liquidation, or 31/12/2024 in the case of those still standing. Only 38 (18%) have generated an annualised return of more than 5%.

So, one way to help avoid extreme losses in investment trusts is to limit investment in trusts where the bulk of the assets are valued on a Level 3 basis. Then again, this could mean missing out on some great opportunities such as the best performers from this sample, which are outlined in Table 18B.

Table 18B: Top performing trusts, holding hard-to-value (Level 3) assets

Investment trust	AIC Sector	Stock exchange admission date / Restructure date	Annualised return %
Literacy Capital PLC	Private Equity	06/2021	30.1
HgCapital Trust Ord	Private Equity	05/1995	17.0
3i Group Ord	Private Equity	07/1994	13.0
ICG Enterprise Trust Ord	Private Equity	09/1981	12.7
3i Infrastructure Ord	Infrastructure	03/2007	10.7

Returns are total annualised shareholder returns, from admission/restructure date to 31/12/2024, expressed in pounds sterling. HgCapital Trust was restructured in May 1995.

Sources: Morningstar, Bloomberg, Regulatory News Service, LSEG.

However, in most cases, it has paid to avoid investment on day one and to wait for a few years of trading history before committing your capital. I think there is a case for waiting to see how some of these alternative trusts fare in their early years before rushing in to buy.

If we analyse the results by sector, the picture is similar, as shown in Table 18C. Only one sector, Infrastructure, has a success rate greater than 50% when it comes to making a positive return for shareholders. The overall numbers are probably skewed by the large amount of new issuance in 2020 and 2021 (22 of the trusts in the sample), so close to the end date of the study. Interest rates rose sharply in 2022 and this contributed to some very poor share price performance amongst alternative investment trusts. However, only time will tell how many of these will ultimately survive and deliver attractive returns.

Table 18C: Sectors holding hard-to-value assets, performance success rates

AIC sector	Sample size	% with annualised returns >0%	% with annualised returns >5%
Property	71	38%	11%
Private Equity	27	41%	37%
Renewable Energy Infrastructure	23	39%	13%
Infrastructure	12	58%	42%

Returns are total annualised shareholder returns, between stock market launch and 31/12/2024, or delisting if earlier. Includes sectors with a sample size of 10 or more trusts.

Data Sources: Morningstar, Bloomberg, LSEG, Company factsheets, Company annual reports, Companies House.

Many trusts holding hard-to-value assets are only suitable for sophisticated investors who have access to the trust's management and the necessary resources to conduct thorough analysis. However, if you are looking for a safety-first approach, there is a lot to be said for limiting your exposure to investment trusts which hold subjectively valued portfolios, particularly in their early years.

If I were to make a general observation at this point to help steer investors, it would be that a high volume of new issues in this space is often followed by more challenging market conditions. When investors demand certain things, such as high income, trust sponsors tend to try to satisfy them by issuing new shares. New issuance of shares is often high during strong markets. The phrase 'when the ducks are quacking, feed them' paints an appropriate picture. This enthusiastic behaviour is possibly mirrored in other parts of the economy. Such economy-wide exuberance can lead to 'hangovers'. This may help to explain why, for example, 68 alternative trusts were launched in 2006/07, just ahead of the Great Financial Crisis and 22 in 2020 and 2021, ahead of the interest rate spike (Source: Morningstar).

Wrapping up

As we have seen, there are several ways to value an investment trust's underlying assets. This, in turn, drives its own valuation and the size of any discount (or premium) to NAV it may attract.

The bottom line therefore is that trusts holding hard-to-value assets are often only suitable for sophisticated investors who may have access to management and the necessary resources to conduct thorough analysis. Others, who may be more risk averse, will usually be better off limiting exposure to trusts which hold subjectively valued portfolios.

As I referred to in Chapter 10 Costs, most investment trusts levy investment management fees based on NAV, not market value. Basing fees on market value represents a much better alignment of interest between trust management and shareholders.

SUMMARY OF KEY POINTS

- IFRS Accounting Standards have established a three-tiered framework, each representing different degrees of reliability for valuing portfolio investments.

- Level 1 valuations are usually referred to as 'marked-to-market'. For example, shares traded on a stock market are marked-to-market in real time by the parties buying and selling.

- Level 2 valuations may rely on recent transaction prices and are relevant for assets such as corporate bonds.

- Level 3 valuations are the most subjective level of the hierarchy and are typically applied to assets for which market data is scarce or non-existent (e.g. private companies).

- The notes to the financial statements of the annual report indicate which basis is used to value investment trust portfolio holdings.

- Most investment trust management fees are levied on the NAV, rather than on the value that is more relevant to shareholders, that is the market capitalisation.

CHAPTER 19

INVESTMENT OBJECTIVES / INVESTMENT STYLES

"If you don't know where you are going, you might wind up someplace else."

—Yogi Berra,
US baseball catcher

To invest successfully, you need to answer one fundamental question – what are you hoping to achieve? Investment objectives vary from person to person, but they can usually be distilled down to one or more of the following broad aims depending on factors such as age, life stage and personal goals:

- Growing capital

- Growing income

- Maximising income

- Preserving capital.

You may have already spotted that these are not all compatible with each other. It is unlikely, for example, that an investment that aims to preserve your capital will also allow you to maximise income. With that caveat noted, what follows is a tour of how different investment trusts set their strategies within this framework and then a look at the respective fund profiles that best correspond to its four core elements.

Defining goals

Investment trusts are required to have clear investment objectives and a set of parameters within which to achieve them. Sometimes they are broad and flexible, perhaps 'To maximise total return from a portfolio of long-term investments chosen on a global basis enabling the company to provide capital and dividend growth.' Or they might be specific, for example, 'To generate capital growth over the long term through investment in a diversified international portfolio of Space Tech businesses.'

When it comes to finding out about a trust's objectives, the annual report provides a clear picture of both what they are and how they will be achieved. The investment trust board should then have the relevant experience and expertise to ensure they are being met.

Building blocks

The resulting underlying investment strategy is likely to involve a combination of the three main asset classes – equities, bonds and cash. In each case, the risk and reward trade-off is different. To see how, I will use the example of a simple bank.

Let's assume the bank raises initial capital from equity investors by issuing them with shares. It then makes a margin by taking money from savers and bond holders (who are both lenders in effect), paying them interest and lending the same funds out to borrowers at a higher rate. The profits that are left, after deducting the costs of running the bank and paying interest to depositors and bondholders, are available to equity shareholders in the form of dividends and a higher share price from reinvested profits.

As such, a basic bank balance sheet, summarising its assets and liabilities, might look like that shown in Table 19A.

Table 19A: Simplistic bank balance sheet

Assets	Liabilities and shareholders' equity (Sources of funding)
Loans	Deposits
	Bonds
	Shareholders' equity

Let's now consider the respective level of risk and reward of the three categories on the right-hand side – deposits, bonds and equities. Logically, bond investors should receive a higher rate of interest on their bonds than depositors receive on their deposits. This is only fair, given that bonds are riskier, in so far as deposits are partly protected by the government and rank ahead of bond holders in terms of a repayment should the bank fail. Meanwhile, equity holders in the bank should receive a higher return than bond holders, as they are taking more risk. After all, bonds come with contractual income payments (rather than variable dividends) and rank more highly in the event of an insolvency.

This can all be summarised as shown in Figure 19A.

Figure 19A: Respective levels of risk and return

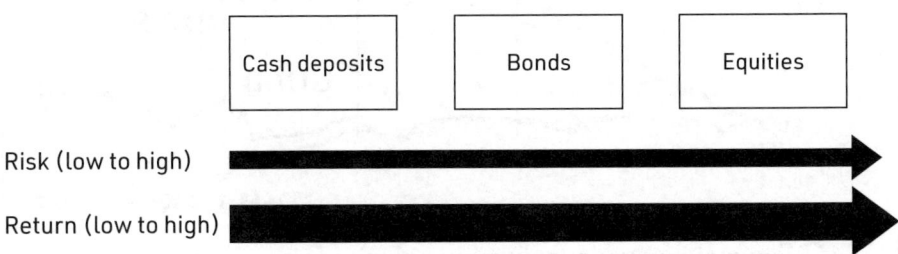

Put simply, we are saying that bonds should outperform deposits over time, and equities should outperform bonds. I use banks as my example as they are one of the few businesses that take deposits, on which they pay interest. At this point, a critic of my simple example might point to the fact that UK bank shares have failed to outperform the equivalent bonds and deposits since the early 2000s. However, that is primarily a function of the failure of a few large UK banks during the last financial crisis in 2008/09. If we widen our view and look at US banks since 1990 (which is as far back as we can go in terms of the Bloomberg Banks Index), the average bank share has outperformed bonds and deposits, albeit at a higher level of overall volatility (aka risk). And once we start taking a very long-term view and look beyond just banks, the case for equities becomes very strong indeed.

Growing capital

The reason equities are so important to long-term capital accumulation becomes clear from Figure 19B. Taken from Professor Jeremy Siegel's book *Stocks for the Long Run* (updated to June 2024, with kind permission from Prof J Siegel, 04/09/2024) it plots the performance of equities against bonds (or bills), gold and the US dollar over more than 200 years. The outperformance of the former is clear from the annualised return data in the middle of the chart.

Figure 19B: Total real return indices

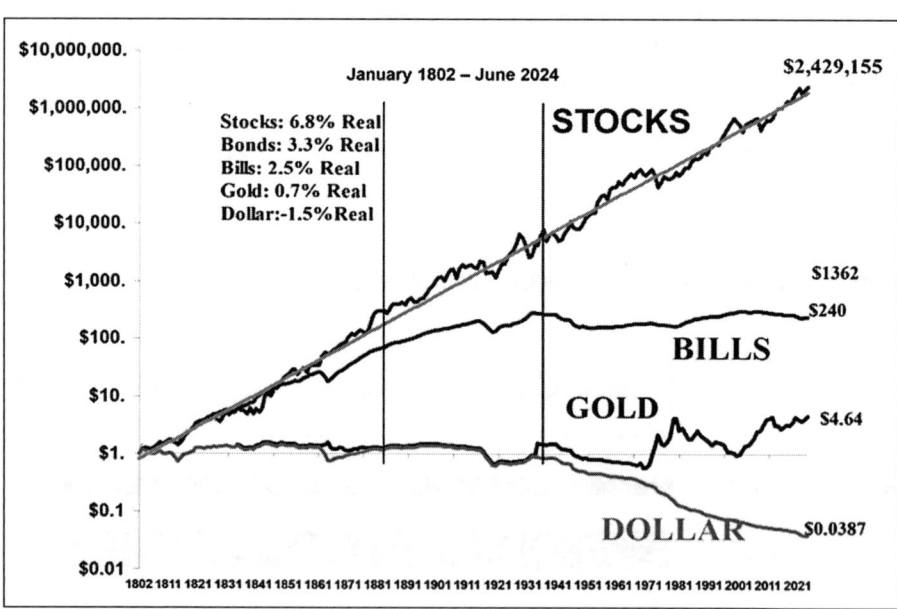

Source: Siegel (2023), with updates to 2024

As for why shares have offered almost twice the return of bonds (6.9% vs 3.6% per Figure 19B), the short answer is that they represent an ownership stake in a business. As such they participate in its growing profits, whether in the form of dividends or their reinvestment, which hopefully underpins long-term share price growth. And for as long as entrepreneurs keep innovating and firms keep expanding, shareholders are likely, on average, to do well.

At this point, I will reference another useful source – the annual Barclays Gilt Equity Study – which tracks the performance of various asset classes. For the UK, for example, it provides a very long-term time series of returns from equities, government bonds (gilts), government inflation-linked bonds, corporate bonds and cash deposits. Importantly, it measures 'real' (i.e. adjusted for inflation) returns. What it reveals, amongst many other interesting things, is that that there has not been a 23-year period for UK equities over which they have failed to deliver a positive real (inflation-beating) return. It also shows that this holds true over most 10-year periods. Both patterns are also in evidence for US equities.

So, if the natural hunting ground for long-term growth is the equity market, where specifically should investors go looking? I think that two types of stocks have delivered strong compounded returns over the long run – quality stocks and smaller company stocks. We will cover these in more detail in Chapter 27. Quality means different things to different investors, but here I use it to refer to companies that have superior profitability and more robust balance sheets than the market average. Chapter 27 cites numerous academic articles that find a positive relationship between profitability and investment returns.

Companies that generate consistently high profits and have relatively low capital expenditure are in a strong position to reinvest those profits and compound them in the future.

Smaller companies, as is also well documented in Chapter 27, tend to outperform larger companies, on average, over time. That said, they cannot be solely relied on in my view, as they can be harder to buy and sell and sometimes struggle to access capital. As such, they can suffer long periods of relative underperformance. For this reason, they should only constitute a minority position in a diversified portfolio.

Growing income

Again, if your objective is to generate an income that beats inflation over long time periods, the best source for it is likely to be equities. In that context, the AIC's dividend heroes list (covered in Chapter 33) is a great reference source.

It contains investment trusts that have raised their dividends for more than 20 consecutive years. Most of the trusts named refer to their dividend hero status in their own annual reports, underscoring the importance they attach to it. It is important to state that this is not a buy list. However, it is a good starting point for those that need a growing income. A further caveat would be that many of them invest in UK equities, so a portfolio constructed exclusively from this list might end up with a large UK bias.

> "The AIC's dividend heroes list (covered in Chapter 33) is a great reference source. It contains investment trusts that have raised their dividends for more than 20 consecutive years."

As such, it is also worth noting that the AIC compiles a second list of the 'next generation' of dividend heroes which have increased their dividend every year for at least a decade. This provides access to a wider range of geographies, including Europe, Asia, North America and China. However, anyone considering a trust from this category should reference the latest Chair's statement in the annual report to gauge the willingness to maintain a progressive dividend policy. It is also worth checking the level of distributable revenue and capital reserves on the balance sheet to ensure that the trust is in a position to supplement future dividends.

Maximising income

What if your priority is to maximise income? In that instance, it is worth considering high yielding equities alongside fixed income and 'alternatives'. By alternatives I mean assets that do not neatly fit into an equity or fixed income classification. Examples of alternatives, in this context, include real estate, infrastructure and various hedge fund strategies. However, always bear in mind the valuation issues that we highlighted in Chapter 18. Given the opaqueness surrounding some alternative investment trusts it is important not to hold positions that can do too much damage to your overall level of income should things go wrong.

Sometimes equity trusts deliberately adopt a high distribution policy. They use accumulated reserves (both revenue and capital) to underpin high yields. These are typically based on a set percentage of NAV at the start of the year. Many investment trusts managed by JP Morgan, for example, have adopted this policy, typically distributing 4% of the start of year NAV as a dividend. We will cover high income trusts in more detail in Chapter 34.

Now for a note of caution – always query any investment trust where the yield is very high. As a guide, anything above 10% is punchy. These 'monster yields' may only be on offer thanks to very high leverage, high default risk or the aggressive use of capital to supplement income. In such instances, it is vital to study the annual report to understand how the yield is being generated and the level of risk that comes with it.

Preserving capital

Last, but certainly not least, we come to capital preservation. Typically, what we are aiming to shelter from is the corrosive effect of inflation. A relatively small number of trusts aim to cater for this, with the most fertile hunting grounds being the Flexible Investment and Hedge Fund sectors. Both sectors contain several trusts that have stated investment objectives containing phrases such as 'To preserve shareholders' real wealth…' or 'To deliver long-term capital growth whilst preserving shareholders capital…'.

Bear in mind though that none of these trusts comes with a guarantee and investors should always take a long-term view. It is also important to check the stated benchmark so that you know what to expect. Trusts in the Flexible Investment sector, for instance, use different benchmarks linked to inflation. These include the 'UK CPI (rolling 5-yr average)' and 'a positive total annual return of at least twice the BOE Bank Rate'.

When considering capital preservers, you should also check the discount control policy. A trust's investment manager may do a decent job of preserving capital at the portfolio level, but if the board does not manage the discount carefully, the trust's shares could suffer material declines during a market sell off, just when you need capital preservation most. We will cover this in more detail in Chapter 35.

Wrapping up

We have seen in this chapter that UK investment trusts encompass a diverse range of objectives and styles, reflecting the dynamic nature of the assets available to them. Therefore, whether you are seeking capital appreciation, income generation or a combination, they can offer a versatile array of solutions.

SUMMARY OF KEY POINTS

- Check the prospectus or annual report to ensure the trust's stated objectives and reference benchmark are consistent with your investment objectives.

- Equities have been the best source of long-term, inflation-beating growth.

- The equities of companies with high and repeatable returns on invested capital and the equities of smaller companies can provide very attractive long-term growth.

- Be wary of very high yields. Ensure you understand, and are comfortable with, how they are generated.

- The AIC's Dividend Hero list is a great source of dependable growing income.

- If one of your priorities is capital preservation, make sure you check the discount management policy as well as the investment policy.

CHAPTER 20

ZERO-DISCOUNT POLICIES

"The best measure of a man's honesty isn't his income tax return. It's the zero adjust on his bathroom scale."

—Arthur C. Clarke,
British science fiction writer

FOR MOST INVESTMENT trusts, discounts are a fact of life. However, a small number adopt a deliberate 'zero-discount' policy in a bid to counter this problem. In this chapter we will take a closer look at how, and when, this benefits investors.

Diving in

In a nutshell, what the board is aiming for here is to keep the share price as close as possible to the NAV per share. This is achieved by issuing shares when the price trades above NAV (to eliminate any premium) and buying them back when it dips below NAV (to close any discount).

Changes to the Companies Act, which became effective in November 1999, allowed investment trusts to buy back shares more tax efficiently than they previously had been able to. Personal Assets Trust was the first investment trust to adopt a zero-discount control policy. It seeks to issue, or buy back, shares when the associated premium, or discount, breaches 2%. It can do this thanks to the liquidity of the underlying portfolio, which tends to have a reasonably high allocation to government bonds and other easily saleable assets. Figure 20A shows how effective this policy has been since it was introduced in late 1999.

Figure 20A: Personal Assets Trust – premium / discount to NAV

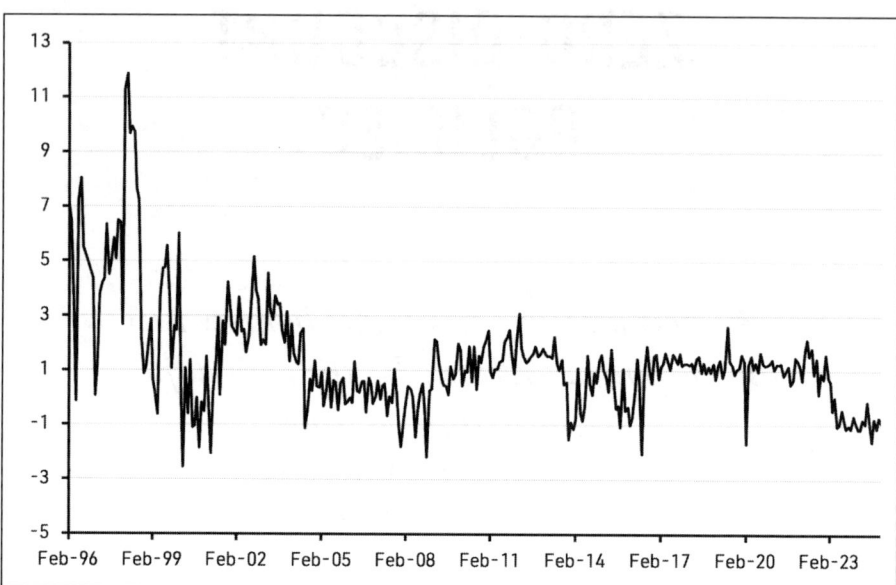

Daily premium (+ve) / discount (-ve) to NAV, 1/1/96 to 31/12/2024.

Source: Bloomberg

One of the key advantages of this approach is that it reduces share price volatility. Portfolios invested in assets that carry any price risk (whether they are shares, bonds or something else) inevitably suffer volatility in their NAVs. The fact that a trust's share price can fluctuate independently then adds a further layer of uncertainty. Reducing the level of divergence between the two therefore helps to calm investors' nerves.

To reinforce the benefits of their approach, here is an explanatory extract from the Personal Assets Trust 2010 annual report:

Investment trusts have long suffered from volatile discounts to net asset value. Sometimes, too, the shares of individual investment trusts may sell temporarily at a significant premium to net asset value. This can put those investing regularly through investment plans at a disadvantage, because they may find themselves buying shares at a sizeable premium which almost certainly will not be sustained, and which will therefore have an adverse effect on the return from their investment.

In view of the disadvantages to shareholders of such discount and premium fluctuations, the Company's policy is to ensure that the shares always trade at close to net asset value through a combination of share buy-backs coupled to the issue of new shares at a small premium to net asset value where demand exceeds supply. This discount and premium control policy is enshrined in the Articles of Association of the Company.

A further benefit is that the mechanical impact of issuing shares at a premium to NAV and buying them back at a discount is to increase NAV per share, an effect that Chapter 26 explores in more detail.

Capital Gearing Trust has enhanced its NAV per share by as much as 2.7% over the five-year period to 31/12/2024, solely through the process of issuing shares at a premium to NAV and buying them back at a discount to NAV.

Getting it right

To operate a zero-discount policy, the board must have the relevant permissions and accounting policies in place. Another trust that follows a zero-discount policy shows what can go wrong when they are missing. In late 2023, an oversight on the part of the board of Capital Gearing Trust meant that instead of trading within a 2% premium or discount to NAV, the share price moved to a 5% discount. That's because the board failed to get the court approval needed in time, to maintain the share buybacks required to enforce the discount control policy. This mistake triggered a wider discount. Once these permissions were put in place a few months later, it duly narrowed back into its usual range. This episode was nonetheless unfortunate for investors who needed to sell at the time. On the flipside, it provided new investors with a more attractive entry level in terms of their subsequent NAV return. Figure 20B shows what happened.

Figure 20B: Capital Gearing Trust – premium / discount to NAV

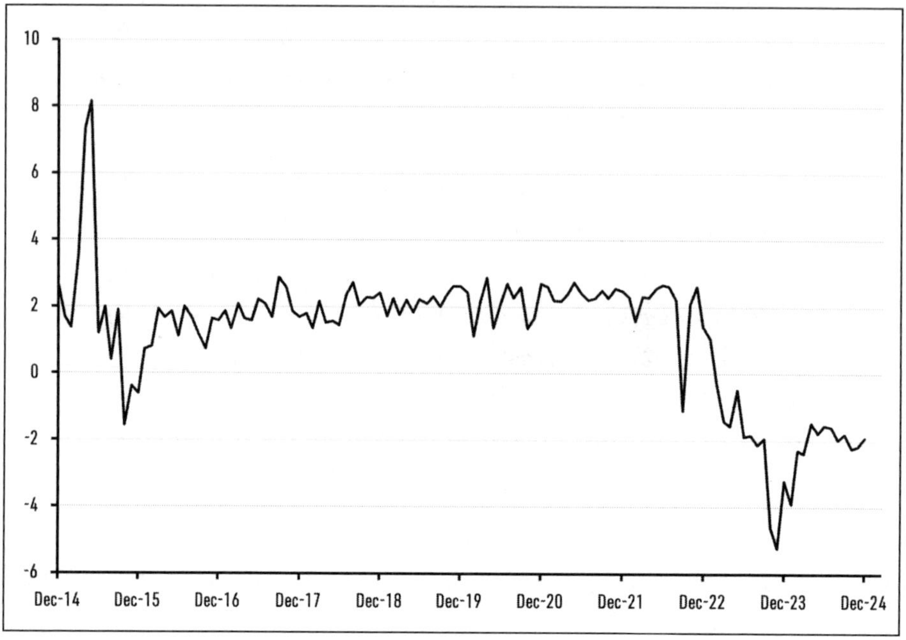

Daily premium (+ve) / discount (-ve) to NAV, 31/12/2014 to 31/12/2024.

Source: Bloomberg

Adopting a zero-discount policy has helped Personal Assets and Capital Gearing to grow their asset bases significantly. In the 10-year period to 31/12/2024, Personal Assets grew its share count from 173m to 321m (adjusted for stock split), an 85% increase, whilst Capital Gearing grew its share count from 2.9m to 19.1m, an increase of more than 550%.

Noting the negatives

But that does not mean this type of policy is a no-brainer for all trusts. For starters, it can be problematic for smaller ones. That is because a prolonged series of sizeable buybacks can dramatically shrink them, and even threaten their existence. For example, in pursuing a zero-discount policy, Troy

Income & Growth (TIGT) bought back many shares during 2023. In total it purchased around £30m, or 16% of its issued share capital. Although the board deserves credit for sticking to its guns in the face of a declining NAV, a subsequent merger with another trust managed by Troy Asset Management, STS Global Growth & Income, was required as Troy Income & Growth's small size made it unviable. STS Global Growth & Income has a similar discount control policy.

Another disadvantage of a zero-discount policy is that the underlying fund manager needs to ensure that cash is always readily available to execute share buybacks and that any proceeds generated from the sale of new shares is invested in a timely manner. For this reason, a zero-discount policy is not suited to all portfolios. For example, it may not work as well for an investment trust investing in smaller companies, given the underlying stocks are less easy to buy and sell and there is a benefit to longer-term holding periods.

It is worth noting, in that context, that another way smaller company trusts can control discounts is via regular tenders. Let's take Diverse Income Trust (DIVI) as an example. It aims to generate income from a portfolio primarily made up of medium and smaller UK companies. Investors are offered the opportunity to get their money back once a year at a price close to NAV via a tender offer. For those that wish to take it up and exit, the board places the equivalent value of assets needed to meet the redemption request in a side-pool and then divests of these assets in a suitable manner to raise the necessary cash. The associated costs are borne by the side-pool. Any knock-on effect, in terms of these sales putting downward pressure on the remaining asset pool, can be influenced by the portfolio manager in identifying which stocks will form part of the tender offer.

This slightly unusual approach seems to work well and DIVI has made this type of tender offer every year since launch in 2011. The discount to NAV may widen at times, but it tends to narrow as the annual tender approaches. This makes it a potential feature for any trust to highlight at its initial launch to gain commitment from investors. However, they should also bear in mind that a redemption facility is not guaranteed as the final decision on execution rests with the independent board. That said, DIVI even honoured its tender in 2020, close to the depths of COVID-induced market weakness. That fact should provide strong reassurance to investors concerned about a wide discount developing in that trust.

Helping investors

Overall, for trusts that want to deliver a low volatility investment return and hold a portfolio of liquid assets, there is a lot to be said for adopting a zero-discount policy. Trusts that aim for smooth portfolio returns but that lack effective discount controls can often disappoint investors. BH Macro is a good example of a trust that reinforces this point. It provides access to several hedge fund strategies with the aim of generating attractive steady returns with low volatility. And, with an average NAV return of 8–9% per annum since inception, it has broadly succeeded.

"For trusts that want to deliver a low volatility investment return and hold a portfolio of liquid assets, there is a lot to be said for adopting a zero-discount policy."

However, its ability to control its discount is another matter. BH Macro's share price dropped from a premium (to NAV) of 19% in September 2022 to a discount of 18% by March 2024. That is a loss of more than 30% over an 18-month period for a vehicle which aims to deliver steady, low-volatility returns.

Wrapping up

Although zero-discount policies may be effective in reducing volatility, they are not commonplace. Neither are they appropriate for all trusts. However, they can be a very useful way of attracting and retaining investors that are uncomfortable with volatile discounts.

SUMMARY OF KEY POINTS

- A zero-discount policy aims to keep the share price as close to the NAV as is practically possible.

- Personal Assets Trust and Capital Gearing Trust are two trusts, which sit within the AIC Flexible Investment sector, that have adopted this practice.

- One of the key advantages of this practice is that it reduces share price volatility.

- Another advantage is that the issue of shares at a premium to NAV and the buying back of shares at a discount to NAV enhances the NAV per share.

- A zero-discount policy is not an option for trusts holding illiquid assets. It is only viable for trusts that hold sufficient liquid assets than can be easily realised at short notice.

PART 3

HOW TO INVEST IN INVESTMENT TRUSTS (STRATEGIES / TECHNIQUES / APPROACHES)

CHAPTER 21

THE POWER OF COMPOUNDING

"Compound interest is the eighth wonder of the world. He who understands it, earns it ... he who doesn't ... pays it."

—Albert Einstein

HAVE YOU EVER created a giant snowball by starting with a handful of compacted snow and then rolling it? As the snowball rolls, its surface area gets bigger, magnifying the effect and enabling the accumulation of even more snow.

Investors know this as 'compounding'.

The concept is so simple that it seems almost unexciting. Yet, within lies a financial superpower capable of turning young investors into millionaires. Compound growth is nothing less than the engine that powers wealth creation.

Investment trusts are engineered to benefit from compounding in three ways: they can reinvest capital profits and 15% of dividends generated by their portfolio (the snowballing effect); they can take a truly long-term view; and they are able to gear, further compounding material growth over time.

In this chapter, we will explore the mechanics of compounding via some examples and reveal what makes it such an essential tool for long-term investors.

Powering growth

For anyone that is new to all this, here are a couple of simple examples that should help convey why the concept of compounding matters so much.

Imagine that you make your own coffee each morning, instead of buying it at a coffee shop, and save £5 a day in the process (at those prices, this coffee shop is obviously in London!). If you decided to invest the amount saved, at a 10% annual return, how much money would you have after 40 years?

The answer is a whopping £808,285. The maths is as follows:

> Annual investment is £5 × 365.25 (to take account of leap years). No interest is applied in year 1, then 10% is applied to start-of-year-capital, plus £5 × 365.25, each year from year 2 onwards.

Let's say a one-off payment of £3,600 was committed to a child's pension by a parent or grandparent when the child was born. Assuming annual compound growth thereafter of 7.5%, how much will the pot be worth by the time that child turns 65?

If we ignore costs, the answer is a handy £390,000.

Overriding our instincts

So, given it is so effective, why do we struggle to master this vital concept? The answer lies in the way our brains are wired. We tend to think in a linear fashion, rather than exponentially. Our ancient ancestors lived in a world where it was more relevant to do so. For example, when hunting or gathering, they had to make simple, linear predictions about where to find food, or how long it would take to reach it. The alternative was starvation.

Exponential thinking, on the other hand, is superficially less useful and cognitively more demanding because it requires us to keep track of rapidly increasing numbers. As such it is less intuitive and, at a first glance, an unnecessary distraction. Even today, many aspects of our daily existence tend to reinforce linear thinking as the default. To fully appreciate the power of exponential returns we must think very long term, and that is not something we find easy to do given we all lead busy daily lives, with so much happening in the here and now. For investors, however, it is an essential skill. Figure 21A should reinforce why.

Figure 21A: Linear vs exponential

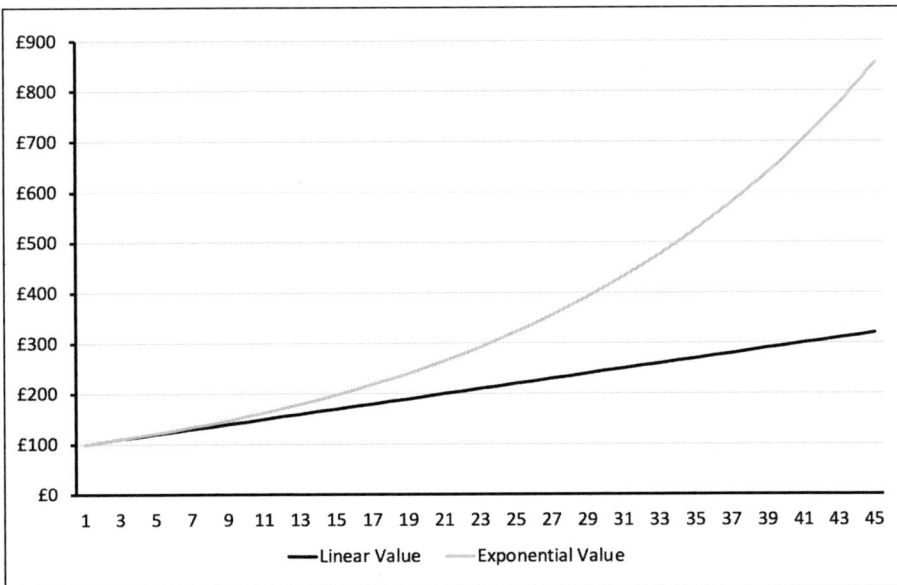

Linear = £100 growing at 5% simple. Exponential = £100 growing at 5% compound.

Figure 21A is showing that if we start with £100 and receive annual interest of 5%, we end year 1 with £105 (our £100 starting capital and our £5 of interest). This is the same in both a linear and compounding scenario. However, repeat this principle and at the end of year 2, a linear scenario leaves us with £110 (£100 + £5 + £5). Compound growth, on the other hand, results in a slightly higher end number of £110.25 (£100 + £5 + £5.25). This comprises our original £100, plus £5 interest in year 1 and then £5.25 in year 2. Why the extra 25p? Because in year 2 we have earned 5% interest not on £100 but rather £105, the difference (£5 × 5%) being £0.25.

This 25p difference may look inconsequential. And over a short period, it is. However, if we keep going, by year 25 this 'interest-on-interest' figure has become £113.64, which is higher than the original £100 of capital. And by year 27 the interest-on-interest in that *one* year (now £138.35) exceeds the entire accumulated amount of simple interest earned to date (£135). That is why the lines in the figure diverge so much as we sweep from left to right. For anyone

183

who wants to see the underlying numbers, Table 21A is a summary for years 1–10 and then 15–27. I have highlighted the ones I just mentioned – note that, for ease of reading, the right-hand column is rounded to the nearest whole number once we get beyond year 2.

Table 21A: Comparison of simple and compound interest

Year	Total value	Simple interest	Interest-on-interest	Total (compound) interest
1	**£105**	**£5**	**£0.00**	**£5**
2	**£110**	**£10**	**£0.25**	**£10.25**
3	£116	£15	£0.76	£16
4	£122	£20	£1.55	£22
5	£128	£25	£2.63	£28
10	£163	£50	£12.89	£63
15	£208	£75	£32.89	£108
20	£265	£100	£65.33	£165
24	£323	£120	£102.51	£223
25	£339	£125	**£113.64**	£239
27	£373	**£135**	**£138.35**	£273

I accept, at this point, that not every reader will want to gauge the potential of compounding via a set of fiddly calculations. The good news is a handy rule of thumb called the 'Rule of 72' can make life easier. It quickly estimates how long it takes for an investment to double based on its annual rate of return.

To apply it, just divide 72 by that rate. For example, if you expect an annual return of 8%, it will take approximately 9 years for your investment to double (72 / 8 = 9). I should point out that it is not foolproof in all scenarios – its accuracy wanes in more extreme ones – but it is useful, nonetheless.

Rules of thumb

So, how can we make the most of this extraordinary force as ordinary savers and investors?

Start early

One of the most profound lessons of compounding is the importance of starting early. Time is the magic that can transform even modest investments into substantial wealth. Let's explore the journey of two individuals: Early Bird Eamonn and Procrastinating Philip to make the point.

Early Bird Eamonn begins investing £2,000 per year at the age of 25 and continues until he is 35, contributing a total of £20,000. After that, he relies on compounding alone. Assuming an 8% annual return, by the time Eamonn reaches 65, his investments will have grown to approximately £340,000 (ignoring costs and taxes).

Procrastinating Philip, on the other hand, delays his investment journey. He doesn't start investing until he is 45. Philip also decides to invest £2,000 per year but from age 45 to 65, contributing a total of £40,000 (twice as much as Eamonn). Given the same 8% annual return, Philip's investments will have grown to approximately £99,000 by age 65.

The difference is stark. Although Eamonn is contributing only half of the amount Philip did, he ends up with a pension that is 3.4x larger. Eamonn's secret weapon was time. By starting early, he allowed compounding to work its magic for a more extended period. Philip, although diligent when it came to his contributions, could not catch up.

Manage risk

For compounding to work effectively, it is also important to avoid taking excessive risk. Gautam Baid, a US-based portfolio manager, highlights why in his 2020 book, *The Joys of Compounding*. Achieving growth at a steady rate beats sharp outperformance for just a year or two. As he writes, "an investor with an 14% average annual return (+20%, +40%, +20%, −50%, +40%) over a five-year period *underperforms* someone with a 9% average annual return if the latter is consistent every year (+9%, +9%, +9%, +9%, +9%)." The point here is that one year's loss of 50% trashes most of the gains that accrued beforehand even if they were earned at a much higher rate.

In the real world

Hopefully, you can now see why the ability to compound an initial sum by earning interest-on-interest is a key driver of investment returns.

However, compounding's enchantment is not just theoretical; it is woven into the fabric of human history, often with astonishing results. From ancient tales to modern financial folklore, its magic has been instrumental in shaping the destinies of individuals, empires, companies and economies.

One of the most iconic examples can be attributed to Benjamin Franklin, a US Founding Father. Before he died, two years before the US dollar was established, he bequeathed £2,000 to Boston and Philadelphia. However, he stipulated that the money could not be touched for 100 years, at which point 75% of it could be distributed with the remainder left to compound for another 100 years. By 1991 the value of the two trusts was $6.5m (Proquest, n.d.). It is therefore fair to say that Franklin understood the power of compounding. His story highlights how it can transform a modest sum into a substantial fortune over a sufficiently long time horizon.

Meanwhile, one of biggest exponents of reinvesting profits at high rates of return is Warren Buffett, often cited as one of the greatest investors of all time. His net worth is estimated to be US$133 billion (*Forbes*, as at 2024), thanks to a lifetime of astute investment decisions. But what is less well publicised is the role compounding played in the creation of this wealth.

Buffett started investing at a young age with a firm belief in what compounding could do. He famously quipped that his favourite holding period for a stock was 'forever'. By keeping investments for decades and continually reinvesting earnings, he was able to harness the full force of compounding. Berkshire Hathaway, the conglomerate he runs and his primary investment vehicle, saw its stock price grow at an annualised rate of more than 19% from 1980 to 2024. £10,000 invested in Berkshire Hathaway in March 1980 would have grown to more than £40 million by 31/12/2024 (Source: Morningstar). That is compounding at work. Berkshire Hathaway has many key characteristics that are shared by investment trusts.

Companies can benefit from compounding by reinvesting profits in productive activities. If a company can consistently make a 10% return on its assets, then there is a strong argument for it to reinvest as much of its profits as possible back into the business and benefit from the effects of compounding.

There are several investment trusts that actively look for companies with this potential to compound their growth over time. Examples include Smithson Investment Trust, European Opportunities Trust and Personal Assets Trust.

Wrapping up

I will close out this chapter with a summary of the key takeaways in the form of a checklist for anyone wishing to exploit what Einstein is believed to have termed 'the eighth wonder of the world'.

Time: This is the primary driver of compounding. The longer your money can grow, the more powerful the effect becomes. Hence the oft-quoted investment quip that the best time to start investing is yesterday, and the second-best time is today.

Rate of return: The rate at which your investments grow is crucial. A higher rate of return will accelerate the compounding process. However, it is important to balance the pursuit of high returns against an appropriate level of risk to achieve maximum consistency. On which note, we come to…

Consistency: Regularly saving and reinvesting interest (or earnings) is essential. Even small investments made consistently over time can generate significant wealth over a sufficiently long time horizon once you harness the ability to earn interest-on-interest.

Patience: Compounding is a long-term effect. It demands the ability to resist the temptation to withdraw money from investments prematurely and to develop a 'jam tomorrow' mindset.

Last, but far from least, we come to:

Diversification: Spreading your capital across a variety of assets can help to manage your overall risk level and improve the consistency of returns over long time periods. It is therefore a crucial component of any successful compounding strategy. So much so, that I will dedicate the following chapter to it.

SUMMARY OF KEY POINTS

- Compound growth is a powerful phenomenon that can dramatically assist wealth creation.

- Human beings tend to think in a linear fashion, rather than exponentially. This helps to explain why so many people fail to grasp the true power of compounding.

- The rule of 72 is a useful way of estimating how long it takes to double an investment, given an expected rate of return.

- Over five years, someone with a consistent 9% annual return (+9%, +9%, +9%, +9%, +9%), outperforms someone with a 14% average annual return (+20%, +40%, +20%, -50%, +40%).

- Benjamin Franklin's £2,000 gift to Boston and Philadelphia compounded to $6.5m by 1991.

CHAPTER 22

THE POWER OF POUND COST AVERAGING

"Successful people are simply those with successful habits."

—Brian Tracy, Canadian-American motivational speaker

REGULAR INVESTING IS a great habit to form. For some people this is the only practical way to invest, as they don't have sizeable amounts of capital at their disposal.

However, even those with large amounts of capital to commit may still wish to consider regular investment. One question is guaranteed to split opinion when it comes to the best way to invest – is it better to commit money all at once, or bit by bit? There is no 100% correct answer to this as it depends on time frames and market movements amongst other things. Investing bit by bit, also known as pound cost averaging (PCA), or dollar cost averaging in the US – has many fans, including me. In this chapter, I want to explore why.

Getting started

The principal behind PCA is that drip feeding each pound into the market regularly, as it follows its inevitable peaks and troughs, ensures that you buy more shares for your money when markets dip (which means they are cheaper) and fewer when they surge (which makes them more expensive). This process smooths the average price paid per share. It also makes for a more comfortable investment journey for another reason – there is no need to worry about trying to time the market. As a 'lock up and leave' investment approach, it takes away a key investment headache and reduces unnecessary prevarication.

The frequency of each payment is usually monthly. Further, the amount invested can be chosen according to your means – it could be £50 per month, or £500. Whatever the commitment, you will benefit from the ability to buy regularly in different market conditions over the long term.

For PCA to be effective, however, the investment that you are dripping money into needs to eventually rise in value. If the entire investment is committed to a single stock there is a risk of losing all your capital should the firm in question subsequently fail. By contrast, the likelihood of this happening to a pooled investment vehicle, such as an investment trust, is considerably lower.

"By promoting a disciplined investment approach, PCA helps investors avoid impulsive decisions based on short-term market movements."

Aside from providing a great way to ride out market volatility, PCA also comes with another big benefit. By promoting a disciplined investment approach, PCA helps investors avoid impulsive decisions based on short-term market movements. A regular investment schedule encourages consistency and helps you to stay focused on your long-term financial goals. That is why PCA is a strategy that I have used personally since the 1990s. As a naturally cautious investor, the steady commitment required helps me to avoid procrastination in the form of, say, waiting for a big market pullback that might not happen for years. Naturally, if I spot a good opportunity to commit extra capital, I will do so, but over and above (not instead of) my PCA baseline amount.

Illustrating the benefits

So, to an example. Table 22A compares a PCA approach (Portfolio A) with an upfront lump-sum approach (Portfolio B) for someone investing in an investment trust. In this comparison, the share price starts the year at £1, then declines to 88p, before recovering to end it at £1.10.

Portfolio B takes the simplest approach and invests a full £6,000 at the start of the year, buying 6,000 shares at £1 each. In doing so, it is exposed to the extent of the rise, or fall, in the market over the subsequent year, and so here it ends up being valued at £6,600 (6,000 shares × £1.10).

Portfolio A, on the other hand, invests the same £6,000 in total, but spread across the year in the form of £500 each month. This approach buys 500 shares in the first month and 568 in May when the price declines to 88p (since £500 at 88p each is 568 shares). By the end of the year, Portfolio B is worth £6,829 (6,209 shares × £1.10), or a full 13.8% more than Portfolio A. This better result is a function of the PCA approach buying shares during a period when they dip considerably below the starting price of £1 (between February and June). As the price recovers, so Portfolio B reaps the relative benefit of buying more cheaply.

Table 22A: Comparison of pound cost averaging versus a lump-sum investment

Month	Investment trust share price (£)	Portfolio A: Investing £500 monthly		Portfolio B: Investing £6,000 upfront	
		Number of shares purchased	Cumulative number of shares purchased	Number of shares purchased	Cumulative number of shares purchased
January	1.00	500	500	6,000	6,000
February	0.95	526	1,026	0	6,000
March	0.85	588	1,615	0	6,000
April	0.79	633	2,247	0	6,000
May	0.88	568	2,816	0	6,000
June	0.96	521	3,336	0	6,000
July	1.01	495	3,832	0	6,000
August	1.03	485	4,317	0	6,000
September	1.04	481	4,798	0	6,000
October	1.04	481	5,279	0	6,000
November	1.05	476	5,755	0	6,000
December	1.10	455	6,209	0	6,000

This can also be shown graphically as per Figure 22A.

Figure 22A: Valuation of Portfolio A versus Portfolio B over one year

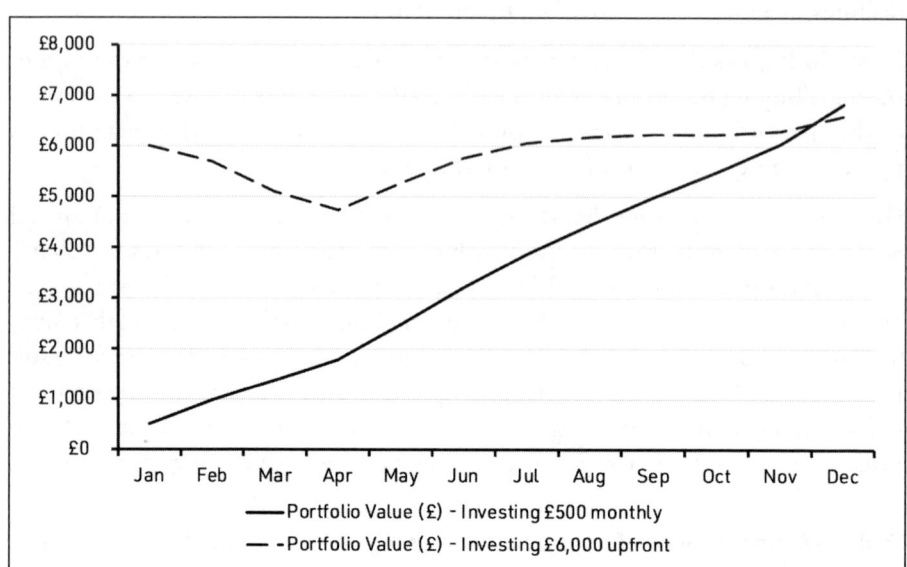

This figure reveals the PCA approach as the winner over a relatively short period of just 12 months. Of course, had the price per share risen consistently throughout the year, a strategy that invests a full £6,000 at the start will come out on top. Later in this chapter, we will see that the longer the investment period the more likely it is that an upfront lump-sum investment approach will prove more profitable. But not always.

Standing back

So far, so good then for PCA investors. However, there are some potential shortcomings with this approach which the scenarios above don't fully address.

The key limitation is that PCA can result in missed opportunities for significant gains in a market that experiences a very prolonged upturn. In a rising market – something which is likely over the very long term if history is any guide – a lump-sum investment at the start should outperform PCA hands down. Further, for PCA to be able to work its magic, markets need to eventually trend upward over the long term.

During prolonged bear markets, or during economic downturns, the benefits will be less pronounced. That said, in practice it is virtually impossible to predict short-term market movements. And besides that, not all investors have sizeable lump sums at their disposal or the discipline to stay invested even if the market tumbles just after they commit capital.

For those who can, however, Table 22B reveals something interesting. It shows the 10 most profitable investment trusts when it comes to regular saving approaches over 25 years since January 2000 at the top. It then also includes figures for the average investment trust and two stock market indices for comparison. The first column with numbers, assumes that £100 is invested each month over the full period. The final column shows the return from an initial lump of £22,361. This has been chosen as being the equivalent of £30,000 (the total amount invested under the regular savings option) but where each of the £100 monthly investments is reduced by 2.5% per year, to adjust for the cost of money (i.e. an approximation of the average Bank of England base rate) since 2000.

Table 22B: Most profitable investment trusts for regular savings since January 2000

Investment trust	£100 per month invested	Lump-sum investment of £22,361
Allianz Technology Trust Ord	335,009	241,965
Polar Capital Technology Ord	318,959	242,867
3i Group Ord	269,877	369,054
HgCapital Trust Ord	263,204	596,481
Scottish Mortgage Ord	241,435	281,590
abrdn Asia Focus plc	204,514	531,459
JPMorgan American Ord	195,635	201,362
Scottish Oriental Smaller Cos Ord	195,493	516,310
Pacific Horizon Ord	170,505	303,406
JPMorgan Global Growth & Income Ord	155,818	165,066
Investment trust average	**109,379**	**153,783**
L&G UK Index I Acc (tracking the FTSE All Share Index	71,367	70,825
L&G Global Equity Index R Inc (tracking the FTSE World TR Index)	103,276	86,599

Performance calculated mid to mid, with income reinvested over 25 years to 31/12/2024.

Source: Morningstar

A key takeaway from the table is that with the regular savings option, the average investment trust has delivered a return of more than three times the total initial outlay over the period. For the average investment trust, this option has also exceeded the returns that could have been achieved by investing in a low-cost index fund, tracking either the UK stock market (FTSE All Share TR Index) or a global stock market index (FTSE World TR Index). These numbers make a strong case for regular savings via investment trusts.

However, although regular saving is an effective strategy, a lump sum usually reaps the biggest return, which is a testament to the power of compounding given that this option sees the largest amount of money invested for the longest possible time. However, this is not always the case. The two technology trusts (Allianz Technology Trust and Polar Capital Technology), produced higher returns from a monthly investment strategy. This is almost certainly due to the fact that technology stocks declined sharply from 2000 to 2002 and took more than 10 years to reclaim their 2000 price levels. This worked well for the patient regular investor but was a frustrating period for the lump sum investor.

These numbers underline how important it is to leave investments to grow and reveal that if you are willing and able to do so, without touching them, the best route is usually to invest as much as possible, as soon as possible. In practice, of course, this may not be feasible – sometimes investors simply don't have large amounts of upfront capital available, or they are forced to withdraw some of it to meet a commitment. Others simply experience a bad short-term performance period and sell up in frustration.

Further, several of the data points in the table show how £30,000 invested over 25 years could have returned anywhere between 4 and 9× the original investment. Indeed, were we to widen the selection, we would see that at least 32 investment trusts achieved this feat. That is a powerful testament to the durability of the investment trust structure, the tailwind provided by gearing (a topic we have addressed earlier in this book) and the power of long-term buy and hold investment strategies in high-growth markets such as technology.

Wrapping up

Hopefully, this chapter has explained why PCA is such a widely used investment strategy. It aims to minimise the impact of market volatility on investment returns via a consistent approach that most of us can achieve fairly easily. Although it can be beaten by lump-sum investments in a rising market over very long periods, in practical terms it nonetheless imposes lower cash flow demands and, arguably, greater investment discipline. As such, it represents a great way to balance risk and reward over different time horizons, whilst mitigating behavioural risk. That makes it a practical and largely stress-free way for many investors to gain an exposure to investment trusts.

SUMMARY OF KEY POINTS

- Pound cost averaging involves drip feeding money into the market regularly, as it follows its inevitable peaks and troughs.

- Pound cost averaging follows a disciplined investment approach, which helps investors to avoid impulsive decisions based on short-term market movements.

- Over shorter time horizons, pound cost averaging can reduce volatility when compared to a lump-sum investment.

- In a continuously rising market, a lump-sum investment at the start will outperform a pound cost averaging approach.

- Pound cost averaging represents a great way to balance risk and reward with modest capital outlay, making it a practical and less stressful way to gain an exposure to investment trusts.

CHAPTER 23

THE DISCOUNT RATE AND WHY IT IS SO IMPORTANT IN FINANCE

"Interest rates are to asset prices like gravity is to the apple. They power everything in the economic universe."

—Warren Buffett

THE DISCOUNT RATE is one of the most fundamental concepts in finance. That's because it plays a crucial role in numerous calculations and decision-making processes. Here, we will explore why, look at some of the ways in which it is used and highlight its relevance to investment trusts.

Back to basics

Let me start by posing a simple question – would you rather receive £100 now or the same amount in a year's time? Assuming there is 5% inflation in the world, the logical answer is '£100 now', as it is worth more. Put another way, inflation will erode the 'purchasing power' of the same sum by 5% over the next year. So, what is the present-day amount that equates to £100 in a year's time if inflation is 5%? The answer is about £95. In other words, £95 is £100 in a year's time discounted at 5% to today. The calculation is £100 / 1.05, or £95.24 to be exact.

Extrapolating this key concept, John Law, the Scottish French economist, once said that "anticipation is always at a discount: £100 to be paid now is of more value than £1,000 to be paid by £10 a year for 100 years" (Chancellor, 2022).

Now let's go a bit further into the mechanics.

Breaking down discounting

In the earlier example we used a simple 5% discount rate to reflect the impact of inflation. However, real-world discount rates have a few more moving parts. You can think of a discount rate as being made up of two factors:

1. the cost of money (i.e. the prevailing interest rate), plus

2. a level of 'compensation' that you would need for taking on the risk of making a particular investment, sometimes referred to as a 'risk premium'.

The rule of thumb that results from this is that the riskier a project, or investment opportunity, the higher the discount rate needed, and vice versa.

Suppose I have an investment which generates an income. I am expecting that to be £100 in one year's time. Let us say the one-year risk-free interest rate (typically the yield I get from holding a safe UK government bond for one year) is 4% and I think that a suitable risk premium for this opportunity is 6% (because I perceive a risk that the amount I receive might be less than £100). My discount rate is then 10% (i.e. an interest rate of 4% + a risk premium of 6%). The receipt of £100 of income in a year's time discounted at 10% is worth £90.91 today (£100 / 1.1 = £90.91).

Analysts and investors normally use this principle when valuing the shares of companies listed on the stock market. We have seen how a change in the discount rate can affect the 'present-day' value of £100 that we expect to receive in a year's time. However, once we consider income received over several years, as well as the capital value of an investment in the future, changes in the discount rate become even more important.

This matters because such changes will have a proportionately bigger impact on shares that generate more income or profitability further into the future. So, although a receipt of £100 in a year's time discounted at 5% is worth £95.23

today (£100 / 1.05 = £95.23), £100 in 10 years' time discounted at 5% is worth a little over £61 today (the maths being £100 / (1.05^10) = £61.39). If we increase the discount rate, because interest rates have gone up, or because the receipt of the £100 in 10 years' time has become much less certain, it will change today's value. For instance, a receipt of £100 in 10 years' time discounted at 6% is worth just under £56 (£100 / (1.06^10) = £55.84). The discount rate has only increased by 1% but this has caused today's estimated value to reduce by about 9% (from £61 to £56).

Keeping it real

In practical terms, it is increases in discount rates that help to explain why the valuations of growth companies, such as Amazon, declined during the period of interest rises between 2020 and 2023. The US 10-year interest rate (i.e. the yield investors would get by buying and holding a 10-year US government bond to maturity) rose from around 0.5% in August 2020 to almost 5% in October 2023. Over the same period the Amazon share price declined by around 18%. This is not necessarily because Amazon became less attractive as a business, but simply that the mechanical impact of higher interest rates, and therefore a higher discount rate, on its future income and profitability translated into a sharply lower value for its shares.

Turning to investment trusts, we can see that Scottish Mortgage (SMT) declined by 25% during this period of rising interest rates. It was holding a portfolio of high-growth businesses such as Amazon, Tesla and Bytedance (the owner of TikTok). Again, the main reason for the decline in the SMT share price was not down to a fundamental change in the fortunes of these businesses, but primarily because of the higher discount rate applied across the board.

Turning to investment trusts

Investment trusts which invest in listed securities use quoted and readily available market prices to determine the trust's overall NAV. Those, on the other hand, which invest in assets that do not have a publicly quoted price have to calculate an NAV in a different way. This normally involves the use of an independent valuer. The resulting valuations usually involve a DCF methodology. This approach discounts future estimated cash flows in the way we have already outlined.

Consider an investment trust that owns a portfolio of income-generating properties. The trust calculates its NAV by estimating the future rental income and other cash flows from these assets. The discount rate, in this case, reflects the level of interest rates as well as the risks associated with the real estate market and wider economic conditions. The trust may apply a higher discount if the properties are in a sub-sector where demand is waning, and there is therefore greater uncertainty.

"A lower discount rate generates higher fees for a trust's manager."

Whilst the interest rate component should be easy to determine, the risk premium element is highly subjective. As we established in Chapter 10 Costs, many investment managers generate fees based on NAV and this is often a function of the overall discount rate. This represents a potential conflict, in so much as a lower discount rate generates higher fees for a trust's managers. Because of this, the role of the independent non-executive board is particularly important in determining a fair and visible discount rate, often with the help of external third parties.

Spotlighting HICL

By way of illustration, we could look at HICL Infrastructure, an investment trust that holds a portfolio of infrastructure projects, predominately located in the UK. These include schools in Derby, a prison in Scotland and a children's hospital in Brighton. If these facilities are available for use, HICL Infrastructure receives regular contractual payments from the government. These are relatively low-risk investments but are certainly not risk free.

Along with most infrastructure investment trusts, HICL discloses the discount rate it uses to value its portfolio. We show the HICL directors' comments on the discount rate from the 2024 annual report. It explains how the interest rate component has increased due to rising long-term rates. It also states that the UK risk premium has increased from 3.4% to 3.9%. There is no further explanation for this beyond a typical industry statement that:

> *In addition to the transaction data, the Investment Manager continues to apply a greater weight to the level of equity risk premium implied by current government bond yields when reviewing and setting the discount rate. In the six months to 30 September 2023, the average 20–30-year UK government bond yields increased by 120 basis points to 4.9% at 30 September 2023 before a small reduction in the second*

half of the year to 4.4% at 31 March 2024. Overall, the UK discount rate has increased by 100 basis points since 31 March 2023. This results in a UK weighted average discount rate of 8.3% at 31 March 2024 (31 March 2023: 7.3%) and a risk premium of 3.9% (31 March 2023: 3.4%). The Investment Manager believes that the risk premium is appropriate for HICL's core infrastructure UK assets.

Unwinding discount rates

That brings us to the final piece of jargon, which I will explain using HICL Infrastructure as an example. The weighted average discount rate for the HICL portfolio (including non-UK assets) at the time of writing is 8.0%. Another way of looking at this is that if everything goes according to plan (i.e. based on management assumptions) the portfolio will grow (including reinvested income) by 8.0% over the next year. So, what was worth £92.59 a year ago (based on an 8.0% discount rate, £100 / 1.08 = £92.59) is now worth £100. That is simply a function of HICL receiving the cash it expected and no longer needing to discount it. It is commonly known as the unwinding of the discount rate.

However, for investors there is still a piece of the jigsaw missing. Whilst the discount rate should be a guide to the level of gross return (i.e. before costs) investors can expect, it reveals the expected gross return on the trust's assets, not on its shares.

To gauge that, we need to consider several other factors, such as ongoing charges, debt levels and whether the shares trade at a discount or premium to the underlying NAV. Fortunately, we can use the various disclosures made by investment trusts to arrive at an expected return on the share price. Analysts at JP Morgan Cazenove were amongst the first to use the term 'steady state' to describe this approach in the context of investment trusts. In short, if everything remains in a steady state – the discount rate, costs, level of debt – then we can establish the return on the share price. If HICL shares are trading at a premium to NAV, the expected return on its shares will be lower than the 8.0% expected return, but if HICL shares trade at a discount, it will be commensurately higher.

In the appendix (which provides a full explanation of the steady state return) we show how HICL's 8.0% discount rate can be converted to a more meaningful steady state return of 8.9% (the future expected return of the share price) by adjusting for ongoing charges, the share price discount to NAV and the sensitivity of the NAV to changes in the discount rate.

Infrastructure trusts and the terminal value

Before we leave the subject of discount rates it is important to mention the terminal value in discounted cash flow valuations and how they relate to investment trusts. We showed earlier in the chapter that £100 to be received in a year's time, discounted at 5%, is worth £95.24 today (£100 / 1.05 = £95.24). In DCF calculations, the discount rate is applied to both cash flows during the investment period and any value that remains at the end of the investment, sometimes referred to as the terminal value. In the case of infrastructure projects, this terminal value is usually zero. This is because the control of the asset associated with an infrastructure concession contract (e.g. school, hospital) is usually returned to the public sector at the end of the project, or the physical infrastructure asset (e.g. a wind turbine) is deemed to have a finite period of useful operation (e.g. 30–35 years) after which it is deemed worthless.

"Why would you invest in something which is worth nothing at the end? The answer is that the value is in the cash flows and that both the cash flow and the zero terminal value are taken account of in the DCF calculation."

The zero terminal value is something a few newcomers to infrastructure investments struggle to get their heads around. Why would you invest in something which is worth nothing at the end? The answer is that the value is in the cash flows and that both the cash flow and the zero terminal value are taken account of in the DCF calculation. Therefore, everything is reflected in the price paid for the contract, or in the case of an infrastructure investment trust, in the NAV.

Let us consider three simple examples:

Project 1 is a contract offering an annual income of £100 with a terminal value of £1,000.

Project 2 is a contract offering an annual income of £100 with a terminal value of £0.

Project 3 is a contract offering an annual income of £200 with a terminal value of £0.

Let's assume that all three contracts carry a similarly low level of risk, so we discount all cash flows and the terminal value by 5%.

Project 1. £1,000 terminal value

Year	1	2	3	4	5	6	7	8	9	10	Total
Cash flow / terminal value	£100	£100	£100	£100	£100	£100	£100	£100	£100	£1,100	received £2,000
Discounted valued	£95	£91	£86	£82	£78	£75	£71	£68	£64	£675	
Net asset value @ 5% discount rate	**£1,386**										

Project 2. Zero terminal value

Year	1	2	3	4	5	6	7	8	9	10	Total
Cash flow / terminal value	£100	£100	£100	£100	£100	£100	£100	£100	£100	£100	received £1,000
Discounted valued	£95	£91	£86	£82	£78	£75	£71	£68	£64	£61	
Net asset value @ 5% discount rate	**£772**										

Project 3. Zero terminal value but higher cashflows

Year	1	2	3	4	5	6	7	8	9	10	Total
Cash flow / terminal value	£200	£200	£200	£200	£200	£200	£200	£200	£200	£200	received £2,000
Discounted valued	£190	£181	£173	£165	£157	£149	£142	£135	£129	£123	
Net asset value @ 5% discount rate	**£1,544**										

We can see that the cash flows and terminal value of Project 1 produce an NAV (we assume no costs and no debt) of £1,386. Project 2 is identical to Project 1 except that the terminal value is nil. This accounts for the lower NAV of £772.

We can also see that despite Project 3 having a zero terminal value, it has cash flows that are sufficiently higher than those of Project 1, that they more than make up for the zero terminal value. Whilst over the entire life of the projects an investor in Project 3 receives the same £2,000 as an investor in Project 1, Project 3 has a higher NAV as more of its cash flow is received sooner.

In these simplistic examples, if both buyer and seller agree on the cash flow assumptions and the discount rate, Project 1 changes hands for £1,386, Project 2 for £772, whilst Project 3 changes hands for £1,544.

The key point in all of this is that a lack of any residual value at the end of the project life is reflected in the NAV. In the case of investment trusts, the board has a responsibility, in conjunction with the investment manager, to monitor the length of project lives. This can help ensure that the trust's portfolio of projects is replenished over time from excess cash flows or new equity capital. Monitoring the portfolio in this way helps to maintain stability in the NAV and share price.

Wrapping up

In conclusion, I have hopefully explained why the discount rate is a pivotal concept in finance, with far-reaching implications for investment valuation, decision-making and risk assessment. In the investment trust sector, its role is central in determining an NAV, market price and yield. As such, investors must be equipped with at least a basic understanding of how it works and the factors that can influence it to make the right decisions about where to invest. Armed with that, we can move onwards to Chapter 24.

SUMMARY OF KEY POINTS

- The discount rate is one of the most fundamental concepts in finance, playing a crucial role in numerous calculations and decision-making processes.

- The discount rate is the interest rate used to determine the 'present value' of an amount to be received in the future.

- The discount rate is made up of the cost of money and a level of 'compensation' needed for taking on a particular risk.

- Many alternative investment trusts determine their NAV using a DCF methodology.

- Another way to view the discount rate is that it is the return the portfolio will achieve if everything goes according to plan.

CHAPTER 24

EXPECTED RETURNS

"Forward-looking indicators such as valuation ratios have a better track record in forecasting future asset class returns than rear-view mirror measures."

—**Annti Ilmanen,** *Expected Return: An Investor's Guide to Harvesting Market Rewards.* **Wiley Finance, 2011**

ONE OF THE most frequent questions investors ask is, 'What return can I expect from my investments?' As with so many questions, the best ones are often the most difficult to answer. But let's try.

As we saw in the previous chapter, the expected return from an infrastructure investment trust is the discount rate, adjusted for costs, discount / premium and other factors.

In the case of fixed interest, if someone has a portfolio of bonds and holds them all the way through to maturity, we can estimate the return with a high degree of confidence. It will be the yield to maturity (i.e. income plus / minus any capital gain / loss) reduced by any defaults. We can make reasonable assumptions about this outcome, and many bond-oriented investment trusts provide us with sufficient information to make reasonable estimates.

However, if we invest in a portfolio of equities, the question of how much we might make back becomes much more difficult to answer with any degree of precision.

An expected return tries to express how much an investor will get back over the term of their investment. If the term of the investment is short, it is more difficult to estimate an equity return with any level of confidence. We saw in Chapter 13 that in any given year UK equity returns have ranged between c. –60% and +100%. Estimating equity returns 12 months ahead is a lottery!

However, estimating returns over longer timeframes is somewhat easier, as more time provides an opportunity for extremes to average themselves out. So how can we estimate returns over longer timeframes?

Let's look at ways this can be done.

Internal rate of return

One approach is to calculate an internal rate of return (IRR). Frequently applied in corporate finance (which deals with how companies raise and structure capital), the IRR estimates the rate of return that will be made on a specific project, or equity investment. In a nutshell, it is the discount rate at which the net present value of a projected series of cash flows equals zero. Mathematically, it can be derived from the formula in Figure 24A.

Figure 24A: IRR calculation

$$\text{Internal Rate of Return (\%)} = \frac{\text{Future Value (FV)}}{\text{Present Value (PV)}}^{\frac{1}{\text{Periods}}} - 1$$

An IRR approach can be applied at an individual company level, based on assumptions about future cash flows and profitability. It can also be applied at a market level based on expected profit growth and market valuation. Such an approach can take consensus (the average analyst view) profit (earnings) growth forecasts, assume that the current market valuation (P/E ratio) will converge to the long term average, and adjust the profit growth forecast accordingly (down if the market is trading above its long term valuation level and up if the market is trading below its long term valuation level) and then add the expected dividend yield. When considering expected returns at a stock market or portfolio level, it can also be helpful to consider the concept of the equity risk premium (ERP).

This is the additional return that investors demand for holding equities compared to risk-free assets, such as government bonds. This premium compensates them for their subordinate position in the capital structure, and for the non-diversifiable risk associated with equities as an asset class, such as exposure to the economic cycle or sociopolitical factors. At the risk of stating the obvious, the ERP is simply an estimate and the actual premium that investors earn can be higher or lower and, in some cases, it can be significantly lower.

Another way to think of a risk premium is as a 'price' for risk. In the case of equities, this is set by supply and demand. When demand is high, it pushes up share prices and reduces the 'price' of the associated risk that investors are willing to accept to buy them. So, the ERP falls. Conversely, when demand for equities is low, it pushes share prices down and increases the 'price' of risk, causing the ERP to rise.

Purely historical ERP

One approach is to use historic data. This involves deducting the risk-free rate from the actual equity return. This approach assumes that the past is largely representative of the future. Interestingly, in the investment classic *Stocks for the Long Run*, the author Jeremy Siegel illustrates that the US equity experience of equities outperforming the 10-year government bond (a positive ERP) has been largely mirrored in 20 other markets over the period 1900–2020. Furthermore, the average ERP of 16 of the markets studied was approximately 3–5%. This implies a relatively stable level of compensation for taking equity risk, (almost) irrespective of the market in question, over a wide range of economic and political environments, over long timeframes.

Valuation-based ERP

There is a relationship between equity valuations and the ERP. During periods of strong equity market returns, equity valuations (e.g. P/E ratios) can expand faster than underlying profits. When the perception of risk is very low, investors accept lower future returns (a lower ERP), resulting in equity markets trading at levels that are materially above their long-term valuation average. You could also have a situation where interest rates decline but the ERP remains constant, pushing valuations above their long-term average. In this scenario, future equity returns are also likely to face a headwind of interest rates increasing in the future, as they normalise towards the long-term average.

Equally, equity markets that are out of favour tend to see their valuations fall.

At an extreme this will be to levels that are materially below their long-term valuation average. From this point, when the perception of risk is very high, investors demand a higher return (higher ERP), resulting in the lower equity valuations. The return they demand is likely to be realised in time, as profits and valuations normalise (improve) in future years. Equally, you could also have a situation where interest rates rise but the ERP remains constant, pushing valuations below their long-term average. In this scenario, future equity returns are also likely to benefit from a tailwind of interest rates declining in the future, as they normalise towards the long-term average.

Taking this principle a step further, some investors will use valuation as a guide to the future ERP. Indeed, this is an approach we use in our team for the fund-based portfolios that we manage. This approach can be used to compare several valuation measures with subsequent returns to help establish relationships between the two.

Our approach is to overweight markets that have higher forward-looking ERPs (i.e. trade on lower valuations) and underweight markets that have lower forward-looking ERPs (i.e. trade on higher valuations). We then get exposure to these markets via funds, which include investment trusts that trade at attractive discounts to NAV.

In his August 2023 paper, 'The Price of Risk: With Equity Risk Premiums, Caveat Emptor!', Aswath Damodaran, a professor at Stern School of Business at New York University, generated a US equity forecast based on the earnings yield (i.e. earnings, or profit, divided by price) of 6.1%. This was based on the relationship between the historical ERP and the earnings yield from 1960 to 2022, a relationship he found to be statistically significant. This is an example of using present-day valuations to forecast future equity returns.

ERP and gearing

As we have noted earlier in this book, investment trusts are able to borrow (gear up) to amplify their exposure to an asset such as shares and potentially enhance returns during periods of rising equity prices.

In that context, the relationship between expected return and the cost of borrowing can provide some insights for investment trust investors:

$$\text{Expected return, after gearing} =$$
$$\text{Expected return} \times (1 + \text{Gearing ratio}) - \text{Cost of gearing}$$

Provided an investment trust can borrow at attractive rates (not too high a margin over government bonds) and provided it remains within its gearing covenants, gearing should enhance returns over time.

Investment trusts and expected returns

How can private investors, without access to the same resources as institutional investors, form a view on expected returns?

One way is to read the important sections of the annual report. Sometimes the investment trust Chair or the investment manager will refer to expected returns. In the case of infrastructure funds this is expressed as a portfolio discount rate. In the case of bond funds, the yield to maturity of the underlying portfolio is often stated in the monthly factsheet.

Equity investment trusts are not as prescriptive in putting numbers on future returns. However, if clues about future returns are contained anywhere, it is likely to be in the investment manager's report. Here is a relevant extract from Aurora Investment Trust's (now Aurora UK Alpha) 2023 annual report:

> *...our low activity level in 2023 was a reflection of our confidence in the portfolio. We entered 2024 with a portfolio that we believe is cheap despite a 2023 return that has taken the NAV to an all-time high. The upside to intrinsic value is 130%, which is attractive in historical terms.*

Whilst most investment managers' reports don't put numbers on their statements, the change in their optimism can be determined by comparing the latest statement with prior ones. Take River UK Microcap for example. In the 2019 annual report the portfolio manager said:

> *...we are in the later stages of a mature cycle ... Given the starting point of relatively high valuations, capital preservation is a key consideration with a focus on well capitalised companies with either, or preferably both, improving return on capital and the potential to grow through the cycle.*

Compare this with the same manager's comments in the 2023 annual report:

The mismatch between valuations and fundamentals – which is evident in our current discount to NAV – has been driven by outflows from open ended funds and a market wide aversion to illiquidity … UK smaller companies are unloved and undervalued, in both absolute terms and relative to the wider market, on extremely attractive, once-in-a-cycle levels. We cannot call the bottom but putting capital to work today on a three to five-year view should be very rewarding.

This illustrates the importance of reading key sections of the annual report. The investment manager's report often contains helpful insights that can help us to determine whether we should be increasing or reducing our exposure.

Wrapping up

The question, 'What return can I expect from my investments?', is an important one. However, in the case of equities, it is difficult to answer with any precision. Over the longer term most equity markets have delivered a return that is 3–5% ahead of the return available from the 10-year government bond issued by the country in question. This provides a very long-term guide.

For a guide over shorter periods (but still greater than 5–10 years) it is helpful to consider equity market valuations. Clues about equity market valuations in general, and portfolio valuations in particular, can sometimes be found in an investment trust's annual report.

SUMMARY OF KEY POINTS

- An expected return is an estimate of how much an investor will get back over the term of their investment.

- The expected return is sometimes expressed as the internal rate of return (IRR).

- The expected equity return over and above that of a risk-free rate is called the equity risk premium (ERP).

- The average equity risk premium over multiple equity markets over very long-term (100+ years) timeframes is approximately 3–5%.

- When equity markets trade materially below (above) their long-term valuation average, future equity returns are likely to be higher (lower) and this is reflected in a lower (higher) forward-looking ERP.

CHAPTER 25

UNDERSTANDING ILLIQUIDITY

"When I hear complaints about less liquidity, remember there is such a thing as too much liquidity."

—Paul Volcker, US economist and former Chair of the Federal Reserve

To introduce this topic, let's imagine two bonds that are both zero coupon (i.e. they don't pay any income during their life and instead are issued at a discount to their maturity value) and identical in all other respects, other than their issue size and tradeable volumes. Both are issued by the same company, with the same maturity date at a redemption price of £100. Yet, the gap between the buying and selling price – the 'bid-offer spread' – for the first bond, which is more frequently traded, is very narrow. Meanwhile, the equivalent for the second, which is less frequently traded, is very wide. This pricing differential generates different trading prices and therefore different yields. If the first bond has a yield to maturity of 5.3%, whilst for the second the equivalent is 7.5%, the yield differential of 2.2% represents what is known as an 'illiquidity premium'.

So, what is this? In short, it represents the compensation due to investors who are willing to bear the risks associated with holding illiquid assets. Liquidity, in this context, refers to the ease with which an asset can be bought or sold without materially affecting its price. Highly illiquid assets, such as privately held equities or property, typically trade less frequently and may require a longer time horizon for liquidation. As such they should attract bigger premiums.

So far, so good. In practical terms, however, investors that can take a long-term view may actively seek out these illiquidity premiums. That is why we will now delve into their dynamics and the implications for investors, with a particular focus on investment trusts.

Looking into liquidity

Illiquid assets have often provided higher returns than their liquid counterparts. This outperformance has prompted investors to explore illiquidity as a theme and a useful source of additional portfolio performance. Several academic studies are worth highlighting in this context.

I will start with the seminal study, 'Asset Pricing and the Bid-Ask Spread' (Amihud and Mendelson, 1986), which laid the groundwork. This study used the difference between the buying and selling price (the bid-ask spread) as a measure of liquidity. The wider the spread, the less liquid the stock. What they found was a revelation. The study observed that the wider the bid-ask spread, the higher the future returns, and that investor returns increased with longer holding periods. In discovering these relationships, the study made the case for the existence of a structural illiquidity premium.

A subsequent study by Amihud in 2002, 'Illiquidity and Stock Returns: Cross-section and Time-series Effects', concluded that if investors anticipate lower market liquidity, they will actively price stocks lower, and this will in turn generate higher returns. Since this affects smaller company stocks to a greater extent than it does larger ones, it helps to explain the higher returns available from smaller companies over time.

Next, 'Liquidity Risk and Expected Stock Returns' (Pastor and Stambaugh, 2003), a paper which extended and broadened the analysis of illiquidity premiums to take account of investment style, size and momentum. The authors duly discovered that expected returns are related to liquidity, having adjusted for all these factors. Over the 34-year period covered in their paper, the average return on stocks with low liquidity exceeded that for stocks with high liquidity by 7.5% annually.

Interestingly, they found that illiquidity premiums are not static and will vary according to market conditions. Changes in investor sentiment, economic conditions or the regulatory environment, for example, can impact the perceived value of illiquidity, thereby influencing the size of any premium.

Unpacking investment trusts

The good news is that investment trusts offer an ideal structure for illiquid holdings and therefore the opportunity to capture any premium. Unlike mutual funds, investment trusts don't have regular unforeseen redemptions that interrupt their investment approach. And, unlike traditional private equity limited partnerships, with their limited life span, or hedge funds offering regular liquidity windows, investment trusts are evergreen.

That means they have an infinite life, provided their shareholders agree, and can therefore take advantage of attractive long-term investments, even where liquidity is poor. That is one reason why certain investment trusts specialising in private equity, such as HgCapital, have been able to generate attractive returns. Real estate, another asset class with poor liquidity, is also to be found in the portfolios of some investment trusts.

Wrapping up

Whilst it is true that closed-ended structures provide investment trusts with flexibility in managing illiquid assets, they are also not immune to redemption calls. Sometimes investors may push the directors to liquidate investments for tenders, share buybacks or full wind-ups. Any of these corporate actions may force a trust to sell less liquid assets at unfavourable prices.

In conclusion, therefore, what we can say is that, once we accept that illiquidity premiums offer investors an avenue for enhancing portfolio returns, investment trusts have often shown themselves to be effective at capturing them. The key to exploiting this observation is to ensure that your time horizon is genuinely long term. That established, you need to make an assessment about how likely it is that the investment trust(s) you choose will match your time horizon. The best indication of this lies in the annual report in the form of the tone of the Chair's statement and the stability of the shareholder register.

SUMMARY OF KEY POINTS

- A study by Amihud and Mendelson in 1986 found a relationship between lower market liquidity and higher stock returns.

- A subsequent study by Amihud in 2002 found that over a 34-year period, the average return on stocks with low liquidity exceeded that for stocks with high liquidity by 7.5% annually.

- Investment trusts offer an ideal structure for holding illiquid assets.

- In contrast to mutual fund managers, investment trust managers do not have to worry about maintaining sufficient liquidity to meet regular redemptions.

- Illiquidity offers investors an avenue for enhancing portfolio returns, and investment trusts have often shown themselves to be effective at capturing them.

CHAPTER 26

CAPITAL ALLOCATION

"Working with Pantheon, we are revising our capital allocation policy, which in the past has not taken sufficient account of the returns to be generated by reinvesting in PIP's [Pantheon International Plc's] portfolio when the discount is high."

—**John Singer CBE,**
Chairman of Pantheon International Plc

THIS CHAPTER WILL deal with an important issue – capital allocation. For trading companies, capital allocation involves investing cash where it can generate a return above a company's cost of capital (the cost that a business incurs to finance its operations), and if it cannot, returning it to its owners (i.e. the shareholders). The cost of capital calculation includes the cost of any debt as well as the cost of equity. The cost of equity is effectively the expected return on a company's shares.

For investment trusts, the expected return on its shares is equivalent to the expected (net of cost) return on its investment portfolio. The investment manager of an investment trust may be able to identify new investments that can generate a higher return than the existing investment portfolio, and therefore above the cost of capital. However, if the trust shares trade at a discount to NAV (a discount to portfolio value) any available cash could be used to buy the entire portfolio at that discount.

This is effectively what happens when excess cash is used to buy back investment trust shares trading at a discount. Applying this logic, any new investment would then need to have a higher expected return than the existing portfolio and the discount combined. The wider the discount to NAV, the less likely it is that the investment manager will identify a sufficiently attractive new investment that can exceed both the existing portfolio return and the discount. Thus, the wider the discount to NAV, the stronger the case for using cash to buy back shares.

Made correctly, such decisions should always pivot on which of the available opportunities is/are likely to provide the best economic outcome. Naturally, there are several factors that need to be carefully weighed to evaluate what might be the best outcome.

Setting the scene

There are two levels at which capital allocation decisions need to be made. Firstly, investment managers must spread money across the various investments available to them. For a UK equity manager, for example, this usually involves considering the merits of around 600 London-listed companies.

The second set of decisions arise at board level. In making them, the directors have a responsibility to consider overall debt levels, as well as interest costs and when principal repayments fall due. They also need to consider the case for doing share buybacks or tenders (where shareholders tender shares for cash at a level close to NAV), and the appropriateness of the current dividend policy. This can all become quite subjective. Where an investment trust share price trades at a premium to the underlying NAV, the board will need to judge whether to issue new shares, thereby raising more capital for investment. They will also need to decide on the correct level of debt to carry. This decision is often based on advice from the investment manager.

Things look rather different when a trust's shares trade at a discount to NAV as the relevant decision then relates to whether to buy back shares at a discount. This can change the overall dynamic of a trust if it results in an NAV per share enhancement via a reduction in the share count. The board needs to consider whether the discount might widen further and the implications for longer-term share price liquidity. Since this is quite a contentious area, I think it warrants a slightly deeper dive.

Breaking down buybacks

With a share buyback the trust instructs a broker to buy its shares in the market and pays for them using the trust's own capital. These shares can then either be cancelled or they can be held by the trust (referred to as holding in treasury) for future reissue. In either case, the shares which have been repurchased no longer qualify for dividends (leaving a smaller number of shareholders to share any available dividend) and are no longer included in the NAV per share calculation (thereby enhancing the NAV per share as the net assets are now assigned to a smaller number of shares).

In the short term, any share repurchase will enhance liquidity because it creates a new source of demand for the shares, the investment trust itself. The flipside is that prolonged buybacks may reduce the share count to a point where liquidity starts to fade, and potential investors are then deterred by a shrinking market capitalisation.

Why would potential investors be deterred from buying smaller trusts? Take wealth management firms, which are a large and important source of demand for investment trust shares. Some of them have grown at pace, typically through mergers and acquisitions. Let's assume as a result that they now have £25bn to invest in funds and wish any investment in an investment trust to be at least 1% of their fund assets (or £250m). Let's also assume that they also do not wish to own more than 10% of the equity of any investment trust. This means that they can only buy trusts with a minimum market capitalisation of £2.5bn. Only 12 investment trusts are currently this big, a fact that puts smaller trusts at a potential disadvantage.

There is, nonetheless, a school of thought which says that if an investment trust holds a liquid portfolio, it should always look to buy back shares whenever they trade at a discount because it enhances NAV per share. To illustrate this, let's say the NAV of an investment trust is £100m and there are 100m shares in issue. The NAV per share is £1 (£100m / 100m) or 100p. If the share price is 80p (i.e. trading at a 20% discount to NAV), the board could choose to spend £8m to buy back 10m shares and then cancel them. All other things being equal (and ignoring any frictional costs), the NAV is now £92m (£100m – £8m). With only 90m (100m – 10m) shares in issue, the new NAV per share is 102.2p (£92m / 90m). So, the share buyback has removed surplus shares from circulation, provided liquidity to the market, and enhanced the value of the remaining shares still in issue – in this case by 2.2% (102.2p/100p – 1).

From the portfolio manager's perspective, a buyback at a 20% discount is akin to acquiring the investment portfolio they have created, 20% cheaper than doing so via the open market. To put it another way, any other new investment under consideration needs to be 25% more attractive than the existing portfolio to justify favouring a new holding over buying back the trust's own stock. The logic behind this is that buying something at 80p, which is worth 100p, offers 25% upside. For that reason, trusts that trade on sizeable discounts shouldn't normally make new investments unless they clearly offer superior returns to shareholders than an equivalent buyback.

"From the portfolio manager's perspective, a buyback at a 20% discount is akin to acquiring the investment portfolio they have created, 20% cheaper than doing so via the open market."

As we saw in Chapter 20, trusts such as Capital Gearing and Personal Assets take the view that they will continue to buy back shares whilst they trade at a discount and issue them when they stand at a premium even when the differences are fairly small (2% or more).

Now for an important nuance. Although most investment trusts simply cancel shares once they have been bought back, in some cases they are held in treasury. This means that the trust continues to own the shares, but they do not count towards NAV calculations or qualify for dividends (discussed later). As such, the impact is the same as if the share count had been permanently reduced, but this route provides the investment trust with the flexibility to reissue the same shares should market conditions change.

Holding shares in treasury may not have as strong an impact on reducing any discount as when they are cancelled. This is because the market may perceive the treasury shares as a potential 'overhang', that is stock that could be sold back into the market at any time, thereby placing downward pressure on the share price. However, views differ on this. Some argue that holding shares in treasury simply makes things easier from an accounting perspective. Some also argue that not holding shares in treasury after a buyback signals to the market that the board has no confidence in the trust trading at a premium / stronger rating in the future.

Next, we need to consider another hotly contested, and related, topic – dividend policy.

Debating dividends

JPMorgan Asset Management, which manages many investment trusts, is clear on where it stands on this topic. It has proposed to the boards of several of its investment trusts that they initiate a 'high yield' policy. That translates into a dividend payout which is typically set at 4% of the start-of-year NAV. So, for example, if that is 100p, the relevant trust should aim to distribute 4p per share in dividends over the course of the following year. Further, when less than 4p per share of income is generated by the portfolio, the investment trust should look to sell some investments and make it up from capital. The portfolio is expected to rise in value over time and thus top-slicing some investments should be an adequate way to supplement, or wholly generate, a dividend.

However, this is not a universal view. Some investment trust purists take a sacrosanct attitude towards capital and income, believing that they should be treated separately. Dividends are taxable as income and therefore at potentially higher rates than capital gains from shares, albeit this matters less where investment trusts are held in a tax shelter such as an ISA or a SIPP.

As we highlighted in Chapter 14, capital and revenue reserves, which are used to supplement portfolio income, are not some sort of special treasure trove of capital. They are simply an accounting convention and are already included in the published NAV.

Another point worth making is that the long-term return from most assets is a combination of capital gain and income. If we look at equities in that context, some will pay high levels of income and deliver relatively low capital growth. Others will do the opposite. That creates a problem for our purists. Let's say the long-term total return from equities is 10%, which includes a dividend yield of 2%. That implies capital growth of 8%. If an equity investor needs an income of 4% and doesn't believe in mixing income and capital, they are likely to avoid high-growth sectors (that traditionally pay low or zero levels of dividends), such as technology, and plump for value stocks with high yields. This can lead to very skewed portfolios. The JPMorgan high yield approach helps to avoid this by setting out a dividend policy that is sufficient to meet investors' income requirements, whilst also giving the portfolio manager the freedom to find total return performance from a wide range of stocks, regardless of their income generation.

There is another argument in favour of this type of high distribution policy. It is that when a trust trades at a discount, a distribution is akin to buying the shares at a discount and then getting part of your investment returned at NAV in the form of a cash dividend. The benefit may be modest, but in the world of investments, every wee bit helps.

Taking stock

All of these considerations resurfaced meaningfully in 2023, when the whole topic of investment trust capital allocation really came to the fore. The sharp rise in interest rates that started in 2022 led to a derating of several investment trusts, especially those specialising in areas such as infrastructure, renewables and private equity. Boards were generally slow to respond to this 'new normal', but those that did won immediate plaudits. In August 2023, the board of Pantheon International, a private equity trust, issued full-year results and announced a share buyback programme. The price duly rose almost 10% in the two-week period that followed, forcing the hand of a number of other investment trusts.

However, the truth is that for investment trusts investing in liquid securities such as quoted equities, a share buyback decision like that tends to be straightforward. If they hold illiquid and hard-to-value assets, on the other hand, the decision is less clear cut, particularly for private equity trusts that have 'follow-on' commitments (i.e. legal commitments to provide further capital in the future to certain investments). These commitments demand a certain minimum level of liquidity to be maintained within the trust. As such, when the board of an investment trust holding illiquid assets decides to initiate a share buyback, it should be seen as a vote of confidence that the underlying NAV is reliable.

"When the board of an investment trust holding illiquid assets decides to initiate a share buyback, it should be seen as a vote of confidence that the underlying NAV is reliable."

However, whilst share buybacks make a lot of sense when an investment trust trades at a discount to NAV, I do not believe it makes sense for alternative asset trusts (those holding illiquid assets) to do so when they have an option to repay floating rate debt instead.

Investors dislike uncertainty. This dislike gets reflected in trust discounts. The greater the uncertainty about future returns the larger a discount is likely to be. Floating rate debt increases uncertainty as it magnifies the range of possible investment returns, both because of the leverage effect but also because the future cost of that debt is subject to market interest rates and is therefore uncertain.

Conversely, reducing this floating rate debt reduces uncertainty. At an extreme, floating rate debt, combined with falling asset values (of illiquid assets), can shift control of trust assets from the board to the lenders. Such a situation could be followed by forced sales and/or dividend cuts, as lenders move to recoup their loans.

Avoiding 'debt distress'

In the past, infrastructure trusts have typically used floating rate debt (usually from a bank credit facility) to finance acquisitions and then subsequently paid this debt down, or off completely, from the proceeds of an equity share issue. That model worked well for years when rates were low and infrastructure investment trusts traded at a premium to NAV. Now that rates have risen, though, raising equity at what is likely to be a discount to NAV doesn't make sense given how dilutive it is for existing investors. In any event, such an equity raise would, in most cases, require shareholder approval.

Most infrastructure trusts currently have floating rate debt on their balance sheet and the cost of this debt has increased with interest rate rises. When it comes to capital allocation my overall preference in the current interest rate environment (late 2024) is to see a trust prioritising paying down any floating rate debt it holds. As stated previously, paying off variable rate debt helps to reduce the impact of future interest rate uncertainty.

Returning capital

Once the 'floating rate debt repaid' box is ticked, the board can then consider how best to return capital to shareholders. Trusts that are popular for their income stream should prioritise maintaining a sustainable dividend. Beyond that, tenders and buybacks are generally preferable to special dividends from a tax perspective.

Capital gains on disposals (via tenders and buybacks) may be offset against allowances or losses to reduce tax, whereas income tax on dividends (ordinary or special) is very difficult to offset. The ideal position from a tax perspective is to remain invested whilst the company carries out a tender or buyback, such that any capital gains tax is deferred until a holding is sold.

Wrapping up

So how does all of this influence an investor?

To get a feel for an investment trust's overall strategy regarding capital allocation, I recommend reading the Chair's statement in the annual report. Then, if you need an income and you wish to build a balanced portfolio which encompasses different equity investment styles such as value and growth, consider trusts that pay enhanced yields (i.e. yields that are supplemented from capital where necessary). I gave the example of JPMorgan earlier, but several others, such as International Biotechnology Trust and European Assets Trust, adopt a similar approach.

As for the question of whether it is better to reduce debt, buy back shares or make further portfolio investments, whilst I have given my view earlier, there are no simple answers as several factors must be weighed up. As a rule, I favour reducing debt first, especially if the cost of servicing it exceeds any expected return on the trust's underlying assets. Thereafter, new investments should normally play a secondary role to buying back shares for as long as an investment trust's shares trade at a steep discount to NAV. The fact that not all investors may agree with me is what makes this topic so interesting, as well as important.

SUMMARY OF KEY POINTS

- Capital allocation refers to the process by which financial resources are distributed across different assets, projects or investment opportunities.

- There are two levels at which capital allocation decisions need to be made for an investment trust – at the portfolio manager level and at the board level.

- In the short term, any share repurchase will enhance liquidity because it creates a new source of demand for the shares, the investment trust itself.

- There are no simple answers as to whether it is better to reduce debt, buy back shares or make further portfolio investments as several factors must be considered.

- When a trust trades at a discount, a distribution is akin to buying the shares at a discount and then getting part of your investment returned at NAV in the form of a cash dividend.

CHAPTER 27

INVESTMENT FACTORS

"To me, style is consistency."

—Adam Ant,
singer, musician and actor

IN THIS CHAPTER I will explain how four prominent investment styles, or 'factors', work – they are known as size, value, quality and momentum.

Let's say you've held a fund for a few years and it has performed very well. Who, or what, is to thank for that? Is it simply a function of market direction? Is it down to the skill of an investment manager? Or is it due to one or more of the investment styles cited above? Let's investigate.

Sizing opportunities

The year 1992 was an important one for investors. Two academics, Eugene Fama and Kenneth French, showed, in a nutshell, that stock price movements are heavily influenced by two specific 'factors', being size (market capitalisation) and value (based on the relationship between their accounting 'book' value and that implied by their market value).

Before we delve any further into this, I should be clear about one thing – the bulk of a diversified equity portfolio's investment returns comes from simply getting broad exposure to the stock market, which has always tended to rise over time.

This 'beta' (discussed in Chapter 15) is one of the reasons that index funds have proliferated in recent years. However, the Fama and French evidence suggested that these two other factors could further enhance performance beyond that.

Let's deal with the size factor first. It posits that smaller companies tend to outperform larger companies over time. This finding was supported by an earlier seminal study by Rolf Banz in 1981.

But why? There are two primary theories. The first revolves around institutional investment behaviour. Large investors, such as pension funds, sovereign wealth funds and insurance companies have huge sums of capital to manage. As such, they need to invest in things that are relatively easy to buy and sell. Smaller companies are not particularly liquid (liquidity is referred to in Chapter 25) in that context and therefore tend to be shunned. This lack of demand gets reflected in lower prices and valuations. This, in turn, plays into the hands of smaller investors.

The second theory relates to the relative lack of analyst coverage. Equity analysts that work for investment banks normally only focus on a relatively small number of companies (often 15–20) in detail. As part of that role, they build models forecasting profitability and provide price targets. Those forecasts, in turn, can have a meaningful influence on share prices. When a profit forecast is boosted for a particular company, the share price tends to rise too, and vice versa.

Smaller companies, on the other hand, tend to attract less interest as the opportunities for the bigger banks to make money by providing ancillary services to those companies tend to be scarcer and transaction volumes in the shares themselves are generally much lower. The upshot is that some very small companies might only have one analyst covering them – typically the company's nominated stockbroker.

This disinterest from the wider community can result in pricing inefficiencies. There are risks, of course, prime amongst which is that smaller companies are more likely to experience financial difficulties and even go bust. However, superior returns from smaller companies could be attributed to the higher returns that investors demand for this higher risk.

That said, smaller companies have failed to outperform larger companies in the UK since 2021, although the performance of the UK size factor in the three decades prior to this was very strong indeed. It should also be noted that the size effect has not been evident in the US for more than a decade.

However, Asness et al. (2018) assert that previous evidence on the variability of the size effect is largely due to the volatile performance of small, low-quality 'junky' companies. By controlling for this, a much stronger and more stable size effect is evident, and it is robust across time. The results of their paper hold in 30 different industries and across 24 international equity markets.

Several smaller company investment trusts offer private investors a way of capitalising on any size effect that might be available in the future. The London market, for example, includes trusts which focus on smaller companies in the UK, Europe, Japan, Asia and the US, as well as some that invest globally.

"Previous evidence on the variability of the size effect is largely due to the volatile performance of small, low-quality 'junky' companies. By controlling for this, a much stronger and more stable size effect is evident, and it is robust across time."

Backing value

So, now let's move on to a related factor. 'Value investing' is a well-established strategy that seeks to identify undervalued securities. Investors in this space tend to focus on companies that are lowly valued. They look for instances where these companies are valued below the market average on metrics such as multiples of profit (P/E ratios) or the ratio of market value to book value (price to book). The underlying theory is that such stocks tend to be overlooked by the market, especially when compared to the opposite 'growth stocks', which offer strong profits growth and are more highly valued as a result. As a result of this demand anomaly between value and growth stocks, plus our human tendency to overprice exciting shares and underprice less interesting ones, opportunities arise.

That said, sceptics suggest that any value effect identified in 1992, when Fama and French made their findings, no longer exists. In that context, the period from the mid-2010s has challenged the idea that value stocks outperform the market even over an extended period. However, one of the reasons for this is the way certain stocks responded to an unusually persistent period of low interest rates. When interest rates fall, the rate used to 'discount' future profits also falls, which boosts valuations. This disproportionately benefits growth stocks which are anticipating a lot of future profitability. Value stocks, on the other hand, tend to generate lower future profits and are therefore less sensitive (in either direction) to changes in interest rates. That is one reason why between June 2007 and August 2020, when US 10-year interest rates declined from over 5% to less than 1%, growth stocks (as measured by the MSCI World Growth Index) outperformed value stocks (the MSCI Value Index) by more than 200%. Once interest rates started to rise, the reverse effect took hold and value stocks started to outperform growth stocks, albeit relatively modestly. And whilst no-one knows what the future holds. We might not see a recurrence of record-low interest rates for many years. Rock bottom valuations for value stocks could well improve as a result.

As for gaining an exposure, several investment trusts employ a value strategy. A notable example is Temple Bar. This investment trust underwent a change of manager in 2020, following the coronavirus outbreak when value strategies had underperformed for quite some time. There was a lot of debate as to whether the board would decide to shelve its value approach and adopt more of a growth style (an approach that had been doing very well at that stage). Fortunately, the board stuck with its approach, albeit under a new manager, a decision largely vindicated by its subsequent performance.

Table 5 in the appendix lists the 25 investment trust portfolios with the lowest price earnings ratio, a proxy for value.

Building momentum

This next factor is built on the observable tendency for investments that have risen, to keep rising and for investments that are falling, to keep falling. Momentum investing involves capitalising on the continuation of existing price trends. So, investors following this strategy buy securities that are exhibiting robust price performance. They are supported by several studies, including one by Lempérière et al. (2014) which looked at the effect of momentum going back to 1800 based on commodities, currencies, stock indices and bonds. One of their key conclusions was that "the existence of trends … is one of the most statistically significant anomalies in financial markets". As for why it exists, human herding behaviour is a large part of the explanation. Once investors see a security rising in value, they act in concert to buy it, and this further perpetuates an upward price trend. Eventually a lack of marginal buyers will see it come to an end. But, in the meantime, it can continue for months and sometimes years.

Another study by Jegadeesh and Titman (1993) also provided evidence of this momentum effect at a stock level. They found that buying stocks which have performed well in the past, and selling stocks that have done poorly, generated significant positive returns over 3–12-month holding periods, independent of other variables, albeit the effect dissipated over the subsequent two years.

Several investment trusts, including Mercantile Investment Trust and River UK Micro Cap, seek to capitalise on share price momentum or earnings (profit) momentum in their investment processes.

Seeking quality

The final factor I want to mention here is quality. This approach is built on backing firms showing strong fundamentals, stable earnings and robust overall financial health. Often, such companies have a durable competitive advantage. Again, it is supported by academic research. For instance, a Novy-Marx (2013) paper suggested that profitability is a robust predictor of stock returns and that companies with high margins tend to outperform their less profitable peers over the long term.

One of the earliest references to 'quality' in relation to stocks is contained in Graham and Dodd's investment classic, *Securities Analysis*, originally published in 1934. It reads, "Securities are selected by the application of standards of quality and yield." It is perhaps unsurprising then that the great US investor Warren Buffett, who studied under Graham at Columbia Business School, has also been drawn over many decades to quality stocks.

These tend to share some common features – they enjoy high, consistent profitability and low levels of debt, often combined with strong competitive advantages. Focusing on companies where this is evidenced by robust financials and sound management increases the likelihood that growth will prove sustainable.

So, how do we quantify quality in a useful and measurable way? In 2013 (and revised in 2017), three academics (Asness, Frazzini and Pedersen, 2017) produced a helpful paper which defined a quality stock as profitable, growing, safe and well managed. Taking each of those briefly in turn:

- Profitability is the profit per unit of book value. It can be measured in several ways including gross profits, operating margins and net earnings – a robust approach will look at a stock's average ranking across all of these metrics.

- Next comes growth, measured as the prior five-year increase in each key profitability measure.

- Safer stocks are defined as those with low price volatility, low levels of indebtedness, low volatility of profits from one year to the next and low credit risk.

- Management strength can then be measured by looking at the relevant payout policies (noting that many growth stocks pay an income too) and how consistently targets are achieved.

Quality companies are often able to enhance returns by reinvesting significant amounts of profit, thereby compounding returns over time at a higher rate. The Asness et al. (2017) paper notes that high-quality stocks carry punchier valuations than the average as a result, but interestingly not by a large margin. It is perhaps thanks to the modest impact of quality on valuation that high-quality stocks generally offer strong risk-adjusted returns.

Other top-tier academic articles that find a positive relationship between profitability and investment returns include Fama and French (2006, 2008, 2015, 2016), Hou et al. (2015) and Ball et al. (2015).

Both Finsbury Growth & Income Trust and Smithson Investment Trust are examples of quality-focused investment trusts. Table 4 in the appendix lists the 25 investment trust portfolios with the highest return on invested capital (ROIC), a proxy for quality.

Wrapping up

Value, quality, size and momentum are just a few of the many factor strategies investors can adopt. And although academic studies provide a robust foundation and offer empirical evidence of their effectiveness, they do not obviate the need for thorough research.

Further, although one or more factors may outperform others over specific time horizons, an investor's best bet is to diversify across a range of different ones. As always, an investment trust's annual report is a useful reference source when it comes to deciding which investment factor a particular manager is focused on and gaining an understanding of their relative performance.

SUMMARY OF KEY POINTS

- Most equity portfolio investment returns come from simply getting exposure to the stock market (beta), but evidence suggests that other factors can further enhance performance.

- Value, quality, size and momentum are all examples of investment factors or investment styles.

- Fama and French's 1992 paper concluded that two factors, size and value, were statistically significant in explaining stock returns.

- There is comprehensive evidence of a size factor, which is that smaller companies tend to outperform larger companies over time.

- Not knowing which factors are likely to do well from one year to the next means it is important to be diversified across a range of investment styles.

CHAPTER 28

PRICE DISCOVERY

"A man of genius makes no mistakes.
His errors are volitional and are
the portals to discovery."
—James Joyce, *Ulysses*

HOW MUCH IS the property that you live in worth? A quick look on a property listings website, such as Zoopla or Rightmove, will give you an estimate based on recent transactions in your area. However, until it is listed for sale and firm offers come in, you won't know what someone else is prepared to pay for it. In short, you will have to discover this. So, although you might think the right number is £350,000, if the best offer you receive is £325,000, then it may not be. This is the process of price discovery – determining the price of something in a marketplace through the interactions of buyers and sellers. However, beyond that broad description, the actual mechanics can vary considerably depending on the asset in question.

Weighing liquidity

Sellers in the housing market, for example, may be tempted to wait for more potential buyers to emerge or for market conditions to improve. With illiquid assets like this the selling process can therefore take time and the pricing process can be quite inefficient. If the seller in this example decides to hold out, then effectively the 'bid-to-offer spread' on the house is £25,000, being the gap between £325,000 (the highest current bid) and £350,000 (the minimum selling price). In an efficient market, these two prices need to converge quickly if a deal is to take place.

An extract from the 2023 interim results of the Aurora Investment Trust (now Aurora UK Alpha) succinctly explains this lumpy process of price discovery in the UK housing market:

An Anatomy of a UK House Price Crash

There are peculiarities of the UK housing market that cause it to correct in a certain way. As it is not possible to walk away from a mortgage in the UK, even if the house is worth less than the loan, and as banks are very reluctant to repossess properties, and in fact are under all sorts of regulatory and political pressure not to do so, there are very few forced sellers in the market.

Price adjustments therefore happen slowly because when told that they need to reduce the price of their house substantially to sell it, most decide not to sell and even not to move. Volumes duly decline.

Price does adjust down gradually though. There is an imprecision about house values but, if we were to think of them like shares, then the bid to ask price is around 10%. In a strong market where buyers outnumber sellers, houses transact on average at the offer side. In a weak market, buyers expect a discount and place lower bids and, within reason, sellers accept those bids. Houses that were transacting for £300k decline to £270k, but only very slowly.

Higher rates are painful for those seeking a mortgage, but a tightly supplied housing market means that there are always occupiers for houses built and we can see that rents are rising rapidly. Housebuilders are therefore now selling more of their product to landlords.

Property is therefore an example of a big, but relatively inefficient, market constantly trying to price an illiquid asset. That's where investment trusts can be useful.

Selling shares

As we saw in Chapter 2, like property, other assets can also be illiquid. Private equity limited liability partnerships, for example, change hands in a secondary market as long as a facilitating agent can match buyers and sellers. In what can be a relatively inefficient market, the bid-offer spread is likely to be very wide, and any deal will take some negotiating.

However, once listed on a public stock exchange, illiquid assets become available to lots of different market participants. Private investors, wealth managers, pension funds and institutional fund managers are all groups that buy and sell investment trusts. This higher visibility improves the price discovery process and narrows spreads. Now you have a much more efficient market in which prices adjust to reflect new information and changing market sentiment. Buyers, motivated by the perceived value of an asset, express their willingness to pay a certain price, whilst sellers, seeking to maximise their return, set the price at which they are willing to part with an asset. These forces of supply and demand eventually converge at an equilibrium price (refer to Figure 28A), reflecting the market's collective assessment of an asset's fair value. This price constantly evolves as conditions change.

Figure 28A: Interaction of supply and demand to determine price

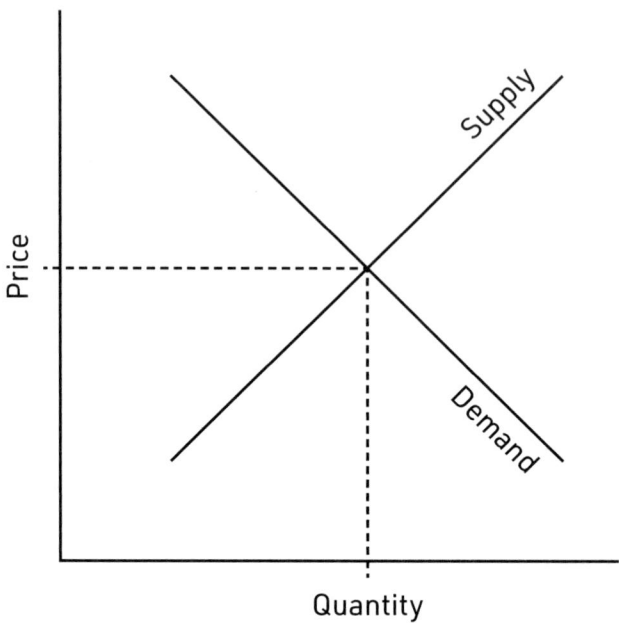

The beauty of investment trusts is that they offer a structure whereby illiquid assets, such as private companies, property, windfarms, infrastructure projects can be held within a vehicle which is listed on the stock market. Investors can then gain exposure by buying and selling shares in it.

That is not to say that all investment trust shares are highly liquid. Far from it. However, this listed structure increases the number and variety of potential buyers and sellers. This provides many illiquid assets with better price discovery than they might otherwise have.

Listing illiquid assets in this way dates right back to the 18th century, when investment trusts focused on emerging market government bonds and US railroads. Now they hold a vast range of private assets.

Creating trust

When a trust holding illiquid assets first comes to market there is, nonetheless, some debate about the right value. That is because early investors, who buy during the initial public offering (IPO), do not have the benefit of full market price discovery. As such, an independent valuer usually helps with the initial assessment. There is always potential for conflict of interest at this stage, in part because the valuer is typically paid by the trust. That said, they have an incentive to value assets fairly if the IPO is to succeed. Indeed, in some cases, they are offered to the market at a discount to help engineer a positive market debut.

Once listed, all market participants have an influence on the subsequent price. That said, some carry more weight than others. One set of participants that can hold sway are the investment banks. These institutions are responsible for bringing an investment trust to market. Many new issues are aborted simply because they are unable to secure sufficient interest from the investment community. Examples are plentiful and, trusts that have never seen the light of day, include the Buffetology Smaller Companies Investment Trust, the Tellworth British Recovery & Growth Trust, The Liontrust ESG Trust, the Cordiant Global Agriculture Income Trust and Welkin China Private Equity.

Once a trust has successfully listed, the issuing bank, often known as the 'house broker', the 'nominated stockbroker' or the 'shop', has a responsibility to make 'two-way' prices, being both a bid and offer price at which it is willing to buy and sell the shares. An analyst from the same sponsor will also typically cover the trust, authoring research as important news is released, such as a set of results or an acquisition.

Other investment banks are also likely to do the same and function as 'market makers' in the shares as well as providing buy or sell recommendations and general opinion. The larger, and more liquid, an investment trust the greater this interest in it and the stronger the element of price discovery.

Understanding value

At this point, it is important to make a distinction between price and value. To quote Warren Buffett, "Price is what you pay. Value is what you get." Valuation relates to the 'fair value' of an asset, whereas price discovery is a pure function of the (sometimes irrational) interactions of buyers and sellers.

Earlier I mentioned that illiquid assets held by an investment trust tend to be priced by an independent valuer. The investment trust board then uses that input to arrive at an NAV. The fact that a divergence can arise between this NAV and the trust's open market share price may sometimes be problematic.

The investment trust's shares may trade at a significant discount to NAV for a prolonged period because the market does not 'believe' the NAV, that is it thinks it is overstated and that the true value is lower. Investors nonetheless usually suffer fees that are based on this more subjective NAV number rather than an arguably more objective market capitalisation, based on the share price.

When an individual trust first comes to market, it may be holding assets that are in demand, but over time that may wane as other trusts enter the same space. So, whereas the initial NAV may be determined by a mathematical valuation method, such as a discounted cash flow forecast, the market price will be influenced by many other factors, including macro-economic conditions, investor sentiment as well as underlying portfolio performance.

Wrapping up

Price discovery is a key concept and central to the efficient allocation of capital across markets. Investment trust prices, which are subject to the forces of supply and demand, can sometimes therefore diverge from the underlying fundamentals.

However, occasional dislocations such as large discounts to NAV provide investors with good opportunities to buy in at an attractive price, provided the shares are subsequently held long term. Any eventual narrowing of a trust's discount, along with an improvement in its underlying NAV, can present a positive double whammy should it subsequently perform well. The reverse is also true, which is why care should be taken when buying trusts at a premium to NAV.

SUMMARY OF KEY POINTS

- Price discovery is the process of determining the price of something in a marketplace through the interactions of buyers and sellers.

- Price adjustments happen slowly in the residential property market.

- In the stock market, through the interaction of buyers and sellers, prices constantly adjust to reflect new information and changing market sentiment.

- Price discovery is not the same as valuation. To quote Warren Buffett, "Price is what you pay. Value is what you get."

- Fees based on NAV can lead to a mismatch between the fees the investment manager is expected to receive and the fees that they actually receive.

CHAPTER 29

INVESTOR PSYCHOLOGY

"When individual investors are optimistic, the demand for these [closed-ended] funds increases and the discount declines. Pessimistic investors sell the funds, and the discount increases."

—John R. Nofsinger,
The Psychology of Investing

NOFSINGER'S OBSERVATION ABOUT closed-ended fund (e.g. investment trust) discounts highlights how useful these measures are in informing us about the mood of investors. They are often a sign of investors' irrationality.

Much of modern finance theory is based on the notion that investors are rational when it comes to decision-making. However, the existence and frequent recurrence of asset bubbles and stock market crashes, as well as extreme discounts and premiums in investment trusts, suggests otherwise. That is why I believe that the psychological aspects of investor behaviour are sometimes not given adequate consideration. Further, a better understanding of them can help to enhance returns. This chapter is therefore all about the mental and emotional 'biases' that play a crucial role in shaping our investment behaviour and ultimately influence the decisions we make. By understanding them, we can counter them and make better choices. The way many investors approach investment trusts in particular can offer some valuable insights.

Explaining our brains

As humans, our thought processes are constrained by factors we often have little direct control over, such as short attention spans, memory lapses and imperfect information processing. These all affect our ability to analyse data rationally. And in order to cope with an increasingly complex world, we have also developed mental shortcuts ('heuristics'). In combination, the result can be that we make expensive mistakes when investing.

As we highlighted in Chapter 27, there are several investment factors (e.g. momentum, value, quality and size) that are widely believed, based on academic evidence, to improve investors' chances of outperforming broad stock market indices. One possible explanation for the effectiveness of these factors is that they 'exploit' behavioural biases.

In summary, some of the best-known systematic errors that many investors are prone to include:

- Performance chasing – buying investments that have already performed well and selling investments that have performed poorly.

- Anchoring – making predictions based on arbitrary, but seemingly important, data.

- Loss aversion – the tendency to prefer avoiding losses over acquiring equivalent gains.

- Disposition effect – a preference for holding on to stocks that have lost value whilst being more eager to sell stocks that have risen in value.

Let's now look at these in more detail in the specific context of investment trusts.

Performance chasing

Buying investments that have performed well and selling investments that have already performed poorly is a prevalent trait amongst both private and professional investors. However, it is particularly commonplace amongst fund investors, including those who focus on investment trusts. Investment trusts that have delivered good NAV performance tend to see their discounts narrow as more investors chase that NAV performance. Equally, investment trusts that have delivered poor NAV performance tend to see their discounts widen as existing investors exit, resulting in wider discounts. There is little evidence that performance chasing leads to superior returns, apart from in the very short term, possibly due to momentum.

> "There is little evidence that performance chasing leads to superior returns, apart from in the very short term, possibly due to momentum."

One of the most prominent studies on this topic was published by Cornell et al. (2017). It found that investors who selected managers on the basis of relatively poor recent performance earned higher returns than those who chose (and chased) the better recent performers. This rather underlines the point, which is regularly reinforced by regulators, that the past is often not a reliable guide to the future.

This also offers the contrarian investor an opportunity to benefit from an improvement in the rating, that is a narrowing in the discount to NAV. By buying an investment trust that has performed poorly for a period and sits at a wider than average discount, there is scope to benefit from both a reversal, that is improvement in NAV performance, as well as a narrowing in the discount.

I am conscious that the idea of contrarian investing, as outlined here, is somewhat at odds with that of momentum investing, which we highlighted in Chapter 27. So let me try to clarify my thinking here. Whilst momentum is a very powerful effect, I am reminded of the adage, "the trend is your friend, until the bend in the end".

> "I see merit in investment strategies employed by investment managers of investment trusts that incorporate share price momentum or earnings (profit) momentum into their investment process to enhance it, rather than relying solely on it."

Yes, trends can be very profitable whilst they last, but at some point they come to an end, the 'bend' referring to a reversal in the price, until the next trend is established. We never know whether we are unfortunate enough to be joining the trend just before the 'bend'. For this reason, I think pure trend following (i.e. simply following price trends) is best exploited by traders or by funds that are specifically calibrated to profit from such trends (and I think these funds serve a useful purpose in portfolios). I do not think pure trend following is a viable investment strategy for the average private investor.

However, I see merit in investment strategies employed by investment managers of investment trusts that incorporate share price momentum or earnings (profit) momentum into their investment process to enhance it, rather than relying solely on it.

Anchoring

In the 1970s two psychologists (Tversky and Kahneman, 1974) described the concept of anchoring in the context of people seeking certainty in an investing world that often offers very little. When it comes to numerical prediction, they established that people are prone to fixing their sights on an initial, often arbitrary, 'anchor' value, such as a purchase price, and adjusting it to produce the eventual answer they want. Then, even if the subsequent performance of the asset in question disappoints, or circumstances change, they will often nonetheless cling on, hoping the price will recover to at least that same level.

This 'break-even bias' was also highlighted in a study by Thaler and Johnson (1990). It asked a sample of economics undergraduates to take a series of two-step gambles using real money. Firstly, money was either given to, or taken from, the student. In the second step, the student was asked whether they wished to take a gamble. After losing some money most of the students were willing to accept a double or nothing bet, even when they were told that the bet was not 'fair' (i.e. they had less than a 50% chance of winning), such was the strength of the desire to break even.

This tendency to cling to an arbitrary price could help to explain why many new issues in the investment trust sector tend to remain above their initiation price, even when the underlying NAV declines during the early subsequent months. In part, this may be a function of the sponsoring investment bank having an incentive to support the share price. However, another reason is likely to be anchoring – the tendency for new investors to anchor their actions around the issue price and demonstrate a reluctance to sell below it.

Loss aversion

Kahneman and Tversky also documented a related bias in 1979. They found that people placed different weights on gains and losses. Specifically, investors feel much more distress at the prospect of losses than they feel happiness about the possibility of equivalent gains. In other words, the thought of a £1,000 gain does not automatically make someone feel twice as good as a £500 gain, yet just thinking about a £1,000 loss makes them feel more than twice as bad as a

£500 loss. Figure 29A highlights this asymmetry. It may go some way towards explaining why investors sometimes find it difficult to crystallise a loss, even if it would be perfectly rational to do so.

Figure 29A: Loss aversion

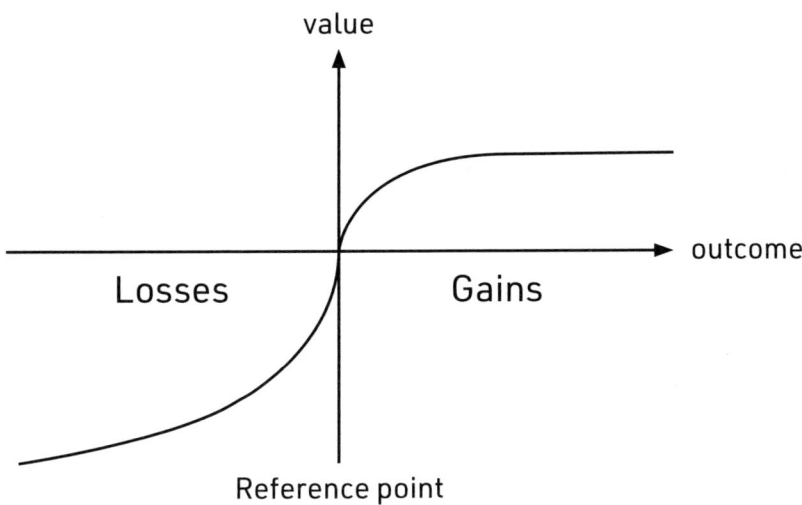

Kahneman and Tversky's important study also found that people will switch from risk aversion to risk seeking when the polarity changes from positive to negative. This implies that investors are more willing to risk £500 in an investment they already hold which has fallen in value from £1,000 (the 'double or quits' mindset) than they are to put £500 of new capital into the same investment, if they don't already hold it.

It doesn't make sense to hold losing investment trust positions purely in the hope that they will recover. Instead, investors should consider in the cold light of day 'knowing what I now know, if I did not already hold this investment trust would I buy it today?' (having taken transaction costs and taxes into account). If the answer to this question is no, the position should probably be sold.

Disposition effect

Two financial economists, Shefrin and Statman (1985), predicted that because people dislike incurring losses much more than they enjoy making gains, as investors they will prefer to hold on to stocks that have lost value (relative to the anchor point of the original purchase) whilst being much more eager to sell stocks that have risen in value.

Portfolio managers are often under scrutiny from investors and commentators. Therefore, with their reputation on the line, taking a realised loss can be embarrassing unless proved correct in due course. Shefrin and Statman called this tendency to run losers and cut winners the "disposition effect". It further supports the argument that investors are sometimes irrationally unwilling to crystallise a loss in order to put their money to work somewhere more attractive and also suggests they often take profits too early. That's an unhelpful double whammy.

Other biases include:

- Recency bias – a tendency to allow recent events (such as an investment trust's strong investment performance) to overly influence our behaviour.

- Availability bias – a preference for information that is familiar or attention grabbing, such as a strong story attached to a shiny new IPO.

- Extrapolation – assuming the past (in many cases, performance) is a dependable guide to the future.

- Overconfidence – believing we are consistently better than the average investor.

- Confirmation bias – lending more weight to evidence that supports our view and less to anything that doesn't.

- The 'house money' effect – a willingness to take more risk with £1 of profit than with £1 of principal.

- Regret aversion – also known as the 'fear of missing out' (FOMO).

Taxing issues

Aside from these psychological challenges, it is worth noting that tax can have an independent influence on investment decisions. For example, capital losses can be offset against future capital gains, or can be carried forward (unused) indefinitely. So, where a £10,000 investment has fallen to £7,500 there is some economic value in the £2,500 loss to the extent that it can be offset against future taxable gains. This creates a clear and separate advantage when it comes to crystallising a loss, all other things being equal and assuming a stock is held outside of a tax shelter.

Indeed, with the reduction in the UK capital gains tax allowance, from £12,000 in the 2022/23 tax year to £3,000 in 2024/25, capital losses have become even more valuable. Investors should therefore consider 'moving' investment trust positions that are sitting on sizeable losses into their tax shelters (ISAs and SIPPs), thereby crystallising those losses for future use. This can be done by selling the trust held within their taxable account and buying it back inside an ISA or SIPP. Equally, it may make more sense to simply sell the position and not repurchase it. The overall point here is that tax can influence investment decisions.

> "Investors should ... consider 'moving' investment trust positions that are sitting on sizeable losses into their tax shelters (ISAs and SIPPs), thereby crystallising those losses for future use."

Diving back into discounts

Now that we have covered much of the theoretical perspectives of investor psychology, let's consider investor psychology in practice and particularly in relation to investment trusts. Earlier, we noted that investment trusts often reflect investor biases as widening discounts and premiums to NAV. Let's now consider in more detail the situation where you are looking to buy a trust that is trading at a wide discount.

The first thing to note is that if the trust holds liquid assets and trades on a particularly wide discount, it may not do so for long. One reason is that activists will seek to take advantage of this situation. We will cover this in more detail in Chapter 39.

To illustrate this let's turn our attention to the European Opportunities Trust, which invests in a concentrated portfolio of listed European equities. It experienced a material decline in its NAV in mid-2020, when its largest holding, Wirecard, the German payment processor, announced that €1.9 bn of its cash was missing. Figure 29B shows the sharp decline in asset value during the COVID pandemic outbreak, followed by a subsequent period of underperformance. Many investors exited after the Wirecard news, resulting in a widening discount. It moved from 5%, a level that it had rarely breached in the prior seven years, to 17% in July 2022, as shown in Figure 29C.

Figure 29B: European Opportunities Trust, share price

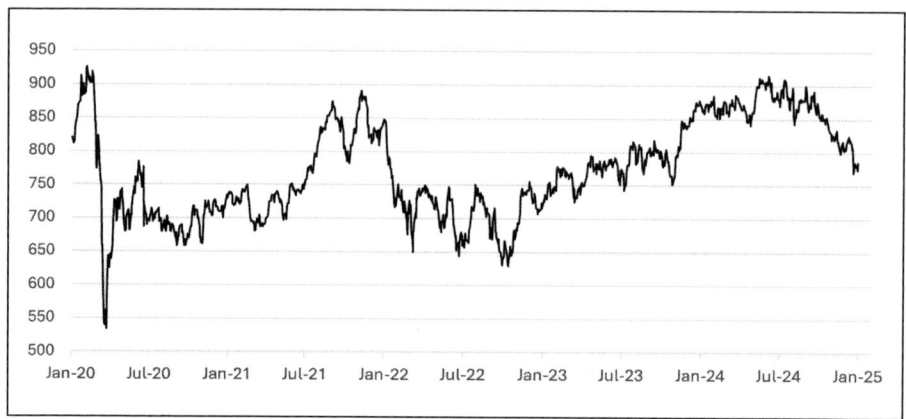

Daily closing price, 01/01/2020 to 31/12/2024.

Source: Bloomberg

Figure 29C: European Opportunities Trust, discount to NAV

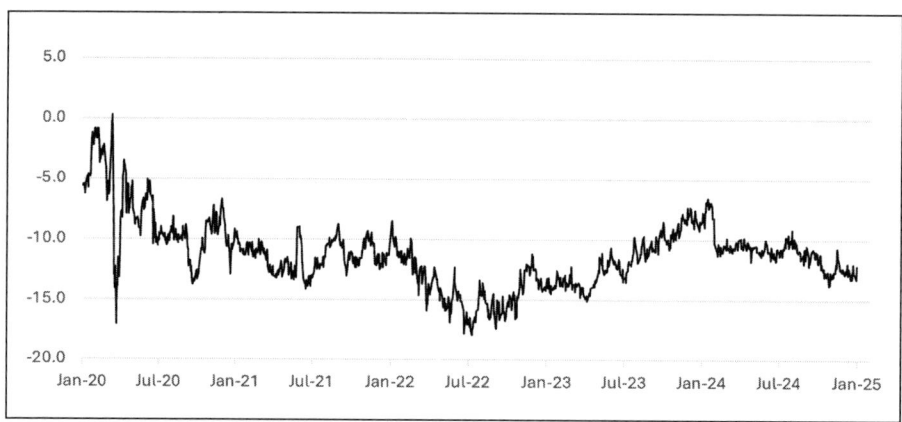

Daily discount (-ve), premium (+ve) to NAV, 01/01/2020 to 31/12/2024.

Source: Bloomberg

For many trusts in situations like this, either the underlying NAV improves and the discount narrows, or someone takes action to try to force the issue. That someone may be the board intervening unilaterally via share buybacks, tender offers or other actions, or it might be the result of investors such as activists piling pressure on them.

In this case, the board started buying back shares in March 2020. However, the level of selling was so high that buybacks failed to soak up the supply. It was not until 2022 (refer to Figure 29C) that the discount eventually started to narrow. Then in 2023, a US activist investor, Saba Capital, declared a stake in European Opportunities Trust and proceeded to request a return of capital. Soon afterwards, the board announced a tender offer to buy back up to 25% of the trust's shares, a move likely prompted by Saba's involvement, and which helped the discount to narrow further.

So, an investor who bought the shares during most of 2022 outperformed the trust's benchmark over the next 18 months, due to the narrowing discount, even though the NAV of the trust saw no discernible improvement over that of the MSCI Europe Index. This discount narrowed to around 7% at the time of the tender and investors that tendered 100% of their shares were able to exit around 35% of their position (because some holders did not tender their shares, leaving some excess capacity above 25% for those that did) at a 2% discount. They were also able to exit the balance of their position in the market at around a 9% discount. The exercise also enhanced the NAV per share for remaining shareholders by around 0.7%.

Therefore buying when a discount to NAV is particularly wide can work to your advantage. However, this approach is best used when you have already decided what underlying asset or market you want to get exposure to and an investment trust exposed to that asset or market happens to be trading at a wide discount.

In the case of European Opportunities Trust, the discount widened after the tender offer and sub-par NAV performance caused it to drift back to about 13% by 31/12/2024. It may well widen further from there. A sufficiently wide discount could provide another buying opportunity, given that it holds a portfolio of quality stocks, generating high returns on invested capital, the activist is still involved, the manager is incentivised to deliver better returns in future and the board is there to act in shareholders' interests.

One final point when buying on wide discounts. I would warn against trying this with trusts with net assets that are hard to value. Stick, instead, to trusts where the underlying assets can easily and reliably be valued ('marked to market') based on their listing on a recognised exchange. Then take a long-term view and be prepared to be patient.

Understanding market moods

Investment trust performance often mirrors market cycles. As such, discounts and premiums can offer an insight into what Benjamin Graham referred to as 'Mr Market's' enthusiasm or fear (Graham, 1973, p. 108). For example, in December 1999, near the peak of the technology boom, the Polar Capital Technology Trust traded at a 19% premium to its asset value. Given that it held quoted equities, this suggests that investors were effectively willing to pay £119 for £100 of assets that could be bought in the open market.

The same trust traded at a 29% discount to asset value in late 2008, at the depths of the Great Financial Crisis. A 'rush for the door' meant that investors were now selling £100 of quoted equities for £71. Neither the extreme levels of premium nor discount were rational, which just goes to show how powerful crowd psychology can be.

Placing constraints on your trading activity

It is important that you know yourself and put rules and guidelines, an investment framework if you will, in place to help avoid these pitfalls. Such guidelines might include not selling an investment that you have bought in the last 12 months (if you know ahead of purchase that you must hold this investment for an absolute minimum of 12 months come what may, you are likely to be more careful in its selection and in the size of investment you make).

Another guideline is to only average down once. Quite often, if your investment continues to decline in value such that it is compelling you to average down, something may well be wrong with this investment. Size your positions carefully. When constructing portfolios, I try to limit certain investment trusts, typically those with more opaque valuations, to a a very small part of a portfolio, ideally 1%.

Wrapping up

What this chapter aims to reveal is the importance of taking a systematic approach to investing and having an awareness of some of the irrational influences on share prices that can see investment trusts swing to large premiums or discounts. Armed with that knowledge, it is easier to make an informed judgement about whether you are looking at a genuine opportunity or about to fall into a trap.

SUMMARY OF KEY POINTS

- Limitations to our mental functioning affect our ability to analyse and can lead to systematic errors that cost us money when investing.

- Systematic errors include recency bias, availability bias, extrapolation, performance chasing, anchoring, overconfidence, confirmation bias, house money effect and regret aversion.

- Investment trusts reflect investor bias in their discounts / premiums (rating) to NAV.

- Investment trust ratings (their discounts or premiums) are often a good barometer of the market mood.

- There is little evidence that performance chasing (buying investments that have performed well and selling investments that have performed poorly) leads to superior returns.

CHAPTER 30

INVESTING TAX EFFICIENTLY

"There's nothing wrong with the younger generation that becoming taxpayers won't cure."

—Dan Bennett, US comedian

BEFORE YOU DECIDE to buy shares in an investment trust, it is important to consider how and where you will hold them. Investment trust shares are liable to tax, in the same way as regular shares, in the hands of a UK taxpayer. Given this, there are several government-approved tax shelters that can be used to house them. These will help reduce the impact of tax on both any profits you make ('capital gains') and income distributed by way of a dividend.

Before addressing these, however, I want to highlight how the taxation of an investment trust itself works, regardless of whether it is held within such a wrapper.

Covering the basics

Investment trusts are subject to corporation tax on their income. However, unlike a regular company, an investment trust is not subject to corporation tax on any chargeable gains that it makes. This means that investments within an investment trust portfolio do not attract tax on capital gains, irrespective of whether these gains are paper gains (i.e. unrealised accounting gains) or realised gains (i.e. where the holding has been sold at a profit). That major advantage is also enjoyed by mutual funds. It enables the holder to benefit from tax-efficient gains from the underlying portfolio.

Importantly, in this context, certain offshore funds are classified by the UK tax authorities (HMRC) as 'Reporting Funds' (RFs). This means that they are treated in largely the same way as onshore mutual funds from a tax perspective. Other offshore funds, by contrast, are classified as Non-Reporting Funds (NRFs) because they don't meet the specified RF criteria.

This is relevant because realised gains on NRFs are usually liable to income tax, rather than capital gains tax, in the hands of a UK taxpayer. By way of an example, most hedge funds are classified as NRFs and so holding them directly can be punitive. Investment trusts, on the other hand, can hold NRFs and, provided they meet certain criteria, they can treat any profits they make from selling the relevant shares as a non-taxable capital gain, rather than taxable income.

Turning to investors

Now let's consider the tax which is potentially payable by individual investors. As we have seen previously, UK investment trusts must distribute at least 85% of their net income (meaning, after the deduction of operating costs) in the form of dividends. These, in turn, may be subject to differing tax treatments, depending on how the relevant trust is held.

A dividend paid by an investment trust within a standard (or 'general') investment account will attract income tax. That said, in 2024/25 UK taxpayers can apply a dividend allowance which means the first £500 is tax free. Beyond that, the rates shown in Table 30A apply, depending on the relevant tax band of the recipient.

Table 30A: UK dividend income tax rates 2024/25

Tax rate	Tax %
Basic	8.75
Higher	33.75
Additional	39.35

It is worth noting that if two spouses are not fully using their individual £500 dividend allowances then investment trust holdings can be transferred between them, such that they are not wasted.

Meanwhile, any disposals of investment trust shares within a regular, or general, account are subject to capital gains tax on the investor. The starting point for any calculation is the difference between the purchase value and eventual sale value. There are a few ways to reduce the resulting tax bill. For example, losses on qualifying asset sales can be offset against gains, and an annual allowance exempts the first £3,000 of any remaining gains in 2024/25. Again, if a spouse is not fully using their allowance, then investment trust holdings can be transferred accordingly to lighten the overall tax burden.

Sheltering income and gains

Beyond these allowances, there are several ways investment trust shares can be protected from tax via the use of wrappers. Here is a summary.

Individual Savings Accounts (ISAs) are a popular, tax-efficient and flexible way to shield investments from both income tax and capital gains tax. UK investment trusts are just one example of the huge range that can be held within a stocks and shares ISA. The current contribution limit (2024/25) is a generous annual £20,000 per person, available to all UK residents, aged 18 or over.

Then there are Junior ISAs (JISAs), available for children under 18. JISA tax benefits are identical to those of a regular ISA, except that contributions of up to £9,000 per child can be made on their behalf by anyone via their parents. Once the relevant child reaches the age of 18, they take control of the account, something donors need to bear in mind. Beyond JISAs there are some other structures, such as 'bare trusts' which can be relatively tax efficient too (in this case, any income or gains are taxed with reference to the recipient). These should be discussed with an adviser.

For some savers, the Lifetime ISA (LISA) may also be suitable for long-term tax-efficient saving where someone is looking to amass a house deposit or save for retirement. The current annual contribution limit for LISAs is £4,000. The government then adds an annual bonus of up to £1,000, provided certain conditions are met. Investment trusts could be suitable holdings in this context, where a LISA is being used to supplement retirement planning over a sufficiently lengthy period. The £4,000 annual LISA allowance forms part of the overall £20,000 annual ISA allowance.

Next, we come to pensions and, specifically, self-invested personal pensions (SIPPs). These wrappers allow someone to accumulate a fund tax free by investing in various assets, which can include UK investment trusts. The big additional win here is that any contributions into such a vehicle receive tax relief at your highest marginal income tax rate. However, on the flipside, strict rules govern withdrawals – the key one being that they are subject to a minimum age being reached, currently 55 (and set to rise to 57 in 2028). The annual SIPP contribution limit is generous and linked to earnings with a current (2024/25) cap of £60,000, plus carried forward unused allowances from the previous three years (subject to limits for higher earners).

A pension can also be set up by a parent or legal guardian for a child under the age of 18. This sort of 'Junior SIPP' arrangement shares many similarities with adult pensions, including attracting similar tax relief and the same age-related limitation on withdrawals. This time, however, the maximum contribution annually is £2,880, a sum then boosted by government tax relief to £3,600.

One of the great advantages of pension fund investing is that it exploits the long-term power of time and the associated ability to tap into compound growth.

Finally, a word about offshore bonds. These are a form of insurance contract which allow money to be put into a variety of assets, including UK investment trusts, inside a tax wrapper which is legally held outside the UK. That means they can offer the potential for tax-deferred growth, but with restrictions on access. As such, they are not suitable for all investors.

As a brief overview, money taken from such a bond is usually liable to income. However, up to 5% per annum of the original investment can be withdrawn (up to a maximum of 100% of the original investment) by a UK taxpayer, with any income tax deferred until a later date. This can be useful to someone who is, say, a UK resident now but may not be by the time they come to fully liquidate the bond. Higher and additional rate taxpayers may also use them to defer taxable proceeds to a point when, perhaps through stopping work, they become a basic rate taxpayer instead. Whatever the potential motivation, seeking professional advice is crucial when considering offshore bonds due to their complexity and cost, plus the fact that the rules could change in the future.

Wrapping up

Successful investing is all about establishing the right long-term strategy and then making it as tax efficient as possible. As we have seen in this chapter, investment trusts, held with the right tax structure, can play a key role in solving both parts of that equation.

SUMMARY OF KEY POINTS

- Investment trusts (like mutual funds) are tax efficient as there is no capital gains tax on the sale of assets within the trust.

- Up to £20,000 can be invested in investment trusts annually within an ISA, thereby avoiding any personal liability to income or capital gains tax.

- Self-invested personal pensions are an ideal home for investment trusts, given the time horizon involved and the power of compounding.

- Offshore bonds can be an efficient way of reducing or deferring tax and most permit the use of investment trusts.

- Investing in investment trusts for children via bare trusts, JISAs and stakeholder pensions can be highly tax efficient.

CHAPTER 31

INVESTING IN IPOS: READING THE PROSPECTUS

*"If it's not a contract I want,
then I won't sign it."*

**—Roy Keane,
former professional footballer**

I F YOU ARE considering investing in a brand-new investment trust at launch, there is one document investors must get to grips with beforehand – the prospectus. This is the legal contract between the trust and the shareholders. It is usually a lengthy document. I used to spend hours wading through the pages of these to find important information. These days they are generally available in PDF format and so searching for relevant sections and key words is relatively easy.

Here is what to look for.

Raising capital

Although investment trusts often raise funds via an IPO whereby new shares are made available to the investing public for the first time, it is worth noting that they can take a couple of other routes. One is an 'offer for subscription', which is an invitation to the public to subscribe for new shares in an investment trust. The other is a 'placing', which involves issuing new or existing shares to selected institutional or sophisticated investors. The latter is often the cheaper method and gives the trust greater control over its target investor base. These two ways of raising capital are often used in combination with one another. In all cases, new shares are offered to investors in exchange for cash, which the issuing trust then uses for investment as pre-agreed.

Investment banks charge investors a capital raising fee. This is typically 1.0–1.5% of the amount raised, with all costs (i.e. including legal, accounting, etc.) usually capped at 2.0%. In some cases, the investment manager may choose to offset some, or all, the costs of a new issue to encourage investors to commit to the investment trust at the outset.

Many investors prefer not to participate in an IPO, in the hope of buying the trust's shares later if and when they are available at a discount to NAV. Clearly, if everyone were to take this approach, an IPO couldn't take place and a trust would fail to launch at all.

That is why new issues occasionally come with warrants or 'subscription shares'. These are ways of encouraging participation via the sweetener of an opportunity to acquire further shares on attractive terms later. By way of an example, subscription shares may entitle the holder to buy ordinary shares, which are issued at IPO at, say, 100p, at 105p within the first year, 110p within the second year and 115p by the end of year three, at which point the deal expires. However, sensible as this may sound, it adds a layer of complication to the trust's capital structure which some investors don't like. As such, it is an approach which is much less common than it used to be.

Testing the water

A more likely route to a successful IPO these days is for the trust's sponsors to sound out key institutional investors early on. The relevant investment bank (or banks) that is arranging the IPO often approaches selected investors that it thinks may be interested in the new offering. These early conversations can lead to potential commitments of capital that might 'cornerstone' the launch (meaning these early pledges may encourage other institutional investors). This process can also be helpful when it comes to determining key terms, such as the related fees and discount control mechanisms (discussed later).

The sponsoring bank is also likely to conduct some 'test marketing'. This usually takes the form of an early pre-prospectus roadshow to gauge the market's appetite for the offer and to gather early indications of interest. If this proves to be fruitful, a prospectus and final pitch document are produced, following numerous meetings with the investment managers and potential investors. Occasionally, the investment trust board participates in this type of roadshow. However, that is rare, which is a pity as it is to the board that investors will turn if they are unhappy with the trust's progress. The bottom line, nonetheless, is that the capital raise is usually driven by the investment managers who will subsequently manage the trust day-to-day, or the investment bank responsible. That's largely because these two parties have the most commercial skin in the game.

Setting out the stall

Now let's turn our attention to the all-important prospectus document on which such decisions are built. It basically serves as a comprehensive guide for potential investors, offering insights into the structure, strategy and risks associated with a given trust. As such, it is a crucial tool for making informed investment decisions, and it can reveal the safeguards that are in place to protect shareholders should things go wrong.

Here is my (non-exhaustive) checklist of the key things I like to find out and weigh up:

- Investment objective and expected returns – are they reasonable and achievable?

- Management contracts – how long are they in place for, what is the notice period and is there a guaranteed termination payment?

- Discount controls – how will the trust avoid a large discount to NAV from developing?

- Leverage – what is the maximum leverage that the trust can employ and is it likely to be fixed or floating?

- Valuation – how will the portfolio assets be valued?

- Index inclusion – is the trust likely to be included in any indices post launch?

- Voting rights – what do they look like for ordinary shareholders?

- Dividends – what is the policy, when does it start and does it rely on any borrowing?

- Currency – what is the reporting currency and are any related strategies (e.g. hedging) deployed?

- Fees – how are they calculated, for example by reference to gross assets, net assets or market capitalisation? Is there a performance fee and how is it calculated?

- Control – does the investment manager have a majority control over voting rights?

- Pre-emption rights – can the board issue further shares without first offering them to existing shareholders?

- Alignment of interests – how much are the board and investment managers investing themselves at launch?

- Board status – does it have sufficient experience and is it fully independent from the management team?

- Capital structure – how many classes of share will be in issue (e.g. voting vs no-voting)?

Here are some key words / phrases to search for in the PDF:

- management contract

- notice

- management fee

- performance fee

- discount control

- voting

- conflict.

Diving deeper

Beyond those basics, in a few specific areas, I strongly recommend finding out as much as possible about each investment trust. Here are some of the more important things to check out in more detail, using the prospectus.

Discount control

Most investment trusts are empowered to buy back up to 14.99% of their issued share capital each year in a bid to limit any discount to NAV. The related clause in a prospectus might read something like 'if the trust's shares trade at a substantial discount to NAV for a significant length of time, the board will consider taking such actions as may seem appropriate to eliminate or reduce the discount'. However, it is worth noting that such actions are usually discretionary and so this type of statement does not provide concrete assurance to shareholders that action will be taken, when or what it will be. That said, investment trusts' boards improve their credibility by being open about what a 'substantial discount' might be, along with clarification around any other potentially ambiguous commitments.

In that context, a specific level of discount might be mentioned in the prospectus, via a phrase such as 'the board will endeavour to limit the discount to NAV to 10% and will consider buying back shares if the discount exceeds this level'. This is helpful in so far as it gives shareholders a way to hold the board to account.

Persistently wide discounts are often triggered by poor performance. However, they might sometimes be a function of something else, such as investor scepticism around asset valuations. Ultimately, the 'nuclear option' with persistent discounts is to wind up the trust. In this scenario, all of the assets are sold, with any proceeds returned to shareholders, less wind-up costs. Within a prospectus, therefore, look for evidence of what is called a 'continuation vote'.

As the name suggests, this gives shareholders the opportunity to vote for, or against, the trust continuing as an entity. The strongest form of such votes requires a majority to vote in favour of continuation. In other words, if less than 50% of those that elect to exercise their vote choose to continue, the trust can be wound up. Alternatively, the prospectus may require a majority to vote against continuation (a 'discontinuation vote'). This is clearly a less powerful clause for minority shareholders. In other instances, a 'super majority' (typically 75%) of voting shareholders may be required to vote for discontinuance. Such a high hurdle is questionable in my view.

Management contract

How a trust is managed matters. So, it is important to understand the minimum period over which a manager has been contracted and the notice period required from the board to end the agreement. This is usually triggered when a trust is wound up or if there is a change of manager. A typical notice period is six months, with 12 possible in some cases. Anything longer than that should be viewed with extreme scepticism.

Voting rights

Make sure you properly understand these. Where there is more than one share class, some of them may not carry voting rights. Anyone subscribing for non-voting shares should receive compensation for doing so, in the form of, say, a higher dividend. The most valuable voting rights will typically relate to the continuation, or otherwise, of the trust.

Fees and expenses

Costs are a key component of any investment decision. So, look at how management fees compare to other, similar trusts. Also, make sure you understand how they are calculated. The gold standard is a management fee based on the lower of NAV and market capitalisation. Very few trusts follow this approach, unfortunately. This is why I want to give a shout-out to some of those that do, namely Baillie Gifford European Growth, India Capital Growth, Lindsell Train, Polar Capital Global Healthcare, TwentyFour Income and TwentyFour Select Monthly Income (albeit some of these also charge a performance fee). Be wary, in particular, of management fees linked to gross asset value as they provide the investment manager with an incentive to maximise leverage.

> "Pay close attention to any hurdle and the performance measurement period. Short ones, measured in quarters, stack things in favour of the manager by giving them lots of regular 'bites at the cherry'."

Performance fees also require scrutiny. These typically enable the manager to be remunerated if the net assets of the trust exceed a stated hurdle. For some trusts, this hurdle is zero, although that is unusual outside of the hedge fund sector. Other performance fees may be linked to a benchmark, for example the NAV outperforming the FTSE All Share Index by more than a certain percentage. My advice is to pay close attention to any hurdle and the performance measurement period. Short ones, measured in quarters, stack things in favour of the manager by giving them lots of regular 'bites at the cherry'. Also check for any 'high water mark'. This is the level the NAV must exceed before any performance fee is paid. Overall, performance fee terms can be complex. My view is therefore that if you have to read them more than a couple of times to understand how they work, maybe it's best to pass on that particular investment trust.

The gold standard in performance fees is: no management fee; outperformance of the reference index over a minimum 12-month performance period, capped so there is not an unlimited upside in the event of a blow-out year; and performance fee paid in shares which are issued at NAV and are subject to a lock-up or clawback for up to three years. Three trusts that meet these gold standard criteria are Aurora UK Alpha, Ashoka WhiteOak India Equity and Ashoka WhiteOak Emerging Markets.

Conflicts of interest

The prospectus should disclose any existing or potential ones that might arise between the investment trust, its management team and any affiliated companies.

Risk management

I would also read everything in the relevant section dealing with risks. Although the majority of this section is often 'boiler plating' prepared by the trust's legal advisers, sometimes you come across something that you may not have considered.

Hitting the market

Once the issue process has happened, new equity-based investment trusts usually commit any initial capital raised over a relatively short period (typically a few months) unless the target assets are particularly illiquid. Some alternative investment trusts may identify a 'seed portfolio' of assets that is ready to be acquired at launch. With many of this type of trust there is an inevitable trade-off for anyone buying at the IPO, or shortly afterwards, in that they may then wait until a trust is fully invested and capable of hitting its yield and total return targets. Investors may also prefer to see whether an investment thesis plays out before backing a new offering. That describes my approach when it comes to trusts that are investing in a very new area – I typically prefer to wait and see how things progress before buying at a subsequent fund raise. Unless a particular trust is exceptionally large from day one, the chances are that it will return to investors for more capital at some point.

One piece of jargon to be aware of when it comes to newly launched trusts is 'cash-drag'. This arises when freshly raised proceeds sit in cash, pending subsequent investment. This tends to reduce potential investment returns until the cash is fully invested. This cash element should be carved out from the rest of the portfolio for fee purposes. However, in some questionable instances this may not be the case and fees may be payable on the cash element as well.

Wrapping up

Ultimately, firms that bring investment trusts to market are commercially driven and spend a lot of time and effort in making sure the process runs smoothly. Abandoning an issue can therefore be costly and a route they will always seek to avoid taking. But, if as a result you only invest in trusts where you can tick *all* the 'good governance' boxes in the prospectus, then you are likely to be limited to a small number of new issues and you may miss out on some good opportunities. In my view, therefore, investors have to accept there is a trade-off between overall governance levels and the size of a position they are comfortable taking in a particular trust within a wider portfolio.

SUMMARY OF KEY POINTS

- Read the prospectus carefully before committing to an IPO.

- Pay particular attention to fees, discount controls and voting rights.

- If there is a performance fee, read the terms carefully and ensure you understand them and that they are fair.

- A search for key words in the PDF of the prospectus can help identify potential pitfalls.

- It is unlikely that all the contractual terms will be perfect for shareholders.

CHAPTER 32

INVESTING FOR GROWTH

"People who chase growth, who chase highfliers, inevitably lose because they paid a premium price. They lose to the people who have more patience and more discipline."

—Seth Klarman, US investor

I N THIS NEXT chapter, I want to address investors who do not need immediate income and have a long-term time horizon. By that, I mean at least five years and ideally more than 10. This sort of period gives equities a good chance to deliver attractive returns and allows compounding a decent opportunity to work its magic.

With the primary objective being to generate capital growth, income will take second place in this section. That said, given that investment trusts must distribute at least 85% of any net income they produce, it is worth noting that even some capital growth-focused trusts may also pay a dividend.

In that context, UK investment trusts are compelling. Firstly, they offer the advantages of diversification, in terms of spreading invested capital across a range of assets, sectors and stocks. This helps to mitigate company- or industry-specific risks and provides a more stable foundation for long-term growth. A closed-ended structure also allows a portfolio manager to think long term because it enables them to invest in less liquid assets. These may have the potential for substantial growth over time, in the absence of any pressure to sell during market downturns. This attribute helps to make investment trusts better suited to long-term capital appreciation than their open-ended counterparts. As we have seen in earlier chapters, investment trusts also have the flexibility to use leverage to try to amplify returns when markets are favourable. Recognising that it can also magnify losses, it needs to be used judiciously.

Since a substantial number of investment trusts aim to achieve capital growth first and foremost, I will narrow the field down to three specific categories. These are 'quality', 'value' and 'smaller companies', investment styles that we have covered in previous chapters. By grouping them like this we can seek complementary investment styles that provide correlation benefits, when combined in the same portfolio.

Looking for quality

Quality means different things to different investors, but here I use it to refer to companies that have superior profitability and more robust balance sheets than the market average. Chapter 27 lays out the evidence for the existence of the quality factor.

Companies with superior profitability (that generate consistently high profits and have relatively low capital expenditure), and with stronger than average balance sheets, are in a strong position to reinvest those profits and compound them in the future. Provided investment managers don't overpay for these quality characteristics, portfolios of such stocks are well placed to compound returns over time. The share prices of such stocks often tend to suffer lower than average declines during market downturns.

Using a database such as Morningstar Direct, profitability, growth and volatility data can be used to assess investment trust portfolios and highlight those that score well. These can then be analysed further to confirm their quality characteristics. Here is a shortlist of trusts that cut the mustard.

The quality trusts

Finsbury Growth & Income Trust (FGT)

FGT aims to generate long-term capital growth along with an element of income, primarily through investment in UK companies (at least 80% of portfolio value). The portfolio is managed by Nick Train of Lindsell Train.

Train runs a concentrated portfolio of companies that have strong brands or other characteristics that provide them with powerful market franchises. Like Warren Buffett, this manager's preferred holding period is forever.

Stock positions are usually only sold or reduced if they are either no longer sufficiently high quality or if they become too large a proportion of the portfolio. The portfolio has a large bias towards branded consumer goods and services (e.g. Unilever) and financial services (e.g. London Stock Exchange Group). The investment process is founded on a belief that the market undervalues durable business franchises with strong cash generation. The approach also seeks to minimise transaction costs with a buy and hold approach preferred. The portfolio's quality is exemplified by its ordinary and preference shareholdings in Europe's greatest football club, Celtic!

The FGT board introduced a share buyback and issuance policy in 2004. Under the policy, the trust normally buys in the shares being offered on the market whenever the discount approaches a level of 5% or more and then holds those shares in 'treasury'. These can then be sold back to the market later, at a premium to NAV.

Smithson Investment Trust (SSON)

SSON aims to generate long-term growth primarily though investment in small and medium-sized companies listed across the globe. Portfolio companies tend to exhibit high returns on invested capital and have low levels of leverage on their balance sheets. SSON therefore provides exposure to both quality and size factors.

The investment manager, Fundsmith, focuses on investing in companies that can compound in value over many years. To achieve this, it selects companies with a track record of success, such as a dominant market position. The manager seeks to invest in companies that exhibit strong profitability that is sustainable over time, and which generate substantial cash flow that can be reinvested back into the business. As with Lindsell Train, the Fundsmith strategy aims to minimise dealing to reduce portfolio expenses.

The SSON prospectus contains a clause that, if the shares have traded at an average discount wider than 10% during the financial year, a continuation vote should be proposed. Such a vote would allow shareholders to vote against the continuation of the trust and, as such, should act as a deterrent to extreme widening of the discount.

Pacific Assets Trust (PAC)

PAC was launched in 1985 and aims for long-term capital growth through investment in selected high-quality companies that are well positioned to contribute to sustainable development in the Asia Pacific region. Investment includes the Indian Subcontinent but excludes Japan, Australia and New Zealand.

The investment manager prefers family-controlled businesses that have been passed from generation to generation and where minority shareholder interests are considered. There is a bias towards companies with business models that can generate sustainably high returns on capital. This is usually achieved because of high barriers to entry but also by having products and services that generate mutually beneficial outcomes for customers, employees and other stakeholders.

The PAC board does not have an explicit discount control policy. It prefers to improve demand for the trust's shares by focusing on marketing the trust to a broader set of investors than the current shareholder base.

Verifying value

The concept of value investing was brought fully into the mainstream in 1998, with a paper produced by Eugene Fama and Kenneth French. This made the case that value stocks could be defined as those that are cheap relative to their balance sheet value. The paper also made the case that value stocks tended to outperform growth stocks (the latter being the opposite, i.e. expensive relative to their balance sheet value) over the period between 1975 and 1995.

In broad investing terms, 'value' these days refers to stocks that are typically unloved and out of favour. As such, they tend to be cheap relative to their 'intrinsic' underlying value. Making money here is based on the principle that the lack of interest in these stocks is often more than reflected in their stock market rating and associated valuation. That's because they have been *deemed* to be 'ex-growth' or are structurally challenged in some way. A few may even be heading towards bankruptcy.

Human nature being what it is, investors often overreact in such circumstances and will happily 'throw the baby out with the bathwater' by dumping any stocks that look suspect. Academic research has shown that this is precisely why they will often reward investors over time, as things transpire to be not quite as bad as many feared. A subsequent rerating can then translate into excellent capital upside.

As for the right investing approach, holding a single value stock is rarely a good idea, as some fail. However, a diversified portfolio, held via an investment trust, is a much safer proposition.

So far, so good. However, as we highlighted in Chapter 27, value investors don't always get things their own way and often need patience. When interest rates are low or falling, for example, growth stocks tend to shine as their superior future profitability potential gets reflected in a higher stock market rating. By contrast, value stocks tend to be shunned. This is one possible reason why they performed very poorly in the 10-year period following the Great Financial Crisis, as interest rates fell to ultra-low levels.

Meanwhile, some value stocks are 'cheap' for good reasons. They deserve to be shunned by the wider market due to factors such as elevated levels of leverage or other 'hidden nasties' that dramatically increase their chances of failing.

Nonetheless, for investors with the right approach, a value-oriented portfolio can generate explosive returns over short periods once the market backdrop is favourable.

One very useful feature of value stocks is that they complement quality well, because in many ways they are the opposite and behave accordingly. This relatively low level of correlation between the two styles aids portfolio construction. When quality stock performance fades, value often picks up the baton.

Several investment trust portfolios exhibit value characteristics, within an approach

> "Value stocks ... complement quality well ... they are the opposite and behave accordingly. This relatively low level of correlation between the two styles aids portfolio construction. When quality stock performance fades, value often picks up the baton."

that can be gleaned from the Chair's statement, and particularly the manager's report with a set of financial statements. Alternatively, you can ask your adviser to provide some aggregate valuation statistics for the last disclosed underlying portfolio. Here are a couple of examples:

Temple Bar (TMPL)

TMPL, one of the oldest investment trusts, will soon celebrate its 100-year anniversary. It aims to provide growth in income and capital and achieve a long-term total return greater than that of the FTSE All Share Index. Most of the portfolio holdings are large and medium-sized UK companies.

It has a distinct and consistent value approach. Morningstar portfolio data goes back as far as 2007 and since then the portfolio has primarily focused on lowly valued UK stocks. The approach has remained consistent despite changes of portfolio manager, a testament to the board's long-term perspective. The current investment manager is RWC Asset Management.

The manager looks to buy attractively valued, out-of-favour companies and hold them for the long term until true value is reflected, or more attractive ideas present themselves. To help avoid mistakes, the manager aims to identify good-quality companies with an emphasis on financial strength because it provides confidence that a company can survive through a prolonged period of lower profitability.

Typically, the portfolio can be broken down into three distinct categories: 1) fundamentally sound but out-of-favour businesses trading below intrinsic value, 2) previously out-of-favour companies still trading below intrinsic value but where fundamentals are improving and 3) companies that are now above intrinsic value and where the manager is in the process of exiting the stock.

North American Income Trust (NAIT)

NAIT has a checkered history, but some board action offers the prospect of a better future. This investment trust aims to provide investors with above-average dividend income and long-term capital growth. The investment process is designed to identify good-quality companies, with good cash generation, that are attractively valued.

The portfolio performed poorly during the 2019–24 period. The board looked to address this poor performance with a change of manager and a new share tender arrangement. The portfolio is now managed by Janus Henderson, with portfolio managers based in the US, following the change of manager from abrdn in August 2024.

Along with the change of manager the board introduced a mechanism for shareholders to redeem part of their shareholding if, after the new manager's first three years, the NAV total return does not exceed the total return of the S&P High Yield Dividend Aristocrat Index, an index that tracks companies with strong dividend growth. The new manager and tender mechanism provide a good set of incentives to encourage better performance over the coming years.

Seeking smaller companies

Now we turn to my final category for achieving growth – smaller ones. Academic research suggests that the market's minnows can outperform their larger peers over the long term, a tendency known, unsurprisingly, as the 'size effect'. It was first documented by Rolf Banz in his 1981 paper 'The Relationship Between Return and Market Value of Common Stocks'. This study found that smaller firms have higher risk-adjusted returns than larger firms. What's more, this phenomenon had been in existence for at least 40 years at that point. The study also found that the smallest companies tended to show the greatest outperformance. Numerous subsequent studies have supported this finding.

One supporting rationale is that smaller companies often fly under the radar of large institutional investors, leading to them being overlooked and potentially mispriced. When this mispricing is eventually recognised, often because of strong revenue and profits growth, the upside can be material.

There is a price for this potential upside, however, as smaller company stocks can be much more volatile than larger-cap equities. You should therefore make sure that your own risk tolerance is aligned with the size of potential short-term fluctuations. For that reason, a long-term investment horizon is essential when targeting a smaller company exposure. Here are some examples…

Baillie Gifford Shin Nippon (BGS)

BGS invests in small Japanese companies, aiming to find hidden gems that can deliver big upside. This means taking risk, and so buyers of this one should strap in for a volatile ride. However, the rewards can be material.

The portfolio, managed by Baillie Gifford, holds 40–80 attractively valued smaller companies that the manager believes offer good growth prospects. Up to 10% of the portfolio can be invested in private companies where the potential rewards, and risk, are greater than those of listed companies.

Many of the companies held in this portfolio have innovative business models and are disrupting traditional Japanese practices. The trust tends to be geared between 10 and 20%, which adds to potential return, and risk. This investment trust taps into the return asymmetry that is available from small, high-growth companies. In other words, the maximum loss from any single position is 100% (i.e. the capital invested), whilst the maximum gain is infinite. This arithmetic, if properly harnessed by the manager, can deliver excellent long-term returns.

The volatility of returns helps to explain why the BGS share price has moved from large discounts to large premiums and back again, over time. Buying at an attractive discount is key.

Scottish Oriental Smaller Companies (SST)

SST holds a portfolio of high-quality smaller companies based in Asia, excluding Japan. Asness et al., in their 2018 paper, 'Size matters, if you control your junk', suggest a definition of a high-quality firm as one that is well-managed, has strong economic and accounting performance, good growth prospects and low risk. These are characteristics that First Sentier Investors (FSI), the investment manager to SST, looks for in the stocks it buys.

FSI's assessment of a business starts with the quality of its majority-owners and management team. It believes that those owners and managers with a track record of treating other stakeholders (e.g. workers, suppliers) poorly will eventually compromise the interests of minority shareholders as well. FSI prefers to invest behind family-owned companies, as families typically take a long-term view of building their businesses and can make counter-cyclical investments.

Many portfolio holdings are simple, predictable businesses which have market-leading positions in underpenetrated categories. Their market leadership in their respective niches can provide strong bargaining power. This should result in a sustainably high return on capital employed, which FSI views as the best reflection of the quality of a business franchise.

Strategic Equity Capital (SEC)

The portfolio management team that helped to launch SEC cut its teeth in the private equity world. It approaches investment in public companies in a similar manner to a private equity investor. In other words, the mindset is to behave in a similar way as that of a majority owner, albeit with minority stakes.

This translates into a concentrated portfolio of 15–25 companies. There is a focus on businesses that can benefit from operational improvements. Companies where debt can be reduced from operational cash flow, thereby increasing equity value, are also favoured. The private equity mindset encourages a sanity check of public market valuations against comparable private market transactions. This helps to ensure attractive entry prices.

Portfolio companies typically have profitable business models, with good cash generation and high operating margins. The investment manager, Gresham House, can support portfolio companies by providing additional capital and facilitating operational improvements.

Given the investment approach, it is unsurprising that SEC portfolio companies tend to receive more than their fair share of takeover bids.

Wrapping up

We have seen how investing for growth via UK investment trusts offers a powerful solution for investors seeking long-term capital appreciation. Features such as diversification, professional management, leverage and a closed-ended structure make them well suited to the task, provided investors are willing to adopt a patient and disciplined approach.

SUMMARY OF KEY POINTS

- When investing for growth, ensure you take a long-term view, ideally 10 years plus.

- Quality stocks reinvest profits, generating high returns – a powerful compounding effect.

- Value stocks have tended to do well over most 10-year periods and complement quality stocks.

- Smaller companies tend to outperform larger companies over time.

- Numerous investment trusts provide exposure to these three key investment factors.

CHAPTER 33

INVESTING FOR PROGRESSIVE INCOME

"It is better to have a permanent income than to be fascinating."
—Oscar Wilde,
Irish poet and playwright

I NCOME IS NICE. When you receive it every year, that's even nicer. And, if it also goes up each year, well, that's close to financial nirvana.

The income-paying flexibility of investment trusts can help us get closer to this financial nirvana. In this chapter we will look at how.

Paying out

Firstly, a recap of a few basics we have touched on in earlier chapters.

Investment trusts are required to distribute at least 85% of their net income (i.e. after costs) to shareholders. The remaining (up to) 15% can be set aside, in the form of a 'revenue reserve', and used to supplement income in future years. This is useful when it comes to smoothing payments over time. In contrast, mutual funds, such as unit trusts and OEICs, must distribute all of their income in the financial year it is received. As such, they are less flexible.

Further, as well as being able to effectively distribute income from previous years out of these revenue reserves, investment trusts are also able to distribute realised capital gains in the form of income. These are recognised in the form of a separate reserve. The combination of revenue and capital reserves gives them huge control over the level of their income distribution.

These features have helped to create a particular category of income-paying investment trusts, known as the 'dividend heroes'. This term, coined by the Association of Investment Companies (AIC), captures investment trusts that have increased their dividend every year for 20 or more consecutive years. Whilst not a buy list, this category of investment trust should appeal to those looking to receive a long-term growing income stream. These trusts have demonstrated a remarkable track record of delivering reliable dividends over consecutive years, showing resilience through various market conditions.

Managing risk

Generating a progressive income over this sort of period is no mean feat, particularly given that the use of capital reserves to supplement income only became an option in 2012. Also, the period since the mid-2000s has witnessed major crises, including the pandemic in 2020 and the Great Financial Crisis of 2008/09.

Given that backdrop, it is remarkable that a few investment trusts have managed to grow their dividend every year for over 50 years. Let's call these the 'golden dividend aristocrats'. This elite group are particularly impressive as they also successfully navigated the early 1980s and early 1990s recessions as well as the mid-1970s oil crisis and inflation shock.

The AIC goes on to highlight a further set of progressive dividend payers, the next generation of dividend heroes. These are the trusts that have increased their dividend every year for at least 10 years, but less than 20. These are next in line to achieve dividend hero status if they continue on their progressive dividend path.

Yet just because a trust has achieved hero status, there is no guarantee that it will maintain it. Take Temple Bar (TMPL), a UK equity income investment trust that I introduced in Chapter 11. Temple Bar started increasing its dividend progressively in 1983. The statement from the Chair included in the 2019 annual report sounded reassuring enough:

> *In spite of this significant [10%] increase the dividend is fully covered by this year's earnings and has not required recourse to the Company's revenue reserves… This will be the 36th consecutive year in which the Company has raised its annual dividend payment, such consistency being reflected in Temple Bar's status as one of The Association of Investment Companies' 'Dividend Heroes'.*

However, those words preceded a significant cut in the dividends received from its portfolio holdings, because of the pandemic. This was exacerbated by an extreme value style (which materially underperformed the market in the three years leading up to TMPL's year end in 31/12/2020). That combination, plus relatively high gearing (never helpful in a falling market) saw it materially underperform subsequently and lose its dividend hero status.

As the Chair's statement in 2020 put it:

> *A consequence of the COVID-19 pandemic was that the majority of our investee companies either significantly reduced the level of their dividend payments or made none at all. This resulted in income generated from the portfolio plummeting from £39.7 million to £12.7 million, a fall of 68%… The total [dividend] payment for the 2020 financial year represents a decline of 25.1% from the dividend paid in 2019. Even this reduced level of dividend has required a significant transfer from revenue reserves… Going forward however, the board hopes to resume dividend growth from this lower level.*

This sudden change of fortunes illustrates the importance of diversifying across multiple dividend-paying investment trusts, such that you are not too reliant on a single market, investment style or board.

Testing dividends

To get an indication about how likely current dividend heroes, or the next generation of dividend heroes, are to continue paying growing dividends, I recommend that investors do a couple of bits of homework as follows:

- Read the Chair's comments about income to see how committed the board is to maintaining its record. References to a willingness to use capital reserves, for example, help to underline the importance of the existing dividend policy.

- Keep an eye on the overall level of revenue and capital reserves to determine what scope the trust has to maintain its record. A consistently growing dividend fosters investor confidence and loyalty. That, in turn, underpins a trust's position as a potential cornerstone of an income-focused portfolio.

Trusts that satisfy both criteria

City of London (CTY)

This UK equity income investment trust can lay claim to having the longest consecutive dividend growth record. It has increased its dividend every year since 1966. As such, it represents the gold standard for a progressive dividend policy.

The trust invests primarily in UK equities, with a slight value bias. It targets a dividend yield that is 10–30% higher than the FTSE All Share Index. Running costs are low – the annual management fee is 0.3% of net assets and the trust uses gearing to good effect.

The CTY annual report makes it clear how important it is to the board that its dividend record is maintained. For example, an extract from the Chair's statement in the 2024 annual report reads, "It should be noted that the capital reserve arising from capital gains on investments sold, which could help fund dividend payments, rose by £1.7m to £346.3 million."

Murray International (MYI)

MYI, launched in 1907, aims for an above average dividend yield, as well as growth in income and capital ahead of inflation. It looks to achieve this by holding a diverse portfolio of lowly valued global stocks along with some modest exposure to fixed interest. The portfolio is managed by abrdn Investments.

The manager considers stocks for the portfolio based on five key attributes. These are the durability of the business model, the attractiveness of the industry, financial strength, capability of the management team and ESG credentials. A global list of stocks is constructed by regional teams of analysts.

The portfolio typically holds 60–80 stocks with position sizes of 1% to 5%. Fixed income positions tend to be smaller. The trust has a good record of dividend growth, having raised the dividend every year since 2004.

Changing tack

Maintaining a progressive dividend policy solely from direct investments in stocks is becoming more difficult. That is because whilst many UK companies used to increase their dividends every year, this consistency faltered during the pandemic. Since then, to give themselves greater financial flexibility, many UK companies have moved to a payout ratio. Under this type of approach, the level of annual distribution is determined using a percentage of earnings (aka profits) rather than by reference to the previous year's dividend.

This sort of policy has been in place across large parts of the world for several years. Asia is a prime example. Rest assured that it has not stopped three Asian equity income trusts from increasing their dividends for at least 15 consecutive years, helped by the selective use of reserves.

Against that backdrop, here are two of the next generation of dividend heroes, where the Chair has stated a commitment to a progressive dividend policy, backed by ample reserves.

Next generation of dividend heroes

Schroder Oriental Income (SOI)

This Asia Pacific equity income investment trust aims to provide a total return primarily through investments in the shares of companies which are based in, or which derive a significant proportion of their revenues from, the Asia Pacific region. The manager also looks for shares that offer attractive yields. As a result, SOI has increased its dividend every year for 18 consecutive years.

This time, the underlying portfolio combines both value and quality elements. Schroders has a network of Asia-based analysts who try to identify companies that are likely to be able to grow over the long term. Specifically, they look for those that can offer high and sustainable free cash flow. The result is a pool of quality stocks that either already pay strong, growing dividends or show the potential to do so.

The annual report highlights this scope for dividend growth and a willingness to dip into reserves when necessary. Here is an extract from the 2024 Chair's statement:

We have continued to grow our own dividend to shareholders progressively for 17 years and the current dividend yield on our share price is approximately 5%. As the global economy begins to slow, we may consequently see some slowdown in dividend growth from our portfolio companies. However, it is important to remember that payout ratios in Asia are modest, so our companies are not under financial pressure and our Manager is not forecasting any notable falls in receipts. The company also has considerable revenue reserves. Any slowdown in dividend receipts is likely to be transitory and we are comfortable, as and when we need to, to dip into our reserves for a short time to maintain or grow our own dividend to shareholders.

Mercantile (MRC)

MRC's investment style doesn't appear consistent with a progressive dividend policy. It invests in growth companies, primarily medium-sized ones in the UK. Facets of the investment process (e.g. identifying stocks with positive earnings momentum) naturally lead towards growth companies and away from yield.

However, the investment trust structure facilitates a progressive dividend policy. The pandemic hit portfolio income hard in 2020, 2021 and 2022, as many companies chose to cut or reduce dividends. Despite this, MRC maintained its dividend growth policy by dipping into revenue reserves. Conditions have improved since 2022 and the dividends paid in 2023 and 2024 have both been covered by portfolio income.

The Chair's statement in the 2024 full year results underlined the importance of dividend growth:

The Company aims to provide shareholders with long term dividend growth at least in line with the rate of inflation over a five-to-ten-year period... the Company has been able to increase the FY24 total dividend by a healthy margin, while also adding a meaningful amount to its reserves, to support dividends in any future lean years.

Wrapping up

We have now seen why investment trust dividend heroes can offer a neat solution to income seekers. Favoured for their commitment to delivering a reliable income, their consistency, long-term focus and diversified portfolios all add to their overall appeal. As investors continue to prioritise stability and visibility of income generation, investment trust dividend heroes are set to maintain their status as useful components of income-focused portfolios.

SUMMARY OF KEY POINTS

- Investment trusts can reserve income and capital to distribute in later years.

- AIC dividend heroes are investment trusts that have raised their dividends for at least 20 consecutive years.

- The next generation of dividend heroes are investment trusts that have raised their dividends for at least 10 consecutive years but less than 20.

- Check the Chair's statement for willingness, and the revenue and capital reserves for the ability, to maintain a progressive dividend policy.

- Just because a trust has achieved dividend hero status is no guarantee that it will maintain it.

CHAPTER 34

INVESTING FOR HIGH INCOME

"Annual income twenty pounds, annual expenditure nineteen nineteen and six, result happiness. Annual income twenty pounds, annual expenditure twenty pounds ought and six, result misery."

—Charles Dickens,
Wilkins Micawber in *David Copperfield*

IN THIS CHAPTER, we will consider high income trusts under three separate headings: 'equity', 'credit' and 'alternatives'. Under the equity label, we will focus on plain vanilla equity trusts that offer a high level of dividend distribution. Credit, meanwhile, will consider trusts that buy credit instruments, such as bonds or loans. Alternatives will then look at trusts that invest in other assets. Before we get to those, though, a bit of context.

Setting the scene

Some people need a decent level of investment income and may require more of it than their asset base can reasonably sustain. Generating it from investment trusts can make sense. However, we should note a few relevant considerations and caveats.

Firstly, to get to their desired income level, investors might need to hold investment trusts that pay distributions from capital. This may reduce potential growth in the future. As we highlighted in Chapter 14, capital and revenue reserves, which are used to supplement portfolio income, are simply an accounting convention. Provided investors are happy to take income at the expense of capital, using these reserves is a perfectly acceptable way of enhancing the trust's natural portfolio income.

Purists might argue that income which is paid from capital is not very tax efficient (since income tax is very difficult to avoid, whereas CGT is easier to reduce via allowances and capital losses). However, a lot of investment trusts are held within tax shelters these days (ISAs and SIPPs primarily), which takes away this issue. Meanwhile, the capital gains tax-free allowance has been reduced dramatically so the CGT argument is less relevant than it used to be.

Secondly, to secure a desired income level, investors may need to look at all three of the sub-sectors mentioned at the start – income, credit and alternatives – whilst not losing sight of the valuation issues we discussed in Chapter 18. That third category may puzzle some readers. However, even trusts that invest in assets that are not typically income generating, such as private equity and venture capital, may choose to pay dividends for two primary reasons:

- It broadens demand.

- If the shares are trading at a discount, then any return of capital enhances NAV per share.

Nonetheless, the opaqueness surrounding the valuation of some alternative investment trusts makes it wise to limit the overall level of exposure to them.

Thirdly, regardless of what is 'under the bonnet', it is important to query unusually high yields. 'Monster yields' of 10% or more are often only possible due to very high amounts of leverage, or default risk, or the use of capital to supplement income. Yields as high as this also imply a higher probability of a future dividend cut. It is therefore vital that you carefully study the annual report to understand how a high yield is being generated, and the level of risk that comes with it. Try to gain a feel, as a minimum, for what would happen to current income if there were no leverage, and therefore how reliant the income is on leverage. For example, high borrowing costs could be a big issue for certain investment trusts that have cheap loans expiring in the coming years. In some cases, it will not make financial sense to take out fresh borrowings at prevailing rates. That probably means that assets will need to be sold to meet the debt redemptions. This shouldn't be any issue for trusts that are primarily invested in quoted equities or tradeable bonds. However, it could be an issue for trusts that hold illiquid assets.

Finally, many investment trusts have holdings concentrated in specific sectors or geographic regions. Economic cycles, regulatory changes and technological disruption can all adversely affect sector performance and, consequently, income generation. Similarly, trusts heavily invested in a particular region face geopolitical risks and currency fluctuations that may undermine income sustainability.

For all of these reasons, it is important not to rely too much on any individual trust to provide you with income. Spread your investments across several trusts with different mandates.

With those words of caution noted, let's now look at the three main income categories in turn.

High equity income

Several equity trusts have adopted a high distribution policy. They use accumulated reserves (both revenue and capital) to maintain yields, which are typically based on a set percentage of NAV at the start of the year. For example, many of the JPMorgan trust range pay a dividend equating to 4% of start-of-year NAV and primarily from capital. When I look for reassurances about how solid this income stream looks, I usually read the Chair's statement for an indication of how committed the board is to maintaining payouts. I also check the level of reserves in the financial statements. Note that with this approach, dividends can vary each year, both up and down, depending on overall returns in the prior year.

In that context, here is an equity trust that currently offers a high yield.

European Assets Trust (EAT)

This trust aims to achieve long-term capital growth via a portfolio of 40–50 smaller European (ex UK) companies. These are often under-researched, which leads to opportunities to buy them cheaply. The investment manager looks to invest in high-quality businesses, which are available at attractive valuations. In this case, 'quality' means an ability to grow sustainably and reinvest solid cash flow into high-return assets.

Although it is difficult to generate a natural income from a smaller company quality and growth portfolio, EAT helps income seekers to gain exposure to these types of stocks via a structured distribution policy. It aims to make payments equating to 6% of end-of-year NAV. The resulting dividend can be funded from a variety of sources, which gives the managers a degree of flexibility. Historically, revenue from dividends has accounted for around a third of the total annual income requirement, supplemented by the selective use of reserves and gearing. Reassuringly, its distributable reserves (refer to Chapter 14) are almost 10× last year's dividend payments.

High credit income

Credit instruments represent a way for companies to borrow. They usually come in the form of bonds or loans. The income paid by these bonds and loans tends to be higher than prevailing government bond yields to reflect the greater risk of default. This can be quantified using a long-term record of default rates produced by one of the rating agencies.

Table 34A shows the historic (from 1981 to 2023) data for a global pool of corporate bonds rated by S&P Global. On average, 1.4% of corporate bonds have defaulted each year. Note that this represents the level of default rather than the amount of any resulting capital loss. Typically, something is recovered from bond and loan defaults, particularly as the related securities usually rank ahead of shares in the event of bankruptcy.

Table 34A: Global corporate debt default rate

Year	Default rate (%)	Year	Default rate (%)
1981	0.2	2003	1.9
1982	1.2	2004	0.8
1983	0.8	2005	0.6
1984	0.9	2006	0.5
1985	1.1	2007	0.4
1986	1.7	2008	1.8
1987	0.9	2009	4.2
1988	1.4	2010	1.2
1989	1.8	2011	0.8
1990	2.7	2012	1.1
1991	3.2	2013	1.0
1992	1.5	2014	0.7
1993	0.6	2015	1.4
1994	0.6	2016	2.1
1995	1.1	2017	1.2
1996	0.5	2018	1.0
1997	0.6	2019	1.3
1998	1.3	2020	2.8
1999	2.1	2021	0.9
2000	2.5	2022	1.0
2001	3.7	2023	1.9
2002	3.5	**Average**	**1.4**

Source: https://www.spglobal.com. S&P Global Ratings Credit Research & Insights. S&P Global Market Intelligence's CreditPro®

The level of yield payable by corporate bonds usually more than compensates investors for default risk. In other words, the level of additional yield available from an average bond is usually more than 1.4% greater than that of an equivalent government bond. Further, some bond and loan issues are relatively small and therefore illiquid. As such, they often pay an additional level of yield to compensate. Unlike their mutual fund counterparts, investment trusts are in an ideal position to buy and hold such bonds and loans due to their closed-ended structure.

Here is a credit trust that offers a high yield.

BioPharma Credit (BPCR)

This trust aims to generate long-term returns, predominantly via sustainable income distributions generated from an exposure to life science businesses. Specifically, it targets a total return that equates to 8–9% of NAV and a dividend of 7% of its original issue price ($1.00).

BPCR primarily invests in corporate and royalty debt of companies that are identifying and developing new drugs but which already have approval on at least one product. The corporate debt is typically a senior loan secured against company assets, with a first priority charge against liquid assets, marketing rights or other intellectual property. Royalty debt is effectively secured against revenues from approved pharmaceutical products. Loans tend to be floating rate and typically are protected against any loss of future coupons from early repayment, or a takeover.

An extract from the 2023 annual report reads:

> *The Company made four dividend payments over the year totalling 11.5 cents per share, referencing net income for the four quarters ending 30 September 2022... and was therefore able to maintain its record of paying a dividend of at least 1.75 cents per share in every quarter since that ending 30 June 2018.*

The company did experience its first default in late 2023 but has recovered the vast majority of this loan at the time of writing and has maintained its dividend throughout.

Note that the underlying assets and the dividend are in dollars. This means the income is likely to fluctuate from one year to the next purely because of the pound sterling / US dollar exchange rate. At the time of writing the trust offers a high single-digit income yield and can do so without any gearing.

High alternative income

Investors should always be slightly wary of alternative asset trusts in my opinion, due to their opaqueness, coupled quite often with a short trading history. That caveat aside, here are two income-generating investment trusts in the infrastructure space.

HICL Infrastructure (HICL)

This trust aims to deliver a sustainable income from a diversified portfolio of investments in core infrastructure. These tend to be assets which are vital to communities, across sectors such as roads, rail, utilities and social infrastructure (i.e., schools, hospitals, etc.). As such, they are positioned at the lower end of the risk spectrum. The bulk of the portfolio is in public-private partnerships (PPP) assets. PPP involves collaboration between a government agency and a private-sector company to finance, build and operate key public infrastructure projects. These range from schools to hospitals and transportation networks. Provided the relevant assets are available for use, the government agency makes payments to the private-sector partner, typically with an annual inflationary increase.

The trust's performance is measured against several key performance indicators (KPIs): an annual distribution equal or greater to the previous year's; a long-term 7–8% internal rate of return (IRR); dividend payments that are covered by cash received; inflation correlation of at least 0.5×; efficient gross to net returns; and, finally, reducing OCR costs where possible.

The 2024 annual report contains the following extract from the Chair's statement:

The impact of high inflation over the past 18 months is increasingly flowing through into higher cash receipts across the portfolio, and is supported by real growth in HICL's demand-based assets, all of which are now making regular distributions. In addition, the asset rotation undertaken in the year has improved the portfolio's yield profile. Together this provides the Board with the confidence that dividend cash cover will continue to improve in the coming years and that a growing dividend will be appropriately supported both by cash and earnings over the long term.

BBGI Global Infrastructure (BBGI)*

BBGI, like HICL, focuses on social infrastructure. Where it differs is in the level of yield (lower) and the level of risk (also lower). BBGI focuses purely on availability-based infrastructure. In other words, it buys concessions to operate schools, hospitals, prisons, etc. but where payments to BBGI depend purely on the facilities being available for use.

So, changes in economic activity shouldn't impact BBGI directly, as they would with volume-dependent infrastructure such as toll roads. The investments receive a contracted income from governments such as Australia, Canada, Germany and the UK. In other words, jurisdictions with stable operating environments and reliable legal systems. The portfolio income stream also benefits from inflation linkage.

BBGI is the only internally managed infrastructure investment trust listed on the London market. The set of management incentives that come with this help to achieve better alignment with shareholders. The management has a significant stake in BBGI shares and operates a long-term share-based incentive plan.

This lower-risk profile comes with a yield that is lower than other infrastructure plays but one that is attractive nonetheless and should grow over time.

Table 34B shows the highest yielding investment trusts (over £100m market cap), along with their valuation basis, which we covered in Chapter 18.

---

* Since writing this there has been a recommended all-cash offer for BBGI from British Columbia Investment Management.

Table 34B: 10 Highest yielding investment trusts

Investment trust	Yield (12 month historic)	Primary IFRS valuation basis (level)
Henderson Far East Income Ord	10.7	1
CQS New City High Yield Ord	8.8	2
M&G Credit Income Investment Ord	8.7	2
TwentyFour Income Ord	9.1	2
TwentyFour Select Monthly Income Ord	8.6	2
NextEnergy Solar Ord	8.8	3
CVC Income & Growth GBP	8.6	3
Real Estate Credit Investments Ord	8.5	3
BioPharma Credit Ord	8.1	3
AEW UK REIT Ord	7.5	3

12 Month historic yield as at 31/12/2024. Excludes trusts listed on the specialist funds market and those with a market capitalisation below £100m.

Data sources: Morningstar, Bloomberg, annual reports.

Wrapping up

As we have seen, UK investment trusts present some good opportunities for high income generation. However, they can also carry risks primarily in the form of equity market volatility, corporate default risk and investment trust discount risk. Whilst growth investors might be able to withstand occasional declines in capital value, declines in income often take longer to recoup. For this reason, diversification is particularly important when building an income portfolio. Don't rely too much on any single investment trust for your income.

SUMMARY OF KEY POINTS

- To generate a very high level of income, be prepared to limit or degrade capital growth.

- Several equity trusts seek a high total return but distribute from capital reserves.

- Yields payable by credit instruments usually more than compensate holders for default risk.

- Be wary of many alternative asset trusts, due to opaqueness and lack of trading history.

- Diversification is even more important than usual when building an income portfolio.

CHAPTER 35

DEFENSIVE TRUSTS

"Unprecedented events occur with some regularity, so be prepared."

—**Seth Klarman, US investor**

IF YOU WORRY about the impact of unprecedented events on the value of your portfolio, you may wish to consider investment trusts with a defensive slant. Some investors focus on growing capital, whilst others prioritise its preservation. If you are in the latter camp, or simply prefer lower volatility and are willing to potentially sacrifice some future gains to achieve it, then this chapter is aimed at you.

Staying flexible

Let's start with a quick tour of the AIC's Flexible Investment sector. As the name suggests, it contains trusts that can invest in a wide range of asset types, which may encompass quoted and unquoted equities, bonds, other debt instruments and property. This investment flexibility enables them to achieve much greater diversification than the average investment trust. This diversification, if carefully employed, can help these trusts to produce steady positive returns in most market conditions.

This sort of return profile appeals to a lot of private investors that are keen to grow their wealth in real (post-inflation) terms, but without feeling the full force of the most extreme market declines that come with pure equity investment. That is why, compared with their peers, defensive trusts in the Flexible Investment sector often employ minimal gearing, or even none at all. This constrains both their potential upside and downside performance.

That said, although they aim to safeguard investors' capital and generate stable returns, nothing is guaranteed in financial markets, and they can also experience losses during extreme conditions.

With investment trusts, it is not enough for the investment manager to operate a defensive portfolio. The board also needs to have an effective discount control policy in place. After all, there is not much point in having a portfolio which avoids large losses during a market drop, if the trust's discount then widens sharply, resulting in a sizeable decline in the share price.

In that context, I am initially going to single out two defensive trusts that share the following useful characteristics:

* a clear investment process, particularly regarding valuations they pay for assets

* good NAV resilience during weak equity market conditions

* an aversion to gearing

* strong discount control mechanisms

* competitive costs and a reasonably narrow bid-to-offer spread.

Then we will take a quick look at some others which I consider also fit the 'defensive' brief, albeit with one or two caveats.

Defensive trusts

Capital Gearing Trust (CGT)

CGT aims to achieve long-term capital growth, in absolute terms, by investing globally across a spread of asset classes. The trust's portfolio may therefore contain equities (typically via ETFs and investment trusts), government and corporate bonds, real estate, infrastructure, commodities and cash. The managers do not, however, use complex strategies, derivatives or short positions. Despite its name, the trust has not employed gearing for many years. This strategy is overseen by the investment team at CG Asset Management. Reassuringly, the founder, Peter Spiller, has managed the underlying portfolio since 1982.

The resulting asset allocation deployed by the investment team is built on two key principles:

- Asset returns 'mean revert' towards their average over the long term, so

- Market timing is therefore possible over a long-term horizon.

The overall philosophy is that there are times when investors should seek strong investment gains and others when they should prioritise avoiding losses. The managers therefore aim to forecast after-inflation asset class returns using models based on long-term datasets. These then drive the underlying asset class exposures.

With an emphasis on capital preservation, they aim specifically to achieve positive returns in any 12-month period, irrespective of market conditions. This focus was severely tested during the pandemic-induced sell-off of 2020, when although the NAV declined by 7.6% peak to trough (during the biggest FTSE All Share peak to trough decline in 2020, 17/01/2020 to 23/03/2020; Source: Bloomberg), this was modest when compared to the FTSE All Share TR Index decline of 35.5%.

The board operates a discount control policy whereby it issues shares at a premium of around 2% to NAV and buys them back at a similar discount level.

Personal Assets Trust (PNL)

PNL aims primarily to achieve capital preservation. Long term growth, above inflation, is a secondary objective. Troy Asset Management has been the nominated investment adviser since 2009. The trust can invest globally in equities, fixed income securities, cash, cash equivalents and gold.

Asset allocation decisions are based on a range of factors, including an analysis of economic conditions, interest rates, inflation and relative valuations. Any equity exposure is focused on high-quality businesses which are perceived to be trading at a reasonable valuation. Given the mandate's emphasis on capital protection, the resulting portfolio often has a defensive bias, with higher-than-average holdings of cash, gold and government debt. The strategy duly delivered on its capital preservation mandate through 2020, with an NAV increase of around 8% even as the FTSE All Share Index declined.

Notably, the board was the first to adopt a zero-discount policy, effectively keeping the share price within a band of a maximum 2% premium or discount to NAV.

Against that backdrop, here are how the two trusts stack up in terms of their long-term NAV, share price total return, downside risk, overall volatility and discount range.

Table 35A: Capital Gearing Trust and Personal Assets Trust – risk and return versus the UK stock market

	NAV TR	Share price / index total return	Maximum drawdown	Worst quarter	Share price / index volatility	Sharpe ratio
CGT	62.5%	57.8%	-15.0%	-4.2%	11.4%	0.81
PNL	66.0%	65.9%	-11.9%	-4.7%	9.2%	0.76
FTSE All Share Index	72.5%	72.5%	-35.3%	-25.1%	18.4%	0.37

All data relates to share price total return, apart from the first data column which is NAV total return. Time frame is since CGT adopted its discount management policy (August 2015), up to 31/12/2024. Maximum drawdown refers to the maximum decline in value of the share price, with income reinvested, from its peak to its trough before a new high is reached, expressed as a percentage of the peak price. The Sharpe ratio is a measure of risk-adjusted performance. The higher the Sharpe ratio, the better the historical risk-adjusted performance. It is calculated by dividing the annualised excess share price total return, over that of the average sterling money market fund return, by the share / index price volatility. 01/08/2015 to 31/12/2024.

Source: Morningstar

Looking elsewhere

Beyond those two, another defensive trust worth considering is Ruffer Investment Company (RICA).

Launched in July 2004, it aims to achieve a positive total annual return of at least twice the Bank of England Base Rate by investing predominantly in equities or bonds. The investment manager, Ruffer AIFM, maintains a diverse portfolio and employs hedging strategies to counterbalance its exposure to equities and credit risk. The resulting portfolio tends to be more esoteric than either CGT's or PNL's and has briefly dipped its toe into areas such as cryptocurrencies. The long-term performance is solid and portfolio volatility tends to be very low.

That said, there is no formal discount management policy. The board aims to purchase shares where, 'discounts of the share price to NAV per share are perceived to be excessive and temporary'. As a result, the long-term range is a 9% premium (in 2010) to a 9% discount (in 2020 during the pandemic), with the average being a 1% premium.

BH Macro (BHMG) is another defensive trust also worthy of consideration. It provides exposure to various hedge fund trading strategies employed by Brevan Howard, a hedge fund management company. For some investors, the phrase 'hedge fund' triggers fear around high costs, loosely defined investment remits and a lack of transparency. BH Macro's running costs (2.05%) are indeed significantly higher than those of CGT (0.69%), PNL (0.65%) and RICA (1.06%). All costs are the actual ongoing costs provided by Morningstar as at 31/12/2024.

Nonetheless, BH Macro operates a credible trading strategy that provides excellent diversification benefits. Indeed, some of the best years, in performance terms, have been delivered during market crises.

However, the trust's discount control policy is not as tight as that of CGT and PNL, in part due to some technical factors that make it more difficult to implement an effective one. Much of the problem with BH Macro's discount control lies with its investment management agreement, which contains a clause whereby, if the trust makes repurchases of shares of more than 5% on an annual basis, it is required to pay the investment manager an additional fee equal to 2% of value repurchased.

BH Macro's share price dropped from a premium (to NAV) of 21% to a discount of 14% between 2022 and 2023. One way of using such discount volatility to your benefit is to simply avoid buying this one on a premium to NAV and look to gain exposure when the discount is relatively wide. This requires some discipline and patience, but the discount has been relatively wide at some point in most calendar years since launch.

Two further trusts in this category are also worth a mention here, although neither employs as robust a discount control mechanism as CGT and PNL. That's partly because they tend to run a sizeable allocation to private equity, which hinders the scope to maintain a consistently tight discount. This looser discount control inevitably translates into much higher share price volatility.

First off, there is RIT Capital Partners (ongoing costs of 2.39%). This self-managed trust aims to deliver long-term capital growth above the level of a relevant benchmark, whilst also preserving capital. Broadly, the board compares NAV performance to the UK's RPI inflation measure +3% and the MSCI All Country World Index.

The portfolio managers focus on macro themes and build a high-conviction portfolio of listed and unquoted stocks around them. Whilst capital preservation is an important part of their remit, the annual report usually discloses the net quoted equity exposure so that investors can gauge how much market risk is being taken on their behalf.

With no formal discount management policy in place, the long-term range (since 2008) is a 13% premium (2011) to a 32% discount (April 2024), averaging out at about a 2% discount.

Last on my list is Caledonia Investments (ongoing costs of 1.61%), which aims to grow 'net asset value total return' by 3–6% above inflation over the short term, in the hope of beating the FTSE All Share Index over the longer term. The result is a balanced portfolio of investments, primed to deliver on three strategic objectives:

1. FTSE All Share outperformance over 10 years, with shorter-term returns between RPI +3% and RPI +6%.

2. An increasing annual dividend.

3. Managed investment risk consistent with long-term wealth generation.

The trust invests in well-managed businesses that combine long-term growth characteristics with an ability to deliver increasing levels of income. It achieves this via a mix of quoted equities, funds and private equity. The trust has historically had little, or no, gearing.

> "'Skin in the game' is a great vote of confidence in the underlying portfolio, and a source of reassurance for external stakeholders, particularly when markets turn turbulent."

One key benefit of this trust's strategy is its scope to co-invest directly in private equity deals without the associated costs of doing so via a fund. Caledonia is also a 'dividend hero', having increased its dividend every year for 57 consecutively. Although the yield is low (currently 2.0%, based on last 12 months distributions) special dividends are sometimes declared when private equity stakes are realised.

There is no formal discount control mechanism or target, but the board has historically bought back shares at discounts ranging between 10 and 35% in most years. It is worth noting that The Cayzer family owns around 49% of the trust's shares. This limits the trust's scope to manage the discount.

One final important feature that all these trusts share is a high level of alignment between the managers, board and investors created by the key participants owning significant stakes themselves. This 'skin in the game' is a great vote of confidence in the underlying portfolio, and a source of reassurance for external stakeholders, particularly when markets turn turbulent. We will revisit this topic in Chapter 38.

Wrapping up

Defensive UK investment trusts, of the sort we have covered in this chapter, can be a valuable tool when it comes to building a resilient portfolio that will help investors to navigate market uncertainty.

SUMMARY OF KEY POINTS

- Some trusts in the AIC Flexible Investment sector prioritise capital preservation over capital growth.

- The most effective trusts in terms of capital preservation are Capital Gearing Trust and Personal Assets Trust.

- They achieve this primarily through asset diversification, low gearing and an active discount management policy.

- BH Macro utilises trading and hedging strategies but has a wide discount range.

- Other trusts aim for a combination of capital growth and long-term capital preservation.

CHAPTER 36

FUND SIBLINGS
AND COUSINS

*"Happiness is having a large, loving, caring,
close-knit family in another city."*

—**George Burns,**
American comedian and actor

SOME INVESTMENT TRUSTS have siblings and some have cousins. I am referring to mutual funds (unit trust or OEICs) that follow a similar investment strategy and are managed by the same investment manager.

Here, I define sibling funds as a pair of funds, comprising an investment trust and a mutual fund, where they share the *same* investment manager, the *same* investment process, have the *same* benchmark and exhibit the *same* style characteristics (e.g. growth, value, size).

I define cousin funds as a pair of funds, comprising an investment trust and a mutual fund, where they share the *same* investment manager, a *similar* investment process, have *similar* benchmarks but exhibit slightly *different* style characteristics.

Those two grammatical sleights of hand should help with navigation in this chapter.

Table 36A compares sibling funds over a comparable performance period of 10 years to the end of 2024. A quick glance reveals that the investment trusts (on the left) have generally performed better than the equivalent mutual funds. Part of the reason is likely to be their ability to gear up in a rising market. Size, as we have already noted, is also likely to have been an influence. Another contributory factor may be the enhancement to NAV per share that can arise from issuing shares at a premium and buying them back at a discount, something an investment trust can do but a mutual fund cannot. The majority (88%) of the investment trusts listed have done better overall, with an average outperformance of 23% (the full methodology is in the appendix).

Table 36A: Sibling funds, 10-year cumulative NAV performance %

Investment trust	%	Mutual fund	%	Relative perfor- mance %
Aberforth Smaller Companies Ord	86.3	Aberforth UK Small Companies Acc	83.8	2.5
abrdn New India Investment Trust Ord	184.1	abrdn-Indian Equity A Acc GBP	128.9	55.2
abrdn UK Smaller Companies Growth Ord	119.5	abrdn UK Smaller Companies I Acc	106.2	13.4
Baillie Gifford Japan Ord	136.3	Baillie Gifford Japanese B Acc	114.72	21.6
Baillie Gifford Shin Nippon Ord	115.7	Baillie Gifford Japan Small Co B Inc	74.1	41.6
BlackRock Income and Growth Ord	76.6	BlackRock UK Income A Inc	72.2	4.3
Diverse Income Trust Ord	80.3	Premier Miton UK Multi Cap Income B Acc	75.6	4.8
Edinburgh Worldwide Ord	118.8	Baillie Gifford Global Discovery A Acc	50.5	68.4
Fidelity Asian Values Ord	154.4	Fidelity Asian Smaller Coms Y-Acc-USD	123.9	30.5
Fidelity European Trust Ord	174.0	Fidelity European Acc	136.4	37.6
Finsbury Growth & Income Ord	120.0	WS Lindsell Train UK Equity Acc	101.65	18.3
Henderson European Trust Ord	153.9	Janus Henderson European Focus A Acc	125.34	28.6
Henderson Smaller Companies Ord	84.9	Janus Henderson UK Smaller Coms A Acc	64.21	20.7

Investment trust	%	Mutual fund	%	Relative perfor- mance %
JPMorgan American Ord	343.1	JPM America Equity A (dist) USD	313.5	29.6
JPMorgan Emerging Markets Ord	115.2	JPM Emerging Markets C Net Acc	86.68	28.6
JPMorgan Global Emerg Mkts Inc Ord	96.6	JPM Emerging Markets Div A (acc) EUR	81.9	14.7
JPMorgan UK Small Cap Growth & Income	142.0	JPM UK Smaller Companies I Acc	121.79	20.2
Jupiter Green Ord	84.9	Jupiter Ecology L Inc	114.68	−29.8
Lowland Ord	58.7	Janus Henderson UK Eq Inc&Gr I Inc	43.6	15.2
Merchants Trust Ord	105.6	Allianz UK Listed Eq Income A Inc	86.8	18.8
Monks Ord	220.1	Baillie Gifford Global Alpha Gr B Acc	193.4	26.7
Pacific Assets Ord	136.9	Stewart Inv Asia Pac All Cap B GBP Acc	140.19	−3.3
Pacific Horizon Ord	231.6	Baillie Gifford Pacific B Inc	172.57	59.0
Personal Assets Ord	68.3	Trojan O Inc	64.67	3.7
Polar Capital Technology Ord	585.4	Polar Capital Global Tech Inc	541.07	44.4
Schroder Asian Total Return Inv. Company	192.4	Schroder ISF Asian Ttl Ret C Acc USD	146.2	46.3
Schroder AsiaPacific Ord	137.8	Schroder Asian Alpha Plus A Acc	115.34	22.4
Schroder Japan Trust Ord	152.9	Schroder Tokyo A Inc GBP	110.3	42.6
Schroder UK Mid Cap Ord	81.2	Schroder UK Mid 250 A Acc	53.1	28.1
Scottish American Ord	213.1	Baillie Gifford Global Inc Growth A Acc	155.55	57.5
Strategic Equity Capital Ord	98.7	WS Gresham House UK Micro Cap A Acc	106.3	−7.7
Templeton Emerging Mkts Invmt Tr TEMIT	94.6	FTF Templeton Global Emerging Mkts W Acc	87.84	6.7
The European Smaller Companies Trust PLC	201.8	Janus Henderson European Smr Coms I Acc	211.38	−9.6

Date range 10 years to 31/12/2024.

Sources: Morningstar, Bloomberg, LSEG, company annual reports, fund factsheets.

Choosing between fund cousins

Now for what I call 'fund cousins'. As a reminder, these are investment trusts and mutual funds that share the same investment manager and adopt a similar investment process and benchmarks, but where the two have slightly different style characteristics. This difference is often due to the investment trust structure permitting greater investment flexibility.

To illustrate this, let's look at the Lindsell Train Investment Trust and Lindsell Train Global Equity, a mutual fund. Both invest in large global stocks, with strong brands. Such stocks tend to be dominant in their industries and exhibit characteristics that are difficult to replicate.

However, the investment trust has one key point of difference when compared to the mutual fund – it holds a stake in Lindsell Train Limited, the investment manager. This stake was valued at £66,600 (666 shares valued at £100 each) at IPO. Now though, thanks to growth in the underlying assets under management and the investment manager's ability to generate profits, that stake was valued at £69m at the 31/03/2024 year end. What's more, it is the largest holding, at 34% of the total portfolio. The result is that the NAV return of Lindsell Train Investment Trust has been materially higher than that of its cousin Lindsell Train Global Equity over the 10-year period to the end of 2024.

This example compares a pair of fund cousins with some very distinct features. The differences between other cousin pairs are more subtle. Take Montanaro UK Smaller Companies and Montanaro UK Income. Both are managed by the same investment manager. However, the investment trust does not have an income yield requirement and invests in much smaller stocks. The UK Income fund, on the other hand, aims to generate an attractive yield and can invest in both smaller and medium-sized companies. The greater diversity of the latter's portfolio helped it to materially outperform its cousin over our 10-year period, particularly during phases when medium-sized stocks and value stocks outperformed smaller quality and growth ones. This just goes to show that the investment trust cousin does not always deliver the superior return.

Aside from investing in slightly different parts of the market, other funds differentiate themselves within a pairing by being able to hold private investments or buying and selling derivatives, such as options. Those private investments can include private company shares, royalty income streams and, in Lindsell Train's case, the business that manages the portfolio. To paint the broad picture, Table 36B shows the relative performances of a few cousin funds over the last 10 years. Again, the full methodology is in the appendix.

Table 36B: Cousin funds: 10-year cumulative NAV performance %

Investment trust	%	Mutual fund	%	Relative perfor-mance %
BlackRock Greater Europe Ord	191.5	BGF European A2	97.93	93.6
F&C Investment Trust Ord	210.6	CT Managed Growth 1 Inc	79.0	131.6
Impax Environmental Markets Ord	176.4	Impax Environmental Mkts Ire A GBP Acc	135.0	41.4
JPMorgan US Smaller Companies Ord	187.1	JPM US Smaller Companies A (dist) USD	149.4	37.7
Lindsell Train Ord	292.7	Lindsell Train Global Equity B GBP Inc	220.9	71.8
Montanaro UK Smaller Companies Ord	52.8	Montanaro UK Income Fund GBP Seed	77.0	−24.2
Polar Capital Global Financials Ord	153.1	Polar Financial Credit I GBP Acc	119.8	33.3
Scottish Oriental Smaller Cos Ord	124.6	FSSA Asia Pacific Equity III USD Acc	134.0	−9.4
Henderson High Income Ord	77.18	Janus Henderson Instl Hi Alp UK Eq I Acc	65.7	11.5

Date range 10 years to 31/12/2024.

Sources: Morningstar, Bloomberg, LSEG, company annual reports, fund factsheets.

Switching horses

Now for a possible opportunity which arises from time to time on the back of our analysis so far. If an investment trust, which is a sibling or cousin, ever commands a particularly large premium to NAV, investors could consider a swich to the equivalent mutual fund. An excellent opportunity to do just this arose with the Lindsell Train Investment Trust in 2019. It traded at a 100% premium to NAV in June 2019. This is despite the Chair's warning in the full-year results released early that same month:

As regular readers of my Chairman's statements will know, any share price premium to the NAV comes with a health warning to new investors. This is because Company shares bought at a high premium can quickly lose substantial value if world stock markets fall and/or the business performance of Lindsell Train Limited deteriorates.

The LTI share price subsequently declined almost 60% from its June 2019 peak to reach its March 2020 low. This is a salutary lesson in the dangers of buying a trust on a very large premium. By comparison, the Lindsell Train Global Equity Fund (B Inc GBP shares) dropped 18% over the same period. That is still painful but much less so. This example may be a little extreme, but it helps me make a key point, which is that the share and unit prices of similar investment trusts and mutual funds can behave in quite different ways.

> "If a wide discount opens up with an investment trust that has an equivalent sibling or cousin mutual fund, it may present an opportunity for a switch into the investment trust and away from the latter. The logic is you may be able to lock in the same underlying portfolio exposure cheaper."

Remember that investment trust shares are driven by supply and demand, meaning that they can drift away from the underlying NAV. When stock market sentiment is poor, for instance, they can move to wide discounts as investors sell. Mutual funds, on the other hand, are not affected in the same way as they are always bought and sold, in effect, at NAV (subject to any entry and exit costs).

As such, if a wide discount opens up with an investment trust that has an equivalent sibling or cousin mutual fund, it may present an opportunity for a switch into the investment trust and away from the latter. The logic is you may be able to lock in a similar underlying portfolio exposure cheaper.

For income-paying funds, such a switch may also result in a higher income. Let's consider sibling funds, where the investment trust and the mutual fund hold similar portfolios yielding 4%. Assuming running costs are the same, if the investment trust is trading at a discount, the yield on its share price will be greater than that of the mutual fund. For example, if the (net of costs) yield is 4%, an investment trust trading at 10% discount offers the equivalent of 4.4%, making it the better bet, all other things being equal.

As a bonus, a mutual fund to investment trust switch may also create a growing income. Two of the trusts in Table 36A are dividend heroes and three are in the 'next generation' of dividend heroes. The growing year-on-year income they generate is something that their mutual fund cousins will struggle to compete with over the long term.

Proceeding with care

There are a few important caveats which I want to end with here. Firstly, with any fund switch, investors should watch transaction costs, including bid-offer spreads, stamp duty and any transaction costs levied by the relevant wealth manager, stockbroker or platform.

Next, it should be noted that very large premiums to NAV, as we saw earlier with Lindsell Train Investment Trust, are rare. Boards usually issue new equity when even a modest premium develops, whereas buying back stock is usually only triggered by a much bigger differential between an investment trust's share price and NAV. As such, the opportunity to switch from a mutual fund to a comparable investment trust trading at a discount is more likely to arise.

Finally, in making a mutual fund to investment trust switch for this technical reason, investors can expect no guarantee about subsequent performance. Where an investment trust is geared, it may dip in the short term, even if the switch to it is subsequently justified over a longer time horizon. As ever, patience is crucial.

Wrapping up

Sibling and cousin funds offer an interesting way to assess the performance differences of investment trusts and mutual funds. By holding constant for investment manager and investment management approach, the performance differential of sibling funds can be examined from the perspective of certain measurable facets. Although the sample size (i.e. the number of trusts that have sibling funds) is small, the 10-year performance numbers help to support the view that the investment trust structure is more conducive to better long-term returns.

Cousin funds are less useful as a direct comparison due to the additional flexibilities and investment powers cousin trusts can employ when compared to their mutual fund cousins. Nonetheless, they are a very useful example of the wider range of investment options that are available within an investment trust structure.

Overall, the reason for categorising funds as either siblings or cousins is it helps investors to compare similar offerings and reach a conclusion about which might be the better long-term opportunity. Using a relatively small sample of funds, we have seen how there may be advantages to making a switch between them in the right conditions, whilst always noting the important considerations that should precede such a move.

SUMMARY OF KEY POINTS

- 'Sibling' funds are two funds which share the *same* investment manager, the *same* investment process and exhibit the *same* style characteristics.

- 'Cousin funds' are two funds that share the same investment manager, a *similar* investment process, have similar benchmarks but exhibit slightly *different* style characteristics or where the investment trust holds some unlisted investments.

- Gearing, ongoing costs, accretive share buybacks / issuance and liquidity help to explain some of the potential differences between sibling funds.

- When the investment trust relative is trading at a particularly wide discount to NAV it can be attractive to switch from the mutual fund cousin to the investment trust.

- A comparison of 33 sibling funds shows that, in this small sample, investment trusts have tended to outperform their mutual fund siblings over a 10-year period.

CHAPTER 37

DO INVESTMENT TRUSTS OUTPERFORM MUTUAL FUNDS?

*"An ounce of performance is
worth pounds of promises."*

**—Mae West,
US actress and singer**

I N THIS CHAPTER I attempt to answer a pretty core question for an investor – which type of fund performs best? In summary, I find that investment trusts ('closed-ended' funds) have tended to outperform their comparable mutual funds ('open-ended' units trusts and OEICs) particularly over very long periods. Let me explain how I reached this conclusion.

Working it out

My starting point was a comparison of consecutive monthly NAVs. Any change in this number is effectively a measure of the average underlying portfolio performance, net of all operating and transaction costs. The full methodology is included in the appendix, so what follows is just a snapshot.

As for my fund selection, I used the Morningstar categories in its Europe / Asia / Africa (EAA) universe. These were established to help investors to make meaningful comparisons. Importantly, they classify funds based on the stocks they hold, rather than simply on their stated objectives or chosen benchmark.

To make my shortlist, specific fund categories had to then meet certain criteria:

- The comparable data was available for at least 20 years, which creates a meaningful performance period.

- Any constituents were invested almost exclusively in quoted equities. This helps to underpin the reliability of the NAV data, as it is largely derived from live market prices.

- At least five constituents were available, which stopped one or two funds dominating overall performance in any given month. The category monthly return is then a simple average.

Making the cut

These criteria combined produced four comparable sectors:

- Europe ex UK Equity
- Global Large-Cap Blend Equity
- UK Flexible Cap Equity
- UK Large-Cap Equity.

However, the results should be viewed with some caution due to small sample sizes. That said, these are always likely to be a constraint when it comes to measuring investment trust performance. This is because any single investment trust sub-sector will contain a relatively small number of trusts at any point in time.

With that caveat noted, Table 37A considers the overall cumulative frequency of monthly outperformance by investment trusts. This was relatively modest. Indeed, across the UK Flexible Cap Category, mutual funds outperformed their investment trusts peers in a slightly greater number of months than their investment trust equivalents (51% and 49% respectively). However, once we look at their relative performance over 10- and 25-year periods, the case for investing in investment trusts over mutual funds strengthens.

Indeed, when we consider very long timeframes (25 years) it does so substantially (refer to Table 37A). The potential reasons for this have been covered elsewhere in detail but include:

- gearing

- accretive share issuance and buybacks

- a greater bias to medium and smaller companies.

Table 37A: Investment trusts versus mutual funds, performance comparison (over monthly, 10- and 25-year periods)

Morningstar category (# of funds at start, end of total period CEF/ OEF)	# Monthly periods	% of months where IT outperforms comparable mutual fund	# Rolling 10-year periods	% of 10-year periods where IT outperforms comparable mutual fund	# Rolling 25-year periods	% of 25-year periods where IT outperforms comparable mutual fund
Europe ex UK Equity (6/41, 5/79)	384	56%	264	100%	85	100%
UK Flex-Cap Equity (5/20, 7/70)	360	49%	241	70%	61	82%
UK Large-Cap Equity (5/14, 7/107)	540	57%	421	91%	241	100%
Global Large-Cap Blend Equity (10/6, 7/162)	504	55%	385	90%	205	100%

Based on average monthly NAV performance, net of fees, with income reinvested, to 31/12/2024. Full methodology is in the appendix.

Source: Morningstar

This comparison of the average investment trust performance against an equivalent mutual fund finds that investment trusts have yielded superior returns in all 10-year observations (between 70 and 100% of the time) and in all 25-year observations (between 82 and 100%). In three categories (Europe ex UK Equity, UK Large-Cap Equity and Global Large-Cap Blend Equity) investment trust performance was superior to that of comparable mutual funds in all (100%) of the comparable 25-year periods.

Table 37B weighs cumulative outperformance over the full observation period. It reveals that investment trusts beat their mutual fund equivalents in each category. Although the annualised performance differential may appear to be relatively low (ranging from 0.7% to 2.0%), when this is compounded over a sufficiently long time the difference in total return is substantial. The fact that many investors may struggle to relate to such long investment horizons in no way invalidates this observation.

Table 37B: Investment trusts versus mutual funds, performance comparison (total return)

Category	First month of data	Last month of data	Total cumulative return on £1,000 (investment trust / mutual fund)	Total annualised return (investment trust / mutual fund)	Difference in annualised return
Europe ex UK Equity	Jan 1993	Dec 2024	£24,212 / £14,276	10.1% / 8.1%	2.0%
UK Flex-Cap Equity	Jan 1995	Dec 2024	£11,096 / £8,733	7.9% / 7.3%	0.7%
UK Large-Cap Equity	Jan 1980	Dec 2024	£67,851 / £34,895	9.8% / 8.1%	1.6%
Global Large-Cap Blend Equity	Jan 1983	Dec 2024	£69,015/ £41,069	10.6% / 9.2%	1.4%

Based on average monthly NAV performance, net of fees, with income reinvested, to 31/12/2024. Full methodology is in the appendix.

Source: Morningstar

Wrapping up

A few caveats notwithstanding, data like this should, at the very least, encourage mutual fund investors to have a closer look at investment trusts. That is especially true for anyone buying and then holding funds over long time periods.

SUMMARY OF KEY POINTS

- The chapter compares the monthly NAV performance of the average investment trust versus that of the average mutual fund.

- Morningstar categories classify funds based on the types of stocks they hold and their portfolio positioning through time, thereby grouping comparable investment trusts and mutual funds.

- The four qualifying categories covered Europe (ex UK), the UK and Global equity funds.

- The results should be viewed with some caution, particularly given the small sample size.

- Based on the data, investment trusts (closed-ended funds) tend to outperform their comparable mutual funds (units trusts and OEICs) for most of the categories analysed, particularly over very long timeframes.

CHAPTER 38

SKIN IN THE GAME

"Don't tell me what you think, tell me what you have in your portfolio."

—Nassim Nicholas Taleb,
a Lebanese-American option trader,
academic and writer

THOSE WORDS ARE from a book, titled *Skin in the Game: Hidden Asymmetries in Daily Life*, by Nassim Nicholas Taleb (2018). The book's title refers to something important in investing – the alignment of different interests. In the world of investment trusts that means the extent to which a board and managers are personally invested in the trust they oversee or manage. That is the topic I will explore here.

Buying in

So, how important is this alignment? I would say 'very'. For instance, would investors have had the same confidence in the fortunes of Amazon, Microsoft, Tesla, Meta and Berkshire Hathaway had it not been for the sizeable shareholdings of their respective CEOs? Probably not.

Meanwhile, there is a reason why directors' dealings in their company shares are regularly disclosed in publications such as the *Financial Times* and *Investors Chronicle*, whilst certain fund managers specifically take this information into account when making decisions. In a nutshell, it is reasonable to assume that if the directors hold a sizeable stake in the business they run, they will be better incentivised to do the job properly and consider any downside risks which may threaten their ability to preserve capital.

> "Investment flexibility afforded to investment trusts and their tax-efficient structure means they are ideal personal investment vehicles for many of the directors and investment managers associated with them."

In that context, it is worth remembering that a trust's investment manager and board are typically best placed to determine how attractive an investment trust portfolio is in the context of current market conditions and other opportunities. This is particularly the case where asset valuations are based on internal models, with limited comparatives. Fortunately, the investment flexibility afforded to investment trusts and their tax-efficient structure means they are ideal personal investment vehicles for many of the directors and investment managers associated with them. And whilst some might argue that career risk already implies some level of skin in the game (i.e. poor performance is bad for a fund manager's future prospects), explicit investment decisions go beyond that. When the managers have a substantial personal investment in a trust, they are more likely to prioritise its long-term success over their interests and the temptation to go for short-term gains that boost their own compensation. This can lead to increased investor loyalty and a stronger reputation for the trust in the market. In that context, it is unsurprising that several of the defensive (capital preservation) trusts that I highlighted in Chapter 35 have large levels of insider ownership.

Digging down

When it comes to finding information about such holdings, the annual report is a decent starting point. It discloses the number of shares held by the directors and the level of their fees, so that investors can compare share ownership to annual compensation.

Some investment trusts have part, or all, of their management or performance fees paid to the relevant manager in the form of shares. This typically comes with a requirement to hold them for a minimum number of years. This structure should encourage a longer-term view. Trusts such as Ashoka India

Equity, Ashoka Whiteoak Emerging Markets, Aurora UK Alpha and Greencoat UK Wind have all adopted just such a policy.

Obtaining shareholding information on the board of directors is straightforward as it's in the annual report. However, finding out the investment managers' level of investment is more difficult. Sometimes the investment manager is also a director of the trust, in which case their shareholding must be disclosed. However, much of the time it is not possible to establish the level of their shareholding.

As for other sources of information, the UK investment banking arm of Investec Securities produces a comprehensive report on insider shareholdings, from time to time. Titled the 'Skin in the Game Report', it covers most investment companies and their disclosable shareholders.

Taking care

So far, so useful. However, there are a few caveats around how an investor should interpret this data. First off, the absolute sum that a director or manager invests isn't the only factor to consider – the relative amount matters too. Someone, for example, with a significant personal fortune might invest a smaller proportion of their own wealth in a trust than a less well-off peer. Further, factors such as a manager's investment philosophy, and the overall structure of the trust's fees and incentives, should be considered to build the full picture.

Meanwhile, although skin in the game is important, it isn't an infallible control on two counts. It may, for instance, still lead to excessive risk taking. Investment managers with significant holdings can still make poor investment decisions and succumb to the perils of overleveraging. For example, despite a management shareholding of more than £35m in JZ Capital Partners, a private equity investment trust, share price performance has been poor, to say the least.

The second problem arises where a single shareholder is sufficiently large (typically with a stake above 25%) to be able to exercise a 'blocking vote'. Specifically, they may resist any action to reduce a wide discount. Several trusts with high levels of insider (director / manager) ownership have suffered from persistently wide discounts with little evidence of any control measures being implemented. Investors should only consider investing in these trusts if they are comfortable taking an incredibly long-term view.

Examples of those with insider shareholdings of more than 25% include Caledonia Investments, New Star, North Atlantic Smaller Companies and RIT Capital Partners although several of these trusts conduct regular share buybacks. At the time of writing, the discounts on these trusts range from 25% to 36%.

Wrapping up

Overall, my view is that when a trust's directors and managers have a significant financial stake in it, they are more likely to act in the best interests of shareholders and focus on long-term value creation. That said, it does not guarantee success. As such, I see it as a helpful starting point for further research.

SUMMARY OF KEY POINTS

- 'Skin in the game' refers to the extent to which the board and managers of an investment trust are personally invested in the trust they oversee or manage.

- Board directors are required to disclose their shareholdings, but getting information on the investment managers' level of investment is more difficult.

- Several investment trusts have part or all their management or performance fees paid to the investment manager in the form of shares.

- Several defensive trusts, highlighted in Chapter 35, have large levels of insider ownership.

- Whilst skin in the game is generally positive, it isn't always so, particularly if it leads to excessive risk taking or is used as a 'blocking vote'.

CHAPTER 39

ACTIVISTS

"Action is the antidote to despair."

—Joan Baez,
US singer-songwriter and activist

THAT IS A fitting way to open a chapter about activist investors. Activists are shareholders who seek change by engaging with company management. They are often the antidote to the despair of long-suffering shareholders in poor-performing trusts. Their aim is to influence anything from decision-making to governance structures and, perhaps of most interest to readers here, the level of any discount to NAV. Let's look at why and how.

Closing valuation gaps

First off, the 'why'. In short, a wide discount offers an opportunity. If an investor can help to narrow it, there is scope to make a profit irrespective of wider market movements and unlock value for all shareholders.

Let's say that an activist investor can buy a trust's shares on a 15% discount to NAV and subsequently help it to narrow to 5%. In effect, they have generated a potential 11.8% return (95 / 85 – 1 = 11.8%). I say 'potential' because it also depends on what happens to the underlying NAV. If there is little change, then the 11.8% return stands as a simple function of the discount narrowing.

However, should the discount narrow while the underlying NAV increases, then investors could make more. Clearly, there is also a risk that the NAV falls in value. To reduce this risk, some investors will take an offsetting 'short' position in the underlying assets, or a proxy for them such as an index.

Despite their potential to improve shareholder returns, the involvement of activist investors tends to split opinion.

Forcing change

To start with the positives, certain activist shareholders spend a lot of time and effort pursuing improved corporate governance and transparency. By engaging with management and advocating for change, they aim to enhance accountability and ultimately improve long-term share price performance.

At this point it is important to note that although activists may advocate for divestitures, share buybacks or changes in the underlying investment strategy to unlock value and narrow any discount to NAV, there are other elements to their role which are equally important. These include their ability to influence fee reductions, performance-related tenders, discount control mechanisms and continuation votes.

A performance-related tender is one where money is returned to shareholders if performance is poor. For example, shareholders could be offered an opportunity to exit 25% of their holding at NAV less costs if the NAV underperforms its benchmark over a five-year period. This makes sense. Provided an investment manager delivers as hoped, outperforming their benchmark over a reasonable medium-term period, their contribution should be reflected in the trust's share price trajectory and related rating. However, a failure to do so saddles shareholders with a double whammy of poor NAV performance combined with a widening discount. In this instance a 'conditional tender' helps to incentivise the investment manager to add value and narrow any discount.

JP Morgan India Investment Trust (JII) is a good example. In JII's case a performance-related conditional tender offer will be made to shareholders for up to 25% of the outstanding share capital at NAV less costs if, over the five years from 1 October 2020, the NAV total return does not exceed the total return of the benchmark (MSCI India Index) in sterling terms plus 0.5% per annum over the five-year period on a cumulative basis.

Meanwhile, a discount control mechanism is a strategy designed to manage or mitigate any discount. A share buyback programme is a good example. Activist engagement with a board may trigger a commitment to repurchase shares in situations when the discount exceeds 10%. If it persists, such that the average discount is greater than 10% for a period of 12 months, then the board may request a continuation vote.

Creating headaches

If this all sounds constructive, don't be fooled – some activist investors have little or no interest in the future fortunes of an investment trust. They simply wish to realise some quick value by closing any discount before moving on to their next target. Further, where the underlying holdings of a trust are transparent and liquid it is possible for them to take a long position (i.e. buy the shares) in the investment trust alongside a corresponding 'short' one in a basket of the underlying shares (i.e. a position that will increase in value as the price of the underlying basket declines). This is a way of encouraging the discount to narrow via something called 'arbitrage'. A key risk is the threat of the discount widening even more, a situation that can lead to losses.

Some activists may go further and seek to force trusts to wind themselves up. The sector has historically been accused of low governance standards, with claims that boards are incentivised (via directors' fees and expenses) to keep underperforming trusts in existence, rather than seeking alternatives such as mergers, wind-ups or tenders. That said, governance has improved markedly. Investors of all types take a greater interest in governance, the 'G' in ESG (environmental, social and governance) these days.

Many investment trusts resist activist demands, a stance which can trigger protracted battles. Some trusts are structured to include what are called 'poison pills'. These are features built into their structure that could block a complete liquidation. Examples include long notice periods on investment manager contracts, a separate class of shares with superior voting powers, or the existence of a large blocking stake in a trust's ordinary shares.

As for whether activist involvement is ultimately good or bad news for other investors, that depends. If they target a trust that you hold, in which you have lost faith or decided you are no longer a long-term investor, then their actions could be helpful. You may benefit from a short-term improvement in the share price and the opportunity to exit at a more attractive level. For ultra long-term investors, however, this may not be particularly important, as a short-term narrowing of the discount may not make a material difference.

Spotting activism

Activism is largely a cyclical phenomenon. When demand for investment trusts is high and many shares trade at premiums to asset value, there is little to attract activist investors. However, when the sector is out of favour and large discounts appear, then they tend to come out of the woodwork.

Take Elliott Advisors, which targeted Alliance Trust in 2015, openly criticising its underperformance and calling for changes to its board composition and investment strategy. Elliot claimed that it could see substantial opportunities to enhance value by improving governance, the cost structure and investment performance.

One group that I think is worth a mention in this chapter is one that does not see itself as an activist in the traditional sense of the word. That group is City of London Investment Management Company (COLIM, not to be confused with City of London Investment Trust). COLIM is a London-listed asset management firm which manages several investment strategies that aim to add value above and beyond traditional market returns through discount narrowing.

"Activist investors are attracted to UK investment trusts primarily because of wide discounts but also because of a favourable regulatory environment for minority shareholders. UK shareholders representing as little as 5% of the company's voting share capital can demand a company's directors call a general meeting."

COLIM tends to operate a relatively low-key form of private engagement with boards, encouraging the adoption of policies and strategies that will reduce discounts whilst improving governance and accountability. It publishes a very useful governance guide which sets out this approach.

One of COLIM's most visible strategies is that of the City of London Emerging World Fund (COLEWF), a Dublin-domiciled OEIC that invests almost exclusively in emerging market investment trusts. The investment manager has trading operations in the UK, US and Asia. This global reach allows it to trade closed-ended funds in several markets. COLEWF has outperformed the MSCI Emerging Markets Index by more than 200% since it launched in 1998 (source: Bloomberg). Much of this has come from discount narrowing in underlying investments. In that context, other activists that should largely be viewed as a welcome addition to an investment trust shareholder register include: 1607 Capital Partners, Asset Value Investors, Lazard Asset Management and AllSpring Global Investments.

Activist investors are attracted to UK investment trusts primarily because of wide discounts but also because of a favourable regulatory environment for minority shareholders. UK shareholders representing as little as 5% of the company's voting share capital can demand a company's directors call a general meeting. However, even those shareholders that hold a single share can voice their support, concerns or make suggestions to the manager and the board at the Annual General Meeting.

Wrapping up

By acquiring stakes in investment trusts and advocating for changes to narrow discounts and improved governance, activists can unlock shareholder value and drive positive change within the sector. In doing so, I think they provide a useful service to the sector despite their detractors.

SUMMARY OF KEY POINTS

- Activist shareholders use their shareholdings to influence board decision-making.

- The main attraction for most activists is the profit opportunity presented by wide discounts to NAV.

- Activists typically acquire stakes in investment trusts at a discount and push for measures to narrow the discount, thereby unlocking value.

- Activism can bring about positive change through initiatives such as fee reductions, performance-related tenders, discount control mechanisms and continuation votes.

- City of London Investment Management Company, although it does not see itself as an activist, has had a key influence on governance standards in the investment trust market.

CHAPTER 40

RESOURCES

*"Listen to everyone's advice
but follow your own."*
—**Irish proverb**

A T THIS POINT, you should feel almost ready to venture into the world of investment trusts. Before doing so, you may want a recap of where you can find further information. There is an abundance of free resources out there, ranging from the Association of Investment Companies (AIC) website to the information, insight and analysis provided by third-party research firms and educational platforms. In this concluding chapter, I will take you on a short tour.

The AIC

As a reminder, the AIC is the trade body for the investment trust sector. As such, it is funded by the investment trust sector and carries out several very useful functions on its behalf. These include issuing guidance to boards on governance issues, lobbying HMRC and the Treasury, conducting research, marketing and managing press relations.

The website (https://www.theaic.co.uk) provides lots of useful information for investors. It contains data on performance, yields and discounts. This can be filtered to help you identify and shortlist investment trusts for further consideration.

It also aggregates investment trust documents, such as annual reports and factsheets as well as third-party research, which I will cover in a moment.

Morningstar

This popular financial information provider offers free access to data on UK investment trusts. Its website (https://www.morningstar.co.uk) allows you to research and compare performance against benchmarks and peers. The relevant data is freely available and includes key metrics plus information about investment styles and portfolio composition. Some of it is similar to that available from the AIC, which also sources it from Morningstar. More detailed underlying portfolio data is available too but at a cost. This is usually too expensive for the average individual private investor, but many wealth managers, stockbrokers and financial advisers may have access to it on their behalf.

Other data providers

Discount information, pricing data and fund filtering options are also freely available at Trustnet (https://www.trustnet.com).

Third-party research

In previous chapters, I have referenced the detailed research produced by the investment banks. However, for various reasons, which include regulatory hurdles, this is generally only available to firms and individuals that are authorised to give investment advice. That said, there are several other sources of third-party analysis.

Wealth management firms, investment platforms, and private client stockbrokers, for example, often produce investment trust research. Since they do not usually have a commercial relationship with specific trusts, they have little interest in recommending one over another. Clients, or potential clients, of wealth management firms should be able to access this research in several ways – directly from an adviser, via the relevant client portal, within the firm's website or by requesting it.

The trusts themselves

Your next stop should be the website of the investment trusts you wish to consider in more detail. Most provide a prospectus, factsheets, interim reports, annual reports and Key Information Documents (refer to Chapter 10 for more on KIDs). Alternatively, the AIC website aggregates most of these documents for ease of use, which can save time if you are looking at more than one trust.

Here is a short summary of what to expect from the various documents:

- The prospectus is the legal contract between the investment trust and investors, which was covered in some detail in Chapter 31.

- Factsheets are usually short (one or two pages) snapshots of key pieces of information about the investment manager, portfolio manager, size of the trust, level of gearing, latest portfolio breakdown and largest holdings.

- Interim reports are provided six-monthly as an update to investors, along with a half-year financial statement.

- Annual reports then offer a more detailed full-year update, along with the year-end financial statements.

- Meanwhile, a KID contains a summary of the ongoing costs of running the investment trust, as well as the transaction costs incurred within the portfolio and any performance-related fees.

From a trust's website, it should also be possible to start forming a picture of its investment objectives, dividend policy and portfolio positioning. However, I find that many investment trust websites fail to clearly explain what their investment philosophy and process are. As obvious as this may seem! For me, this is much more important than how much experience the portfolio manager might have or how they are positioned right now.

Current positioning is information with limited shelf life. It is much more important to understand the investment process as this should inform you about the type of stocks or investments the trust is likely to hold both now and in the future. You can 'hold' this process against future portfolio information to check for consistency and look out for style drift (where a portfolio drifts from its stated style and positioning into other, possibly new, areas). If a clearly stated investment process is not available on the trust's website, then a good place to look for such information is via a third-party research provider.

Several third-party research providers offer information that is freely accessible to private investors. Examples are Kepler Partners (www.trustintelligence.co.uk), Marten & Co (https://quoteddata.com), Edison Group (www.edisongroup.com) and Hardman & Co (www.hardmanandco.com). This research is normally paid for by the investment trust and so any opinions that it contains should be read with that caveat in mind. However, it can be useful for anyone looking for structured factual content. The Kepler website has a particularly extensive database of investment trust research notes.

The AIC website aggregates research notes from all of these third-party research providers. This is usually a more efficient way when searching for information on a specific trust.

The Money Makers podcast

This was launched in 2020 and each episode usually appears once a week. It is hosted by Jonathan Davis, a journalist and editor of the *The Investment Trusts Handbook*. The latter is released annually and provides commentary from various portfolio managers, analysts and commentators about the investment trust sector.

As for the podcast, I think it offers an excellent roundup of newsflow from the sector, as well as context about what is happening in global capital markets. It also contains an interview with a guest – usually an investment trust analyst, portfolio manager or board director. This is all pretty useful content for anyone (with an hour to spare each week) who wants to get a better understanding of what is driving returns in the sector.

The media

Several newspapers and magazines make regular references to investment trusts as they make a good topic for money and investment-related columns.

One of the key sources of breaking news in the investment trust sector is Citywire (https://citywire.com/). You can subscribe for free to receive emails containing the latest news stories. The Citywire site also has a dedicated investment trust section – Investment Trust Insider – designed for investment trust enthusiasts, whether private or professional. It contains news, commentary, videos, discussion forums and other useful data.

Investors Chronicle (IC) also runs regular features on this sector, along with key themes and data via the Tools & Data section of its website (https://markets. investorschronicle.co.uk/data). Several IC journalists, such as Dave Baxter and Val Cipriani, are well versed on the investment trust sector and produce topical content in both print and podcast form.

Beyond these, the wider media will often highlight investment trusts that may not be on the main radar of retail investors, as well as flagging those that may have undeservedly drifted out of favour. *The Telegraph*'s Questor column and the Tempus column in *The Times*, for example, are widely read sources of ideas around individual stocks and investment trusts.

Wrapping up

Hopefully, you now appreciate the full suite of resources available which can get you started on your investment trust journey and help you to make informed decisions.

Good luck!

SUMMARY OF KEY POINTS

- The AIC (www.theaic.co.uk) provides lots of useful information including data on investment trust discounts, performance and yields.

- Morningstar (www.morningstar.co.uk) allows you to compare performance against benchmarks and other trusts, including investment style and portfolio composition. The freely available data includes metrics and investment style and portfolio composition.

- Several third-party research firms provide information that is freely accessible to private investors and is paid for by the investment trusts.

- The Money Makers podcast (https://money-makers.co/money-maker-podcasts) is an excellent weekly roundup of movers and shakers in the investment trust sector.

PART 4

APPENDICES

APPENDIX TO
CHAPTER 10

COSTS

Cost comparison of equity-based investment trusts and mutual funds

Methodology

THE STUDY CALCULATED, using the Morningstar Direct database, both management fees and total ongoing charges for all available equity investment trusts and a large sample of equity mutual funds. The management fee is the most recently reported actual percentage that was deducted from an investment's average net assets to pay the investment's management. This is typically taken from the latest annual report.

The ongoing charge figure represents total ongoing operating costs but excludes performance fees, transaction costs and financing costs. It includes management fees, as well as costs relating to administration, custodian, legal and any other fees that will usually not vary from year to year. The data is reported as a percentage of average net assets.

The investment trust sample (of 121 trusts) included all UK listed equity (based on Morningstar's Global Broad Category Group) investment trusts, which provide daily NAVs. The mutual fund sample (of 2,797 funds) included all UK-domiciled equity (based on Morningstar's Global Broad Category Group) UCITS (Undertakings for Collective Investment in Transferable Securities) funds, pricing in sterling. Index funds were excluded. Share classes that are only accessible with special access (e.g. to other funds of the same group) were excluded by removing share classes with ongoing costs and management fees of less than 0.1% per annum. Some share classes with obvious data errors were removed.

Limitations

The ongoing charges figure does not include performance fees. Some funds charge lower base management fees along with a performance fee. If such funds represent a greater proportion of the investment trust cohort, this could understate the true operating cost of investment trusts compared to mutual funds.

Several share classes of the same mutual funds were included in the sample. If the aggregate level of fees from such funds was greater than it would have been if we had only included the lowest cost share class available to retail investors, this may overstate the true total ongoing costs of the mutual fund cohort.

All mutual funds with ongoing charges of 0.1% per annum or greater were included in the sample. Some mutual funds with very low (but not below 0.1%) ongoing costs may not be available to private investors. Including such funds may understate the true total ongoing costs of the mutual fund cohort.

No account was taken of minimum investment sizes. Some low-cost (but with ongoing charges of more than 0.1%) mutual funds may have very high minimum investment levels and/or may not be available on fund platforms and therefore may not be available to most retail investors. Including these funds in the sample may understate the true total ongoing costs of the mutual fund cohort.

Several investment trusts enhance their NAV per share by buying back shares at a discount to NAV and issuing shares at a premium to NAV. Although this has the economic effect of reducing the cost burden to investors, it is not taken account of in the cost data disclosed.

Some of the data quality was poor and certain funds needed to be removed.

Results

When I compare a wide range of equity-based investment trusts with equivalent mutual funds, from a cost perspective I find a noticeable difference in management fees but little difference in overall operating costs – refer to Table A10A.

The management fee, which is usually the largest single cost item, is somewhat lower for investment trusts (average 0.69%, median 0.70%) than for mutual funds (average 0.87%, median 0.75%). I think this is primarily due to the efforts of independent boards in negotiating better terms for shareholders and, partly because of those efforts, the economies of scale enjoyed by several larger trusts.

Table A10A: Cost comparison of equity-based investment trusts and mutual funds

	Investment trust	Mutual fund
Average management fee	0.69%	0.87%
Median management fee	0.70%	0.75%
Average ongoing charge	0.98%	0.98%
Median ongoing charge	0.90%	0.90%
Sample size	131	2,455

Based on all available equity investment trusts and a large representative sample of actively managed mutual funds. Management fee is the actual percentage deducted from an investment trust's average net assets to pay for the investment trust's management, based on numbers from the latest annual report. The ongoing charge is the total ongoing operating expenses, including the management fee, expressed as a percentage of the average net assets based on numbers from the latest annual report.

Source: Morningstar, 31/12/2024.

When I include other running costs in the total ongoing charges figure, both investment trusts and mutual funds show the same average ongoing charge (0.98%), and the same median ongoing charge (0.90%).

Comparing fees based on asset value with fees based on market capitalisation

We have established that there can be a material difference between a trust's market value and its NAV. This differential is particularly important when it comes to the fees that investment trusts incur.

The established norm in the investment trust world is that the investment manager is remunerated based on the value of the assets that they manage, usually the total NAV. However, the investor doesn't buy and sell the NAV, they buy and sell the share price of the trust. In this respect, basing fees on the market value (i.e. share price) of a trust represents a better alignment of interests between the investment trust and the shareholder.

When the shares trade at a premium to NAV, having the investment management fees linked to market capitalisation rather than NAV still represents a better alignment of interest between trust management and shareholders.

It may also be that the premium to NAV needs to be much higher to justify fresh equity issuance. Issuing 10% more shares, when trading at a 10% premium, increases NAV per share by 0.9%, a figure that goes a long way to offset a year's worth of fees), compared to increasing the share count by 10% at a 2% premium, which increases NAV per share by a mere 0.2%.

A problem arises when an investment manager receives fees based on an asset value which is higher than the trust's market valuation. Investors can become understandably unhappy, especially if this situation persists. So, how widespread is this issue?

To help answer this question, I carried out an exercise comparing management fees if they were based on asset value versus the comparable fees if they had been based on market capitalisation.

Data

I used the Morningstar Direct database as my data source. This database contains historical information on virtually the entire universe of investment trusts through the 31/12/24 year end. The study included all closed-ended funds listed on a UK exchange, but excluding non-surviving funds (a total of 349).

Methodology

The study calculated monthly management fees in pounds sterling. This was based on the product of 1/12 of the management fee and the total NAV (or GAV) of each trust each month and compared with the product of 1/12 of the management fee and the total market capitalisation of each trust each month. Month-end total NAVs, or GAVs, and market capitalisation values were used.

In compiling Table A10B, trusts were removed if their management fees were not calculated as a percentage of NAV or GAV. Such fee structures included trusts where fees were based on market capitalisation, or where fees were based on the lower of NAV and market capitalisation.

Limitations

The fee calculation was based on month-end NAVs, GAVs, and market capitalisations. Many trusts calculate their fees at intervals that are not based on month ends and so the estimated fees in this study are likely to differ from the actual fees levied.

The monthly fee, expressed in pounds sterling, was compounded over the five-year period in question. This may overstate the level of some management fees and it may understate the level of other management fees relative to total shareholder return.

Some of the data quality was poor and certain funds needed to be removed.

Results

The fees based on asset value and fees based on market capitalisation, both expressed in pounds sterling, are shown in Table A10B as is the difference between the two, expressed as a percentage of the fee based on asset value. Trusts are ranked (high to low) on the percentage difference.

Table A10B shows the 5 trusts where the fees' differential was the greatest.

Table A10B: Comparison of (estimated) investment management fees based on asset value vs scenario where investment management fees are based on market capitalisation

Investment	Estimated fees on NAV – 5 years	Estimated fees on GAV* – 5 years	Estimated fees on mkt cap – 5 years	Differential as % of fee based on NAV (or GAV in case of JZ Capital Partners)
JZ Capital Partners*		£20,049,024	£8,653,696	70%
Riverstone Energy	£35,128,778		£19,351,206	45%
EPE Special Opportunities	£9,380,504		£5,379,677	43%
Ground Rents Income Fund	£4,533,666		£2,590,374	43%
Phoenix Spree Deutschland	£24,022,438		£14,492,001	40%

Data covers five years to 31/12/2024. Estimates are based on actual management fee rate, as published by Morningstar, pro-rated on monthly NAV or GAV and market cap. Calculations are based on calendar years, rather than financial years. * JZ Capital Partners levies management fees based on gross asset value (GAV).

Source: Morningstar

We can see that shareholders have paid between 40 and 70% more in management fees because of an asset value basis, compared to what the situation would have been on a market value basis.

APPENDIX TO
CHAPTER 18

VALUATION

Investment trusts primarily valued on an IFRS Level 3 basis

THE PURPOSE OF the study in Chapter 18 is to compare the performance of investment trusts where the bulk of the assets are hard to value and so an IFRS Level 3 valuation basis is used.

Data

The fund data used in this study came from Morningstar Direct. This database contains virtually the entire universe of closed-ended funds listed on a UK exchange, including non-surviving funds (a total of 1,248 trusts).

Methodology

The study uses total annualised shareholder return between inception and liquidation, or to 31/12/2024 if the trust was still listed at the end of 2024.

Morningstar does not have a filter for valuation basis, so NAV valuation frequency was used with those trusts with NAVs valued less frequently than monthly taken as a proxy for a Level 3 valuation basis. VCTs, warrants, subscriptions shares and trusts with obvious data errors were excluded. This reduced the universe to 224 trusts.

The return calculation used was shareholder total return. In Morningstar this return basis is referred to as 'Market Return', defined as: "an exchange-traded or closed-ended fund's total return based on market prices, as opposed to NAV". Morningstar calculates the market price return by taking the change in the fund's market price, reinvesting all income and capital gains, distributions during the period, and dividing by the starting market price.

The data is analysed at the aggregate level as well as at the AIC sector level. AIC sectors were split out where there were at least 10 constituents, namely Private Equity, Renewable Energy Infrastructure and Infrastructure. All AIC Property sub-sectors were aggregated into a single Property category.

Limitations

The number of categories that fit the selection criteria in certain AIC sectors is relatively small. Some of the data quality was poor, particularly for trusts that were in realisation mode, and these were removed. Most of these trusts delivered very poor performance and so their removal likely flatters the results compared to reality.

The overall numbers are likely skewed by the large amount of new issuance in 2020 and 2021 (23 of the trusts in the sample), as this is very close to the end date of the study and so only considers a very short time period. Interest rates rose sharply in 2022 and this contributed to some very poor share price performance amongst alternative investment trusts.

Results

The findings show that of the 217 trusts in the sample, less than half (84 or 39%) generated a positive return between launch and liquidation, or 31/12/2024 in the case of those still standing. Only 40 (18%) generated an annualised return of more than 5%.

The trusts, with the highest annualised returns, which were still trading as at 31/12/2024 are shown in Table A18A.

Table A18A: Top performing trusts, holding hard-to-value (Level 3) assets

Investment trust	AIC Sector	Stock exchange admission date / Restructure date	Annualised return %
Literacy Capital PLC	Private Equity	06/2021	30.1
HgCapital Trust Ord	Private Equity	05/1995	17.0
3i Group Ord	Private Equity	07/1994	13.0
ICG Enterprise Trust Ord	Private Equity	09/1981	12.7
3i Infrastructure Ord	Infrastructure	03/2007	10.7

Returns are total annualised shareholder returns, from admission/restructure date to 31/12/2024, expressed in pounds sterling. HgCapital Trust was restructured in May 1995.

Sources: Morningstar, Bloomberg, Regulatory News Service, LSEG.

No sector has a success rate greater than 50% when it comes to making a positive return for shareholders. The sector results are shown in Table A18B.

Table A18B: Sectors holding hard-to-value assets, performance success rates.

AIC sector	Sample size	% with annualised returns >0%	% with annualised returns >5%
Property	71	38%	11%
Private Equity	27	41%	37%
Renewable Energy Infrastructure	23	39%	13%
Infrastructure	12	58%	42%

Returns are total annualised shareholder returns, between stock market launch and 31/12/2024, or delisting if earlier. Includes sectors with a sample size of 10 or more trusts.

Data sources: Morningstar, Bloomberg, LSEG, Company factsheets, Company annual reports, Companies House.

APPENDIX TO
CHAPTER 20

ZERO-DISCOUNT POLICIES

Calculating NAV per share enhancement due to changes in share count, that is issuing at a premium to NAV and buying back at a discount to NAV

THE MECHANICAL IMPACT of issuing shares at a premium to NAV and buying them back at a discount to NAV, is to increase NAV per share.

Issuing 10% more shares, when trading at a 10% premium, increases NAV per share by 0.9% (Table A20A) a figure that goes a long way to offsetting a year's worth of fees), compared to increasing the share count by 10% at a 2% premium, which increases NAV per share by a mere 0.2%.

Table A20A: NAV per share accretion (%) from new equity issuance

Premium to NAV	Size of share issue (as % of equity in issue)	NAV per share Accretion (%)					
		1%	5%	10%	15%	20%	25%
1%		0.01%	0.05%	0.09%	0.13%	0.17%	0.20%
2%		0.02%	0.10%	0.18%	0.26%	0.33%	0.40%
5%		0.05%	0.24%	0.45%	0.65%	0.83%	1.00%
10%		0.10%	0.48%	0.91%	1.30%	1.67%	2.00%
20%		0.20%	0.95%	1.82%	2.61%	3.33%	4.00%
25%		0.25%	1.19%	2.27%	3.26%	4.17%	5.00%
50%		0.50%	2.38%	4.55%	6.52%	8.33%	10.00%

$$NAVps \text{ accretion from share issue} = \frac{NAVps_{new}}{NAVps_{old}} - 1$$

Where

$NAVps_{new} =$

$$NAVps_{new} = \frac{NAV_{old} + (New \ issue \ share \ price \times \#_{new \ shares})}{\#_{old \ shares} + \#_{new \ shares}}$$

and

$NAVps_{old} =$ NAV per share immediately prior to the issue of new shares.

Table A20B: NAV per share accretion (%) from share buybacks

		NAV per share Accretion (%)					
Discount to NAV	Size of Buyback (as % of equity in issue)	1%	5%	10%	15%	20%	25%
1%		0.01%	0.05%	0.11%	0.18%	0.25%	0.33%
2%		0.02%	0.11%	0.22%	0.35%	0.50%	0.67%
5%		0.05%	0.26%	0.56%	0.88%	1.25%	1.67%
10%		0.10%	0.53%	1.11%	1.76%	2.50%	3.33%
20%		0.20%	1.05%	2.22%	3.53%	5.00%	6.67%
25%		0.25%	1.32%	2.78%	4.41%	6.25%	8.33%
50%		0.51%	2.63%	5.56%	8.82%	12.50%	16.67%

$$NAVps \ accretion \ from \ share \ buyback = \frac{NAVps_{new}}{NAVps_{old}} - 1$$

Where
$NAVps_{new} =$

$$NAVps_{new} = \frac{NAV_{old} - (Buyback \ share \ price \times \#_{shares \ bought \ back})}{\#_{old \ shares} - \#_{shares \ bought \ back}}$$

and

$NAVps_{old} =$ NAV per share immediately prior to the share buyback.

APPENDIX TO
CHAPTER 23

THE DISCOUNT RATE AND WHY IT IS SO IMPORTANT IN FINANCE

CHAPTER 23 EXPLAINS how discount rates are used to arrive at present-day valuations of future cash flows and asset values. It refers to a steady state methodology which is widely used to calculate the expected returns from trusts where there is sufficient disclosure of the inputs.

The methodology is explained below.

Whilst the discount rate should be a guide to the level of return investors can expect, it reveals the expected return on the trust's assets, not on its shares.

To gauge the return on a trust's shares, we need to consider several other factors, such as ongoing charges and whether the shares trade at a discount or premium to the underlying NAV. Fortunately, we can use the various disclosures made by investment trusts to arrive at an expected return on the share price. Analysts at JP Morgan Cazenove were amongst the first to use the term 'steady state' to describe this approach in the context of investment trusts. In short, if everything remains in a steady state – the discount rate, costs, level of debt – then we can establish the expected return on the share price. If HICL Infrastructure shares are trading at a discount to NAV, the expected return on its shares will be higher than the 8.0% expected return, inferred by the average discount rate in the 2024 Annual Report (see below), but if HICL shares trade at a premium, it will be commensurately lower.

Calculating the steady state return involves multiple inputs. However, it is possible to make a reasonable estimate of the steady state return using a few readily available ones. These are outlined below, using HICL Infrastructure as an example.

A = The average discount rate

B = Ongoing charges

C = The NAV per share

D = Sensitivity of the NAV per share to a 1% increase in the discount rate

E = Current share price

We get inputs A to D from the HICL 2024 Annual Report, and we use the 31/12/2024 share price:

A = 8.0% (page 48)

B = 1.14% (page 18)

C = 158.2p (page 113)

D = −15.6p (−7.8p is the sensitivity to a 0.5% increase, so we multiply by 2, page 50)

E = 118.8p (share price as at the 31/12/2024)

F = Premium to NAV

We then need to calculate the premium (or discount) to NAV per share. Using the 31/12/2024 share price of 118.8p we arrive at a premium of −24.9%. The shares trade at a 24.9% discount to NAV, so we express this as a negative percentage value (i.e. −24.9% premium) for the calculation:

$$= \frac{E}{C} - 1$$

$$= \frac{118.8}{158.2} - 1$$

$$= -24.9\%$$

G = Sensitivity of the NAV to an increase in the discount rate expressed as a percentage.

We then need to adjust for the size of the premium (or discount). Firstly, we change the sensitivity to changes in the discount rate to a percentage by dividing D by C to get –9.9%. So, if the discount rate goes up by 1%, the NAV declines by 9.9%:

$$D / C = -15.6 \div 158.2 = -9.9\%$$

Bringing all that together, the steady state return is then calculated as:

$$((1 + A) / (1 + B) - 1) \times 100 + ((F / (G))$$

$$((1+0.08) / (1+0.0114)) - 1) \times 100 + (-24.9\% / -9.9\%) = 8.9\%$$

As the shares trade at a discount to NAV (of 24.9% in this case), this increases the expected annual return from 8.0% (expected return on the NAV) to 8.9% (expected return on the share price). We can use this approach to compare different trusts even though they have different discount rates and trade at different premiums or discounts to NAV.

Adjusting in this manner accounts for the fact that the portfolios of different investment trusts will have differing weighted average asset lives and therefore differing cash flow durations. Trusts with longer (shorter) duration cash flows will have higher (lower) sensitivity to a rise or fall in discount rates.

To keep things simple, we have not taken inflation assumptions into account. Neither have we taken debt or cash balances into account. In this example HICL Infrastructure has almost no debt or net cash on its balance sheet. However, where there is cash or debt on the investment trust balance sheet, then to arrive at a more accurate expected return, you need to adjust the expected return up (in the case of debt) or down (in the case of cash) to take account of this. This can be done by scaling up the discount rate by the debt level expressed as a percentage of net assets or by scaling down the discount rate by the cash level expressed as a percentage of net assets.

To arrive at a more precise expected (steady state) return you can also adjust for any cost of debt or benefit from interest income. This latter point may involve making some assumptions based on disclosures in the annual report.

Discount rates are ultimately influenced by human judgement and are therefore subjective. Estimates of future cash flows are just that, estimates. They are often based on inputs (e.g., long-term estimates of wind speeds and solar irradiation, asset lifespans, long-term power prices, expected revenues, profit margins and inflation), some of which come from third-party forecasters, who can employ different assumptions.

APPENDIX TO
CHAPTER 36

FUND SIBLINGS
AND COUSINS

Definitions

I DEFINED SIBLING FUNDS as a pair of funds, comprising an investment trust and a mutual fund, where they share the *same* investment manager, the *same* investment process, have the *same* benchmark and exhibit the *same* style characteristics (e.g. growth, value, size).

I defined cousin funds as a pair of funds, comprising an investment trust and a mutual fund, where they share the *same* investment manager, a *similar* investment process, but have *different* benchmarks and/or slightly *different* style characteristics.

Data

I used the Morningstar Direct database as my data source. This database contains historical information on virtually the entire universe of funds up to the 31/12/24 year end. The study included all closed-ended funds listed on a UK exchange, using only surviving funds (a total of 273) and all mutual funds that are registered for sale in the UK. Where there was more than one share class I used the oldest share class, excluding non-surviving funds (a total of 12,169).

Methodology

I used the 'Manager Name' field to cross-reference the 273 investment trusts with the 12,169 mutual funds for matching purposes. This field names individual portfolio managers. Where a match was returned, this was checked, and the Manager History field was used to establish a common start date between the investment trust and the mutual fund. Month-end start dates were used.

In certain cases, annual reports and historic factsheets were used to verify common start dates. The study considered the investment management team, rather than a single named portfolio manager, to assess continuity of management. Some subjective judgement was required here due to a lack of standardised data.

The resultant paired funds were checked for style consistency and similarity of benchmark. Where a pair of funds had a common style (as defined by the Morningstar style box field) and shared the same benchmark, they were classified as sibling funds. Where a pair of funds, sharing the same investment management team and a similar investment process, did not have a common style (as defined by the Morningstar style box field) or did not share the same benchmark, they were classified as cousin funds.

Performance is measured in NAV total return terms with income reinvested. This measures the total return based upon changes in fund NAV assuming reinvestment of all income and capital gain distributions. Returns are net of the funds' expense ratios and portfolio transaction costs but are not adjusted for front-end fees on mutual funds or bid-offer spreads on investment trusts. All returns were measured in GBP.

Limitations

The resultant pairs of sister (54) and cousin (24) funds that fitted the selection criteria were relatively small. I cross-checked Morningstar performance data with that of Bloomberg and LSEG. Some of the older data quality was poor and certain funds needed to be removed from both cohorts. The resultant number of sister pairs and cousin pairs that had a common 10-year performance history was even smaller, reducing the sample to 33 (sisters) and 9 (cousins) respectively. This is too small a sample size to derive any results that are statistically significant.

Using the oldest mutual fund share class could mean selecting a higher cost share class than is subsequently available to retail investors. This could understate possible mutual fund returns versus the investment trust returns.

The performance comparison did not consider entry and exit costs, including stamp duty costs and bid-offer spreads when purchasing investment trust shares, or bid-offer spreads, swing prices and anti-dilution levies when buying and selling mutual funds. This may have modestly overstated investment trust returns relative to mutual fund returns.

The performance comparison does not take account of volatility. Carrying out the same performance comparison on a risk-adjusted basis is likely to improve the relative attractions of mutual funds relative to comparable investment trusts.

Results

Table A36A compares the performance of sister funds that have a comparable performance period of 10 years to 31/12/2024. A quick glance reveals that the investment trusts (on the left) have generally performed better than the equivalent mutual fund. Part of the reason is likely to be the ability to gear in a rising market. Size, as we have already referred to, could also be an influence. Another contributing factor is likely to be the enhancement to NAV per share from issuing shares at a premium and buying them back at a discount.

However, not all the investment trusts have outperformed their sibling. That said, the majority (88%) of the investment trusts have delivered superior performance, with the average outperformance being 23% over the period.

Table A36A: Sibling Funds, 10-year cumulative NAV performance %.

Investment trust	%	Mutual fund	%	Relative performance %
Aberforth Smaller Companies Ord	86.3	Aberforth UK Small Companies Acc	83.8	2.5
abrdn New India Investment Trust Ord	184.1	abrdn-Indian Equity A Acc GBP	128.9	55.2
abrdn UK Smaller Companies Growth Ord	119.5	abrdn UK Smaller Companies I Acc	106.2	13.4
Baillie Gifford Japan Ord	136.3	Baillie Gifford Japanese B Acc	114.72	21.6
Baillie Gifford Shin Nippon Ord	115.7	Baillie Gifford Japan Small Co B Inc	74.1	41.6
BlackRock Income and Growth Ord	76.6	BlackRock UK Income A Inc	72.2	4.3
Diverse Income Trust Ord	80.3	Premier Miton UK Multi Cap Income B Acc	75.6	4.8
Edinburgh Worldwide Ord	118.8	Baillie Gifford Global Discovery A Acc	50.5	68.4
Fidelity Asian Values Ord	154.4	Fidelity Asian Smaller Coms Y-Acc-USD	123.9	30.5
Fidelity European Trust Ord	174.0	Fidelity European Acc	136.4	37.6
Finsbury Growth & Income Ord	120.0	WS Lindsell Train UK Equity Acc	101.65	18.3
Henderson European Trust Ord	153.9	Janus Henderson European Focus A Acc	125.34	28.6
Henderson Smaller Companies Ord	84.9	Janus Henderson UK Smaller Coms A Acc	64.21	20.7
JPMorgan American Ord	343.1	JPM America Equity A (dist) USD	313.5	29.6
JPMorgan Emerging Markets Ord	115.2	JPM Emerging Markets C Net Acc	86.68	28.6
JPMorgan Global Emerg Mkts Inc Ord	96.6	JPM Emerging Markets Div A (acc) EUR	81.9	14.7
JPMorgan UK Small Cap Growth & Income	142.0	JPM UK Smaller Companies I Acc	121.79	20.2
Jupiter Green Ord	84.9	Jupiter Ecology L Inc	114.68	−29.8

Investment trust	%	Mutual fund	%	Relative performance %
Lowland Ord	58.7	Janus Henderson UK Eq Inc&Gr I Inc	43.6	15.2
Merchants Trust Ord	105.6	Allianz UK Listed Eq Income A Inc	86.8	18.8
Monks Ord	220.1	Baillie Gifford Global Alpha Gr B Acc	193.4	26.7
Pacific Assets Ord	136.9	Stewart Inv Asia Pac All Cap B GBP Acc	140.19	−3.3
Pacific Horizon Ord	231.6	Baillie Gifford Pacific B Inc	172.57	59.0
Personal Assets Ord	68.3	Trojan O Inc	64.67	3.7
Polar Capital Technology Ord	585.4	Polar Capital Global Tech Inc	541.07	44.4
Schroder Asian Total Return Inv. Company	192.4	Schroder ISF Asian Ttl Ret C Acc USD	146.2	46.3
Schroder AsiaPacific Ord	137.8	Schroder Asian Alpha Plus A Acc	115.34	22.4
Schroder Japan Trust Ord	152.9	Schroder Tokyo A Inc GBP	110.3	42.6
Schroder UK Mid Cap Ord	81.2	Schroder UK Mid 250 A Acc	53.1	28.1
Scottish American Ord	213.1	Baillie Gifford Global Inc Growth A Acc	155.55	57.5
Strategic Equity Capital Ord	98.7	WS Gresham House UK Micro Cap A Acc	106.3	−7.7
Templeton Emerging Mkts Invmt Tr TEMIT	94.6	FTF Templeton Global Emerging Mkts W Acc	87.84	6.7
The European Smaller Companies Trust PLC	201.8	Janus Henderson European Smr Coms I Acc	211.38	−9.6

Date range 10 years to 31/12/2024.

Sources: Morningstar, Bloomberg, LSEG, company annual reports, fund factsheets.

Table A36B shows the relative performances of several cousin funds over the last 10 years.

Table A36B: Cousin Funds, 10-year cumulative NAV performance %

Investment trust	%	Mutual fund	%	Relative performance %
BlackRock Greater Europe Ord	191.5	BGF European A2	97.93	93.6
F&C Investment Trust Ord	210.6	CT Managed Growth 1 Inc	79.0	131.6
Impax Environmental Markets Ord	176.4	Impax Environmental Mkts Ire A GBP Acc	135.0	41.4
JPMorgan US Smaller Companies Ord	187.1	JPM US Smaller Companies A (dist) USD	149.4	37.7
Lindsell Train Ord	292.7	Lindsell Train Global Equity B GBP Inc	220.9	71.8
Montanaro UK Smaller Companies Ord	52.8	Montanaro UK Income Fund GBP Seed	77.0	−24.2
Polar Capital Global Financials Ord	153.1	Polar Financial Credit I GBP Acc	119.8	33.3
Scottish Oriental Smaller Cos Ord	124.6	FSSA Asia Pacific Equity III USD Acc	134.0	−9.4
Henderson High Income Ord	77.18	Janus Henderson Instl Hi Alp UK Eq I Acc	65.7	11.5

Date range 10 years to 31/12/2024.

Sources: Morningstar, Bloomberg, LSEG, company annual reports, fund factsheets.

APPENDIX TO
CHAPTER 37

DO INVESTMENT TRUSTS OUTPERFORM MUTUAL FUNDS?

CHAPTER 37 SUMMARISES the findings of a comparison of investment trust and mutual fund NAV performance over various timeframes. The methodology is explained below.

Data

The Morningstar Direct database contains historical information on virtually the entire universe of funds up to the 31/12/2024 year end. The study included all closed-ended funds listed on a UK exchange, including non-surviving funds (a total of 1,248) and all UK-domiciled open-ended funds, including index funds. Where there was more than one share class I used the oldest share class, including non-surviving funds (a total of 6,284).

The next step was to establish comparable categories. I used Morningstar categorisations. Morningstar developed the Morningstar categories to distinguish funds by what they own, as well as by their prospectus objectives and styles. Whilst the prospectus objective identifies a fund's investment goals based on the wording in the fund prospectus, the Morningstar category identifies funds based on their actual investment styles as measured by their underlying portfolio holdings.

The study uses Morningstar categories for funds in its Europe / Asia / Africa (EAA) universe. These categories were established to help investors make meaningful comparisons between investment funds.

In summary, the data is drawn from Morningstar categories where:

1. There is at least 20 years of data.

2. The constituent funds invest primarily in quoted equities.

3. There is consecutive NAV performance data, derived from at least five investment trusts and at least five mutual funds constituents each month across the entire observation period, which is a minimum of 20 years.

4. Morningstar has comparable categories for both investment trusts and mutual funds.

These criteria produced four comparable sectors:

- Europe ex UK Equity

- Global Large-Cap Blend Equity

- UK Flex-Cap Equity

- UK Large-Cap Equity.

Methodology

The average monthly return is a simple average from the available funds each month, rather than being weighted by fund size. The study considered all funds that came under the relevant Morningstar category in each month, including funds that are no longer available, thereby avoiding survivorship bias.

The returns relationship was investigated by segmenting the sample by fund category and testing the mean NAV returns of the two cohorts. The data in all four categories meet the conditions for a parametric test. Namely, they are normally distributed, have equal variances, no outliers and are independent.

A paired samples t-test was used to test the hypothesis of no significant difference in monthly mutual fund and investment trust NAV returns, over the longest possible period which met the data and category criteria. Time periods vary for each category with the start date established by the first full calendar year in which each cohort (investment trust and mutual fund) had at least five constituents each month, and at least five each month thereafter through to December 2024.

Data

I looked to ensure that the performance data was based on NAVs that were derived from live market prices. For this reason, I only considered categories that invested, almost exclusively, in quoted equities.

Several investment trust sectors contain a relatively small number of constituents. To avoid one or two investment trusts dominating the performance in any given month I chose categories that had at least five constituents in every single observable month.

Finally, I wanted to ensure that the categories were comparable across both investment trusts and mutual funds.

The Morningstar categories are based on the following principles: **Proper Evaluation:** Every rated category should form a benchmark against which a manager's ability to add value relative to peers with similar investment exposures can be meaningfully measured. **Transparency:** The rules defining each category should be clearly stated such that asset managers and investors can easily determine the rationale for a fund's classification. **Independence:** A fund's classification is based on Morningstar's independent analysis of its holdings, objective, and performance. **Stability:** Except for a clear change to a fund's strategy which will be addressed at such time as the change is evident, a fund's categorisation is based on its positioning through time with the trailing three years the default period evaluated. This enhances the stability of the classifications and is aligned with the interests of fund investors, who generally use funds as longer-term investments.

The categories that met the criteria were:

Europe ex UK Equity: Europe ex UK funds invest principally in the equities of companies in continental Europe. These funds may also include smaller positions in the region's smaller markets, including the emerging markets of Eastern Europe. These funds invest at least 75% of their total assets in equities; and invest at least 75% of equity assets in European equities, with less than 10% in the UK. Morningstar MPT Category Index: Morningstar DM Eur xUK TME NR.

UK Flex-Cap Equity: UK Flex-Cap Equity funds invest in equities across the market-cap spectrum from the UK. Although they may at times favour a particular market-cap range, they do not display a clear, sustained bias to large-cap or small-cap issues that would qualify them for another category. A mandate that permits the fund to invest across the market-cap spectrum is not sufficient to qualify for this category in the presence of a clear, sustained bias to large-cap or small-cap issues. At least 75% of total assets are invested in equities and at least 75% of equity assets are invested in UK equities. Morningstar MPT Category Index: Morningstar UK All Cap TME NR.

UK Large-Cap Equity: UK Large-Cap Equity funds invest principally in the equities of large-cap UK companies. Equities in the top 70% of the European equity market (including the UK) are defined as large-cap. At least 75% of total assets are invested in equities and at least 75% of equity assets are invested in UK equities. Morningstar MPT Category Index: Morningstar UK All Cap TME NR.

Global Large-Cap Blend Equity: Global Large-Cap Blend Equity funds invest principally in the equities of large-cap companies from around the globe. Most of these funds divide their assets among many developed markets and invest at least 20% of equity assets in North America and 15% in Greater Europe. Equities in the top 70% of the capitalisation of each of the seven regional Morningstar style zones are defined as large-cap (the style zones are Europe, US, Canada, Latin America, Japan, Asia ex-Japan, and Australia / New Zealand). The blend style is assigned to funds where neither growth nor value characteristics predominate. At least 75% of total assets are invested in equities.

My criteria for selecting comparable categories included several considerations. Firstly, I wanted to ensure that I could compare performance over multiple 10-year (and longer) periods, across a range of market and economic conditions. For this reason, I selected categories where there was comparable data that was at least 20 years long.

Limitations

The number of categories that fit the selection criteria is small and the number of constituent funds in each cohort is small in several monthly observations. Even a cohort of five funds represents a small sample size. Some of the older data quality was poor and certain funds needed to be removed from both cohorts. The study only used months of consecutive performance data, derived from at least five investment trusts and at least five mutual funds after any data cleansing.

Results

Return is the monthly total return computed based upon changes in fund NAV assuming reinvestment of all income and capital gain distributions. Returns are net of the funds expense ratio and portfolio transaction costs but are not adjusted for front-end fees on mutual funds or bid-offer spreads on investment trusts.

The results are summarised in Tables A37A and A37B.

Table A37A: Investment trusts versus mutual funds, performance comparison (total return)

Category	First month of data	Last month of data	Total cumulative return on £1,000 (investment trust / mutual fund)	Total annualised return (investment trust / mutual fund)	Difference in annualised return	Paired comparison t-test (p value, <0.05 is significant)
Europe ex UK Equity	Jan 1993	Dec 2024	£24,212 / £14,276	10.1% / 8.1%	2.0%	0.021
UK Flex-Cap Equity	Jan 1995	Dec 2024	£11,096 / £8,733	7.9% / 7.3%	0.7%	0.350
UK Large-Cap Equity	Jan 1980	Dec 2024	£67,851 / £34,895	9.8% / 8.1%	1.6%	0.015
Global Large-Cap Blend Equity	Jan 1983	Dec 2024	£69,015/ £41,069	10.6% / 9.2%	1.4%	0.029

Based on average monthly NAV performance, net of fees, with income reinvested to 31/12/2024.

Source: Morningstar

Table A37A shows the total cumulative performance over the respective time periods. The investment trust cohort has outperformed the mutual fund equivalent in each category. Table A37B considers the frequency of monthly outperformance, as well as relative performance over rolling 10-year and rolling 25-year periods. In other words, the first 10-year period for the Europe ex UK Equity category is from January 1993 to December 2002 inclusive. The second 10-year period is from February 1993 to January 2003 inclusive, and so on.

The t-test p value is statistically significant (<0.05) for three of the four sectors (Europe ex UK Equity, Global Large-Cap Blend Equity, UK Large-Cap Equity) but not for the other sector (UK Flex-Cap Equity).

Table A37B: Investment trusts versus mutual funds, performance comparison (over monthly, rolling 10-year and rolling 25-year periods)

Morningstar category	# Monthly periods	% of months where IT outperforms mutual fund	# 10-year periods	% of 10-year periods where IT outperforms mutual fund	# 25-year periods	% of 25-year periods where IT outperforms mutual fund
Europe ex UK Equity	384	56%	264	100%	85	100%
UK Flex-Cap Equity	360	49%	241	70%	61	82%
UK Large-Cap Equity	540	57%	421	91%	241	100%
Global Large-Cap Blend Equity	504	55%	385	90%	205	100%

Based on average monthly NAV performance, net of fees, with income reinvested to 31/12/2024.

Source: Morningstar

Table A37B shows that the *frequency* of monthly investment trust outperformance is modest. Indeed, in the UK Flexible Cap Category mutual funds outperformed in a greater number of months than their investment trust equivalents. However, when we consider 10-year periods, the case for investing in investment trusts over mutual funds is strong. When we consider very long timeframes (25 years) the case for investment trusts is powerful.

However, the results should be viewed with some caution due to small sample sizes. Only four categories meet the criteria and even a cohort of five funds represents a small sample size. However, small sample sizes are always likely to be a constraint in measuring investment trust performance. I have attempted to deal with this challenge by using very long data sets and then comparing both cohorts over multiple subsets of this data.

Notwithstanding the relatively small number of categories and small number of constituents, in the categories that met the criteria, I find that investment trusts (closed-ended funds) tend to outperform their comparable mutual funds (units trusts and OEICs) for most of the categories analysed, particularly over very long timeframes. All four of the categories analysed had at least 30 years of data. When comparing the average investment trust performance with the average mutual fund performance over all possible 25-year periods, for these four categories, I find that the investment trusts yield superior returns in at least 82% of the instances and for three of these categories in all (100%) of the comparable 25-year periods.

PART 5

TABLES

Table 1: The 25 oldest investment trusts

Investment trust	Ticker	AIC sector	Market capitalisation	Inception date
F&C Investment Trust	FCIT	Global	5,346,460,632	1868-03-19
Investment Company	INV	UK Smaller Companies	6,779,286	1868-11-14
Dunedin Income Growth	DIG	UK Equity Income	370,317,571	1873-02-01
Scottish American	SAIN	Global Equity Income	880,604,029	1873-03-31
JPMorgan American	JAM	North America	2,022,371,780	1881-06-18
Mercantile	MRC	UK All Companies	1,804,095,625	1884-12-08
JPMorgan Global Growth & Income	JGGI	Global Equity Income	2,969,068,659	1887-04-21
Henderson Smaller Companies	HSL	UK Smaller Companies	602,978,760	1887-12-16
Bankers	BNKR	Global	1,299,726,100	1888-04-13
Alliance Witan	ALW	Global	4,979,010,256	1888-04-21
The Global Smaller Companies Trust	GSCT	Global Smaller Companies	751,790,329	1889-02-15
Merchants Trust	MRCH	UK Equity Income	817,821,127	1889-02-16
Edinburgh Investment	EDIN	UK Equity Income	1,085,801,226	1889-03-01
AVI Global Trust	AGT	Global	1,070,801,094	1889-07-01
Law Debenture Corporation	LWDB	UK Equity Income	1,184,061,768	1889-12-12
City of London	CTY	UK Equity Income	2,130,582,656	1891-01-01
abrdn Diversified Income & Growth *	ADIG	Flexible Investment	130,598,790	1898-01-05
TR Property	TRY	Property Securities	991,721,813	05/05/1905
BlackRock Smaller Companies	BRSC	UK Smaller Companies	640,035,146	02/05/1906
Baillie Gifford China Growth Trust	BGCG	China / Greater China	132,486,323	24/01/1907
Murray International	MYI	Global Equity Income	1,553,057,739	18/12/1907
Scottish Mortgage	SMT	Global	11,952,075,258	17/03/1909
Hansa Investment Company Ltd	HAN	Flexible Investment	96,400,000	01/01/1912
Murray Income Trust	MUT	UK Equity Income	831,248,317	07/06/1923
Finsbury Growth & Income	FGT	UK Equity Income	1,376,878,149	15/01/1926

Please note that several of the names have changed since inception. * In managed wind-down.

Source: Morningstar, 31/12/2024.

Table 2: The 25 largest investment trusts

	Investment trust	Ticker	AIC sector	Market capitalisation (£)
1	3i Group	III	Private Equity	34,691,591,231
2	Scottish Mortgage	SMT	Global	11,952,075,258
3	Pershing Square Holdings	PSH	North America	7,330,363,157
4	F&C Investment Trust	FCIT	Global	5,346,460,632
5	Alliance Witan	ALW	Global	4,979,010,256
6	Polar Capital Technology	PCT	Technology & Technology Innovation	4,119,101,748
7	Tritax Big Box	BBOX	Property – UK Logistics	3,291,858,988
8	JPMorgan Global Growth & Income	JGGI	Global Equity Income	2,969,068,659
9	3i Infrastructure	3IN	Infrastructure	2,928,461,250
10	Greencoat UK Wind	UKW	Renewable Energy Infrastructure	2,878,214,302
11	RIT Capital Partners	RCP	Flexible Investment	2,845,635,890
12	Petershill Partners	PHLL	Growth Capital	2,776,556,411
13	Monks	MNKS	Global	2,489,709,218
14	HgCapital Trust	HGT	Private Equity	2,467,156,615
15	HICL Infrastructure PLC	HICL	Infrastructure	2,379,943,598
16	International Public Partnerships	INPP	Infrastructure	2,275,339,876
17	City of London	CTY	UK Equity Income	2,130,582,656
18	Renewables Infrastructure Grp	TRIG	Renewable Energy Infrastructure	2,114,174,914
19	JPMorgan American	JAM	North America	2,022,371,780
20	HarbourVest Global Priv Equity	HVPE	Private Equity	1,986,093,247
21	Smithson Investment Trust	SSON	Global Smaller Companies	1,937,021,704
22	Caledonia Investments	CLDN	Flexible Investment	1,876,925,330
23	Mercantile	MRC	UK All Companies	1,804,095,625
24	Templeton Emerging Mkts Invmt Tr TEMIT	TEM	Global Emerging Markets	1,723,395,860
25	Worldwide Healthcare	WWH	Biotechnology & Healthcare	1,600,100,532

Source: Morningstar, 31/12/2024

Table 3: The 25 lowest cost investment trusts

	Investment trust	Ticker	AIC sector	Annual report ongoing charge (%)
1	Scottish Mortgage	SMT	Global	0.35
2	City of London	CTY	UK Equity Income	0.37
3	JPMorgan American	JAM	North America	0.38
4	JPMorgan Global Growth & Income	JGGI	Global Equity Income	0.43
5	Monks	MNKS	Global	0.44
6	Aurora UK Alpha *	ARR	UK All Companies	0.45
7	Henderson Smaller Companies *	HSL	UK Smaller Companies	0.45
8	Capital Gearing	CGT	Flexible Investment	0.47
9	Mercantile	MRC	UK All Companies	0.47
10	Manchester & London **	MNL	Global	0.47
11	F&C Investment Trust	FCIT	Global	0.49
12	Law Debenture Corporation	LWDB	UK Equity Income	0.49
13	Ashoka India Equity Investment *	AIE	India/Indian Subcontinent	0.50
14	Bankers	BNKR	Global	0.50
15	Murray Income Trust	MUT	UK Equity Income	0.50
16	Murray International	MYI	Global Equity Income	0.53
17	Edinburgh Investment	EDIN	UK Equity Income	0.53
18	BlackRock Throgmorton Trust *	THRG	UK Smaller Companies	0.54
19	Merchants Trust	MRCH	UK Equity Income	0.55
20	Temple Bar	TMPL	UK Equity Income	0.56
21	Scottish American	SAIN	Global Equity Income	0.58
22	Castelnau Group *	CGL	Flexible Investment	0.59
23	Mid Wynd International Inv Tr	MWY	Global	0.60
24	Finsbury Growth & Income	FGT	UK Equity Income	0.61
25	Alliance Witan	ALW	Global	0.62

Latest annual report ongoing charge, expressed as a percentage of net assets. Includes all ongoing operating costs but excludes any performance fee.

*Trust levies a performance fee.

**Trust has performance-related management fee.

Source: Morningstar, 31/12/2024

Table 4: The 25 investment trust portfolios with the highest ROIC (a proxy for quality)

	Investment trust	Ticker	AIC sector	Equity portfolio ROIC (%)
1	Manchester & London	MNL	Global	49.0
2	Finsbury Growth & Income	FGT	UK Equity Income	35.5
3	Baillie Gifford UK Growth Trust	BGUK	UK All Companies	30.9
4	Allianz Technology Trust	ATT	Technology & Technology Innovation	29.0
5	Polar Capital Technology	PCT	Technology & Technology Innovation	27.2
6	JPMorgan American	JAM	North America	25.3
7	Martin Currie Global Portfolio	MNP	Global	25.1
8	JPMorgan Global Growth & Income	JGGI	Global Equity Income	24.1
9	BlackRock Greater Europe	BRGE	Europe	23.1
10	European Opportunities Trust	EOT	Europe	22.4
11	JPMorgan UK Small Cap Growth & Income	JUGI	UK Smaller Companies	22.1
12	F&C Investment Trust	FCIT	Global	22.0
13	Personal Assets	PNL	Flexible Investment	21.7
14	Montanaro UK Smaller Companies	MTU	UK Smaller Companies	21.4
15	Smithson Investment Trust	SSON	Global Smaller Companies	21.1
16	Scottish American	SAIN	Global Equity Income	19.8
17	Edinburgh Investment	EDIN	UK Equity Income	19.8
18	Mercantile	MRC	UK All Companies	19.5
19	Dunedin Income Growth	DIG	UK Equity Income	19.3
20	Montanaro European Smaller	MTE	European Smaller Companies	18.9
21	Monks	MNKS	Global	18.5
22	Mobius Investment Trust	MMIT	Global Emerging Markets	18.5
23	Mid Wynd International Inv Tr	MWY	Global	18.5
24	JPMorgan Emerging Markets	JMG	Global Emerging Markets	18.4
25	Pacific Assets	PAC	Asia Pacific	18.2

The Return On Invested Capital (ROIC) numbers in the table represent the asset-weighted average trailing twelve month ROIC of the underlying equity holdings, where ROIC data is available, expressed as a percentage. Stocks from the Financial Services and Real Estate sectors are excluded. Some of the trusts in the table hold other assets in addition to quoted equities. These other assets are excluded from the ROIC calculations. ROIC = NOPAT / Invested Capital. NOPAT (Net Operating Profit After Tax) is calculated as Operating Income * (1 - Tax Rate). Invested Capital is the total capital invested in the business, including debt and equity. ROIC is an indication of the efficiency of a company at allocating its capital to profitable investments. Trusts with a market capitalisation of less than £50m are excluded.

Source: Morningstar, 31/12/2024

Table 5: The 25 investment trust portfolios with the lowest price / earnings ratios (a proxy for value)

	Investment trust	Ticker	AIC sector	Equity portfolio price to earnings ratio
1	Temple Bar	TMPL	UK Equity Income	8.3
2	Fidelity Asian Values	FAS	Asia Pacific Smaller Companies	8.6
3	Fidelity China Special	FCSS	China / Greater China	8.7
4	Merchants Trust	MRCH	UK Equity Income	8.8
5	Fidelity Special Values	FSV	UK All Companies	8.8
6	Diverse Income Trust	DIVI	UK Equity Income	9.0
7	Aberforth Smaller Companies	ASL	UK Smaller Companies	9.0
8	BlackRock Frontiers	BRFI	Global Emerging Markets	9.2
9	Lowland	LWI	UK Equity Income	9.2
10	abrdn Equity Income Trust	AEI	UK Equity Income	9.2
11	Henderson Far East Income	HFEL	Asia Pacific Equity Income	9.5
12	CQS Natural Resources G&I	CYN	Commodities & Natural Resources	9.5
13	Aurora UK Alpha	ARR	UK All Companies	9.6
14	Ruffer Investment Company	RICA	Flexible Investment	9.9
15	Templeton Emerging Mkts Invmt Tr TEMIT	TEM	Global Emerging Markets	10.2
16	Vietnam Enterprise	VEIL	Country Specialist	10.3
17	City of London	CTY	UK Equity Income	10.3
18	Henderson High Income	HHI	UK Equity & Bond Income	10.4
19	Law Debenture Corporation	LWDB	UK Equity Income	10.4
20	Schroder UK Mid Cap	SCP	UK All Companies	10.5
21	Hansa Investment Company Ltd 'A' Class A	HANA	Flexible Investment	10.5
22	JPMorgan Claverhouse	JCH	UK Equity Income	10.7
23	JPMorgan UK Small Cap Growth & Income	JUGI	UK Smaller Companies	10.9
24	Schroder Income Growth	SCF	UK Equity Income	11.1
25	JPMorgan Global Emerg Mkts Inc	JEMI	Global Emerging Markets	11.2

The Price To Earnings (PE) numbers in the table represent the asset-weighted average forward looking PE of the underlying equity holdings, where data is available, expressed as a percentage. The PE for the underlying stocks is the ratio of the company's 31/12/2024 share price to the company's estimated earnings per share (EPS) for the current fiscal year, at that date. If a third-party estimate for the current year EPS is not available, Morningstar calculates an internal estimate based on the most recently reported EPS and average historical earnings growth rates. Some of the trusts in the table hold other assets in addition to quoted equities. These other assets are excluded from the ROIC calculations. Trusts with a market capitalisation of less than £100m are excluded.

Source: Morningstar, 31/12/2024

BIBLIOGRAPHY

Adams, A.T. (ed.) (2005) *The Split Capital Investment Trust Crisis*, Wiley Finance.

Amihud, Y. (2002) 'Illiquidity and Stock Returns: Cross-section and Time-series Effects', *Journal of Finance Economics*, 5(1), pp. 31–56.

Amihud, Y. and Mendelson, H. (1986) 'Asset Pricing and the Bid-Ask Spread', *Journal of Financial Economics*, 17(2), pp. 223–249.

Asness, C.S., Frazzini, A. and Pedersen, L.H. (2017) 'Quality Minus Junk'. Available at https://papers.ssrn.com/sol3/papers.cfm?abstract_id=2312432

Asness, C.S., Frazzini, A., Israel, R., Moskowitz, T.J. and Pederson, L.H. (2018) 'Size Matters, If You Control Your Junk', *Journal of Financial Economics*, 129(2018), pp. 479–509.

Baid, G. (2020) *The Joys of Compounding: The Passionate Pursuit of Lifelong Learning*, Columbia University Press.

Ball, R., Gerakos, J., Linnainmaa, J. and Nikolaev, V. (2015) 'Deflating Profitability', *Journal of Financial Economics*, 117(2), pp. 225–248.

Banz, R.W. (1981) 'The Relationship Between Return and Market Value of Common Stocks', *Journal of Financial Economics*, 9(1), pp. 3–18.

Berkshire Hathaway (2022) 'Share Price Returns'. Available at www.berkshirehathaway.com/2022ar/2022ar.pdf

Bessembinder, H. (2018) 'Do Stocks Outperform Treasury Bills?' *Journal of Financial Economics*, 1293(3), pp. 440–457.

Brands, H.W. (2010) *The American Colossus: The Triumph of Capitalism, 1865–1900*, Doubleday.

Chambers, D., Dimson, E. and Foo, J. (2015) 'Keynes the Stock Market Investor: A Quantitative Analysis', *The Journal of Financial and Quantitative Analysis*, 50(4), pp. 843–868.

Chancellor, E. (2022) *The Price of Time: The Real Story*, Penguin.

Chopra, N., Lee, C.M.C., Shleifer, A. and Thaler, R.H. (1993) 'Yes, Discounts on Closed-End Funds Are a Sentiment Index', *The Journal of Finance*, 48(2), pp. 801–808.

Cornell, B., Hsu, J. and Nanigian, D. (2017) 'Does Past Performance Matter in Investment Manager Selection?' *The Journal of Portfolio Management*, 43(4), pp. 33–43.

Crittenden, E. and Wilcox, C. (2008) *The Capitalism Distribution: Fat Tails in Motion*, Blackstar Funds.

Damodaran, A. (2023) 'The Price of Risk: With Equity Risk Premiums, Caveat Emptor!' Available at https://pages.stern.nyu.edu/~adamodar/pdfiles/blog/PriceofRisk2023.pdf

Davis, J. (2023) *The Investment Trusts Handbook*, Harriman House.

Dodd, D. and Graham, B. (1934) *Securities Analysis*, McGraw-Hill.

Esteves, R. and Chambers, D. (2013) 'The First Global Emerging Markets Investor: Foreign & Colonial Investment Trust 1880–1913', *Explorations in Economic History*. Available at http://dx.doi.org/10.2139/ssrn.2024921

Fama, E.F. and French, K.R. (1992) 'The Cross-Section of Expected Stock Returns', *The Journal of Finance*, 47(2), pp. 427–465.

Fama, E.F. and French, K.R. (2006) 'Profitability, Investment, and Average Returns', *Journal of Financial Economics*, 82(3), pp. 491–518.

Fama, E.F. and French, K.R. (2008) 'Dissecting Anomalies', *Journal of Finance*, 63(4), pp. 1653–1678.

Fama, E.F. and French, K.R. (2015) 'A Five-Factor Asset Pricing Model', *Journal of Financial Economics*, 116(1), pp. 1–22.

Fama, E.F. and French, K.R. (2016) 'Dissecting Anomalies with a Five-Factor Model', *Review of Financial Studies*, 29(1), pp. 69–103.

F&C (2023) *Annual Report and Accounts*. Available at https://www.fandc.com/document-library/?filter=annual-report-and-accounts

Fisher, L. and Lorie, J. (1970) 'Some Studies of Variability of Returns on Investments in Common Stock', *The Journal of Business*, 43(2), pp. 99–134.

Forbes (n.d.) 'Warren Buffet Wealth'. Available at https://www.forbes.com/real-time-billionaires/#371bfe0b3d78

Frazzini, A., Kabiller, D. and Pedersen, L.H. (2018) 'Buffett's Alpha', *Financial Analysts Journal*, 74(4), pp. 35–55.

FTSE Russell website: https://www.lseg.com/en/ftse-russell

Galbraith, J.K. (1954) *The Great Crash 1929*, Penguin. (This was first printed in 1954 and I'm not sure who the publisher was but reprinted with revisions in 1975, and subsequently reprinted by Penguin in 1992, which is the version I have referenced.)

Garner, B. and Pratt, K. (2024) 'How to Survive a Stock Market Crash', Forbes. Available at https://www.forbes.com/uk/advisor/investing/how-to-survive-a-stock-market-crash/

Graham, B. (1973) *The Intelligent Investor*, Harper Business, fourth revised edition, p. 108.

Hou, K., Xue, C. and Zhang, L. (2015) 'Digesting Anomalies: An Investment Approach', *Review of Financial Studies*, 28(3), pp. 650–705.

iamkate.com (n.d.) 'Historical UK Inflation Rates and Price Conversion Calculator'. Available at https://iamkate.com/data/uk-inflation/

Ilmanen, A. (2011) *Expected Return: An Investor's Guide to Harvesting Market Rewards*, Wiley.

Investment Trust Association website: https://www.theaic.co.uk/

Jegadeesh, N. and Titman, S. (1993) 'Returns to Buying Winners and Selling Losers: Implications for Stock Market Efficiency', *The Journal of Finance*, 48(1), pp. 65–91.

Kahneman, D. and Tversky, A. (1979) 'Prospect Theory: An Analysis of Decision Under Risk', *Econometrica*, 47(2), pp. 263–291.

Land Registry website: https://landregistry.data.gov.uk/app/ukhpi/

Lempérière, Y., Deremble, C., Seager, P., Potters, M. and Bouchaud, J.P. (2014) 'Two Centuries of Trend Following', *Journal of Investment Strategies*, 3(3), pp. 41–61.

Meli, J. and Rajadhyaksha, A. (2024) *Barclays Capital Equity Gilt Study 2024*. Available at https://www.ib.barclays/news-and-events/equity-gilt-study-2024.html

Morecroft, N. (2017) *The Origins of Asset Management from 1700 to 1960*, Palgrave Macmillan.

Newlands, J. (1997) *Put Not Your Money In Trust*, AITC.

Novy-Marx, R. (2013) 'The Other Side of Value: The Gross Profitability Premium', *Journal of Financial Economics*, 108(1), pp. 1–28.

Pastor, L. and Stambaugh, R.F. (2003) 'Liquidity Risk and Expected Stock Returns', *Journal of Political Economy*, 111(3), pp. 642–685.

Proquest (n.d.) *Benjamin Franklin's Gift to Boston & Philadelphia*. Available at https://www.proquest.com/openview/e3aebca1b25597bd667bfcbaf5c02d22/1 ?pq-origsite=gscholar&cbl=18750&diss=y

Scratchley, A. (1875) 'On Average Investment Trusts and Companies Dealing with Stock Exchange Securities', Shaw. Available at https://catalog.hathitrust. org/Record/006124330

Sharpe, W.F. (1991) 'The Arithmetic of Active Management', *Financial Analysts Journal*, 47(1), pp. 7–9.

Shefrin, H. and Statman, M. (1985) 'The Disposition to Sell Winners Too Early and Ride Losers Too Long: Theory and Evidence', *The Journal of Finance*, 40(3), pp. 777–790.

Siegel, J. (2023) *Stocks for the Long Run*, 6th edition, McGraw-Hill.

S&P Dow Jones Indices website: https://www.spglobal.com/ratings/en/

Statista (n.d.) 'Total Net Assets Under Management (AUM) of Active and Passive Mutual Funds in the United States from 2000 to 2023'. Available at https://www.statista.com/statistics/1263822/active-passive-mutual-funds-total-net-assets-usa/

St. Louis Fed (n.d.) Website: https://fred.stlouisfed.org/series/LTCYUK

Taleb, N.N. (2018) *Skin in the Game: Hidden Asymmetries in Daily Life*, Allen Lane.

Thaler, R.H. and Johnson, E.J. (1990) 'Gambling with the House Money and Trying to Break Even: The Effects of Prior Outcomes on Risky Choice', *Management Science*, 36(6), pp. 643–660.

Tversky, A. and Kahneman, D. (1974) 'Judgment under Uncertainty: Heuristics and Biases', *Science*, 185(4157), pp. 1124–1131.

Walker, C.H. (1940) 'Unincorporated Investment Trusts in the Nineteenth Century', *Economic History*, 4(15), pp. 341–355, Royal Economic Society.

LIST OF KEY ABBREVIATIONS AND ACRONYMS

AGM – Annual General Meeting

AIC – Association of Investment Companies

AIFM – Alternative Investment Fund Manager

AIM – Alternative Investment Market

AMC – Annual Management Charge (also referred to as Annual Management Fee)

BOE – Bank of England

Bps – Basis points

BPS – Book value per share

BV – Book value

Capex – Capital expenditure

CGT – Capital Gains Tax (also the stock market ticker for Capital Gearing Trust)

CFD – Contract For Difference

CPI – Consumer Price Index

DCF – Discounted cash flow

EPS – Earnings per share

ERP – Equity risk premium

ESG – Environmental, social & governance

ETF – Exchange Traded Fund

FCA – Financial Conduct Authority

FCF – Free cash flow

FSI – First Sentier Investors

FV – Future value

HMRC – His Majesty's Revenue & Customs

IFRS – International Financial Reporting Standards

IPO – Initial public offering

IRR – Internal rate of return

ISA – Individual Savings Account

KID – Key Information Document

KPI – Key Performance Indicator

LLP – Limited liability partnership

LP – Limited partnership

LPE – Listed Private Equity

LSE – London Stock Exchange

MSCI – Morgan Stanley Capital International

NAV – Net asset value

NAVps – Net asset value per share

NFR – Non-reporting fund

OCR – Ongoing charges ratio

OEIC – Open-Ended Investment Company

PCA – Pound cost averaging

PDF – Portable Document Format

PEG – Price earnings to growth

PEP – Personal Equity Plan

PIP – Pantheon International Plc

PPP – Public Private Partnership

PRIIPs – Packaged Retail Investment products and Insurance-based Investment Products

PV – Present value

REIT – Real Estate Investment Trust

RF – Reporting Fund

ROIC – Return on invested capital

RPI – Retail Price Index

RNS – Regulatory News Service

S&P – Standard & Poor's

SFM – Specialist Fund Market

SFS – Specialist Fund Segment

SIPP – Self Invested Personal Pension

UCITS – Undertakings for Collective Investment in Transferable Securities

VCT – Venture Capital Trust

ZDP – Zero Dividend Preference Share

INDEX

ABOUT THE AUTHOR

MICK GILLIGAN IS a partner at Killik & Co, the award-winning wealth management firm. He joined Killik & Co in 2001 and became a partner in 2004. He is part of Killik & Co's research team and is responsible for the firm's Managed Portfolio Services, discretionary management services that are invested in funds. Prior to joining Killik & Co, Mick was a fee-based Independent Financial Adviser with The John Lamb Partnership. He is a CFA Charterholder, a Chartered Fellow of the Chartered Institute for Securities & Investments, a Certified Financial Technician and holds the Certificate in Investment Performance Measurement. Mick manages portfolios using a fund-based approach and is a specialist in investment trusts. He is frequently quoted in the financial press regarding investment trusts. He lives near Killik & Co's Esher branch in Surrey, with his wife and two daughters.

Killik & Co's fund research team provides research to clients and advisers on a wide range of funds. The team also manages portfolios that are predominantly invested in funds.